LIVING LARGE IN AMERICA

The Life and Times of
The Family Ginsburg (*pronounced* Du Pont)

BY
ERIC ROBESPIERRE

Special thanks go to the brilliance of the three who made this publication possible. Sarah Coots and Stephanie Wardach, my understanding editors, and to the equally simpatico Victoria Jamieson, who designed the cover and the interior.

Library of Congress Control Number: 2012905150
ISBN 978-0-615-66397-5

Published by Eric Robespierre
www.Ericrobespierre.com

All rights reserved. Without limiting the rights under copyright reserved above, no part of this publication may be reproduced, stored in or introduced into a retrieval system, or transmitted, in any form, or by any means (electronic, mechanical, photocopying, recording, or otherwise) without the prior written permission of both the copyright owner and the above publisher of this book.

This is a work of fiction. Some names, characters, places, brands, media, and incidents are either the product of the author's imagination or are used fictitiously. The author acknowledges the trademarked status and trademark owners of various products and published music lyrics referenced in this work of nonfiction, which have been used without permission. The publication/use of these trademarks is not authorized, associated with, or sponsored by the trademark owners.

Amazon Edition License Notes

This ebook is licensed for your personal enjoyment only. This ebook may not be re-sold or given away to other people. If you would like to share this book with another person, please purchase an additional copy for each person you share it with. If you're reading this book and did not purchase it, or it was not purchased for your use only, then you should return to Amazon.com and purchase your own copy. Thank you for respecting the author's work.

"I know, my dear Watson, that you share my love of all that is bizarre and outside the conventions and humdrum routine of everyday life."

Sherlock Holmes

LIVING
LARGE
IN AMERICA

The Life and Times of
The Family Ginsburg (*pronounced* Du Pont)

And She Who Brings Forth Life, the Great Baleboosteh Ginsburg (*pronounced* Eleanor of Aquitaine) blessed them, and She Who Brings Forth Life, the Great Baleboosteh Ginsburg (*pronounced* Eleanor of Aquitaine) said unto them, Be fruitful, and multiply, and replenish the earth, and subdue it: and have dominion over the fish of the sea, and over the fowl of the air, and over every living thing that moveth upon the earth.

Genesis 1:28 Ginsburg (*pronounced* Du Pont) Version

JANUARY 1ST, 2005

From: Cheryl.G@Ourmail.us
Date: Saturday, January 1, 2005, 11:06 a.m.
To: US@Ourmail.us
Subject: *Bollettino di festa del Cheryl del cugino* (Cousin Cheryl's Holiday Newsletter)

Mi estimada familia: (My dear family)
Joyeux Nouvel An! (Happy New Year!)

Another year has come and gone, and so much has happened during the 365 grand and glorious days of the year 5764 (*pronounced* 2004).

Of course, you all know about Monroe's Nobel Peace Prize, Grant's Academy Award, Tyler's Pulitzer, Washington's Medal of Honor, Madison's appointment to the Supreme Court, and, naturally, Clinton's meeting with Goddess (he received a beautiful Hermes tie, and of course, the additional, five commandments). So let me start with Eisenhower, who just turned two and, you know, has quite the pair of lungs.

Well—the Little Mister (as I love to call him) was just invited to join the Three Tenors in Blackface on their Mississippi Delta Slave Arias and Other Favorite Songs of the Old South Tour. It will be the first time the little fella's been away from home, but *la mia famiglia* (my family)—i.e., the boy's mistake for a father (the polo-playing low-life), his cheap whore-secretary, the whore's crack-fiend husband (posing as her brother—what a laugh—ha!), my girlfriends from the D.O.D. (a.k.a., Daughters of Darkness, a.k.a., the Anne Rice Stake and Ale Investment Club), and of course, yours truly—figured it was the kind of thing that would look good on the old résumé when the Little Mistake (oh, excuse me—I meant the Little *Mister*) applies to Harvard.

So, I said, why not let the tiny tyke sing a little blues, which is only fair, since his coming into my life that's all I've ever done.

Oh yes—since the Little Mister's been born, a night doesn't go by I don't cry myself to sleep asking the Dapper Dipper in the sky the eternal question—why are all women suckers for men in uniform?

OK, so maybe hubby-to-be number six wasn't the first guy in silks, *but he was the tallest* to impregnate my sacred body after lathering me up in a bathtub full of Cristal and Vanilla Häagen-Dazs. (By the way, don't ever let a polo player tell you that ceremony completely takes the place of the morning-after pill.)

Did I mention Monroe's Nobel Peace Prize, Grant's Academy Award, Tyler's Pulitzer, Washington's Medal of Honor, Madison's appointment to the Supreme Court, and, of course, Clinton's meeting with Goddess? It makes a mother proud, doesn't it? *Certamente!* (It certainly does!)

I know, I say this every year, but this year (I swear) I am definitely going to build more cabinets. As we speak, all shelves are jam-packed with the children's sporting trophies: Grant's Olympic Gold in the triathlon, Tyler's *two* Tour de France triumphs, Washington's *three* MVP Super Bowl trophies, Clinton's NBA and MLB Rookie of the Year and MVP awards, and of course, Madison's *five* Ironwoman trophies. Oops-a-daisy—I meant *four*. I forgot she gave one to Jodi. After all, weren't they roommates up at Yale, and every Thursday evening don't they still have sleepovers and watch *Silence of The Lambs?*

Oops–a–daisy again! What about the Little Mister's *two* Grammys and his La Scala's Golden Throat Award? Can't forget those—, no siree, bobcats.

Of course, when I'm talking about their awards, I'm leaving out their college, high-school, and elementary-school trophies that fill the second- and third-floor bedrooms, not to mention the five fully illustrated pages in *The Guinness Book of World Records*. The only thing missing in my trophy case is the head of hubby number six (the polo-playing, low-life). *Un qué pinchazo!* (What a prick!)

I'm a Ginsburg (*pronounced* Du Pont) Girl, well-endowed with Ginsburg (*pronounced* Du Pont) genetic gifts so magnificent in size and shape men (and some women) have been throwing themselves at them (*me*) since I first wore sweaters. (If you have to know, I was twelve.)

I'm fluent in all the romance languages and some that want to be. I have an MBA in Banking and Finance from the London School of Economics, a PHD in Molecular Biology from Stanford, and—*and*—everybody mistakes me for a young Katie Couric. So you tell me—why am I putty in the hands of brutally handsome men?

Did I really have to have *six* husbands to realize that the *A* in a married man's DNA stands for *morally unacceptable asshole?* (OK, OK, . . . so I'm putty in the hands of brutally handsome men.)

Looking back on the courtship of the Little Mister's Father (the polo-playing low-life), I wonder why I chose to make love in the bathtub instead of the sauna. *Quelle erreur*! (What a mistake!)

I never told anyone, but giving birth to the "Devil's Baby" nearly did me in. I thank Google for directing me to UnloadYourPain.com, or else I never would have met Pope John II, the blogger who saved my life.

We spent four glorious days sailing the Greek Isles, drinking vintage San Pellegrino and singing "Big Girls Don't Cry." When we docked, "Elvis" (that's the secret name I call my playful pontiff) gave me a signed copy of the book he secretly penned during our voyage (in Latin with three-color illustrations and on papyrus, don't you know).

"Girl with the Swollen Belly" (that's the secret name he called me) . . . *"I wouldn't be caught dead in your shoes for all the tea in China. Kiss, kiss—Elvis."*

How is that for an inscription?

Another thing—if you want to learn how to keep a secret, this book is a must-read.

Every morning, for my own inspiration, I open *A Walk on the Wild Side: How the Holy Father Dealt with his Love Child and Kept Other Dirty Secrets from* the Enquirer (I just love saying the entire title—it's *so, so* meaningful) and read the opening sentence that, to this day, still gives me goose bumps (*"Admit nothing, even if they have pictures."*), and I say to myself, *Cheryl, why hasn't this classic been turned into a major motion picture with Brad Pitt playing the Pope and Scarlett Johansson playing you?*

When I returned from the Greek Isles, my darling next-door townhouse neighbor (another UnloadYourPain.com blogger) was there to comfort me, and to point out that even though he watered my plants every day, the Dieffenbachia still had the white gooey stuff all over it. *Quanto tragico!* (How tragic!)

"Dr. Phil" (that's the secret name I call Dr. Phil) immediately sensed how deeply distressed I was and never left my side, except to buy lottery tickets. The man is a living goddess and has the patience of a saint.

That first tortuous night away from Elvis (Pope John II), Dr. Phil stayed up with me until dawn, stroking my upper thigh and crocheting. Only after we each made five-dozen pairs of baby socks that he so generously filled with discount coupons for his new vitamin line (I gave Tenderly the web site, so I know you all have it), did he finally leave so he could buy more lottery tickets.

Unfortunately, when I ran out of meds, things spiraled out of control. I know—I should have saved the Prozac for labor, but how can anyone get through pregnancy on just bar nuts and double lattes? *Sono di destra o sono di destra?* (Am I right, or am I right?)

In a last-ditch effort to take my mind off my pregnancy, I put together a weekend for my pal Tony Robbins (who not only shares my birthday, but my shoe size).

Have Group Sex with the Tallest Self-Help Guru and Make Money from Your Home Forever broke all records for Agoraphobia Conventions held via phone from the Marriott Marquee. The show resonated with the disturbed, and struck such a popular chord with these heretofore-disenfranchised phobics that "Big Foot" (that's the secret name I call Tony) figured he could guest host for Leno. *Ché tipo, huh?* (What a guy, huh?)

Even though I was headed home (with five signed copies—'Big Foot' always pays in books, which I donate to Suze Orman's Readers Club), when I passed Bergdorf's (I always pass Bergdorf's no matter where I'm going) I seriously considered going up to the fur department, wrapping myself in a white, full-length Natural Royal Crown

Russian Sable coat (yum, yum), and giving birth then and there.

Of course, we Ginsburg (*pronounced Du Pont*) Girls won't do anything that foolish, because that worked *only once* (with my baby Madison). Since then, Bergdorf's made me *persona non grata* (person not wanted). Out of spite, management gave those hateful women (they call themselves sales associates—*please* . . .) my photo and promised each a fifty-dollar gift certificate if they catch me walking out with a white, full-length Natural Royal Crown Russian Sable (yum, yum). But I already have one, by the divine right of "She whose placenta stain marks the lining, gets to keep it."

Sure, my girlfriends from the D.O.D. (a.k.a., Daughters of Darkness, a.k.a., Anne Rice Stake and Ale Investment Club) wanted to cover my theft by impaling Kate Moss at the entrance, but I didn't want to draw attention to the unbelievable sales in Chanel.

One piece of advice I learned the hard way: when you're going into labor, having an affair with your personal trainer, daughter's fiancé, teenage son's roommate, or best friend's husband is a no-no. (They will never come with you to the hospital.) *Qué bastardos!* (What bastards!)

Dear, darling *famille* (family), all is not lost! Thoughts are things! Out of crisis comes change. To get control is to give up control. Let me explain, *por favor* (please). If you believe you're guided (no—it's not the drugs talking), a guide will show up when you need them most and show you the path—show you that what *is best*.

That's why I wasn't at all surprised when I stared into my white chocolate mocha Frappuccino and saw the face of my darling daughter, Reagan, staring out from the foam mouthing the words, *Order me one.*

Reagan—my exquisitely scented candle that will always light up the darkest and most demented corners of my brain; the bell that will always chime the most harmonious one-note melodies; the little girl-child who Goddess, in her infinite wisdom, didn't want me to have—who will one day order her own Starbucks . . . (Although, it's been two heartbreaking years since I received that smeared and mangled postcard from Laos: MET A NICE WARLORD—LEARNING TO USE A MACHETE—COME VISIT ANYTIME . . .)

She always had a way with words, didn't she? Why it was written in block letters with that horrible smudgy purple lipstick when I gave her that fabulous Mont Blanc for her fifth birthday—, well, *wer zum Teufel weiß!* (Who the hell knows!)

As one of my court-appointed shrinks (who was sadly addicted to bad puns and the Food Channel) was fond of saying, "It was the yeast of times and it was the wurst of times." Can you imagine, the schmuck's a regular on *Good Morning America. Quel monde!* (What a world!)

Of course, you all know about Carter's record-breaking flight across the Atlantic on the back of a paper airplane, Jefferson's reincarnation, Lincoln's coronation, Kennedy's abdication, and of course, of course, Ford's sainthood. (Children born out of wedlock are so special, aren't they?)

I just can't wait for 5766 (*pronounced* 2005). *Fino all'anno prossimo!* (Until next year!)

Cousin Cheryl, A Very Proud Mom!

P.S. Remember . . . *El amor nos guardará juntos.* (Love will keep us together.)

SING IT LOUD! SING IT PROUD! SING IT NOW!

From: Bubbeh.E@Ourmail.us
Date: Saturday, January 1, 2005, 2:23 p.m.
To: Cheryl.G@Ourmail.us
Cc: US@Ourmail.us
Subject: Bubbeh Esther's (*pronounced* Granny Smith Apples) *Naches!*

Mein darling Cheryl,

I just want to say, once and for all, I get so much *naches* from seeing how far my wonderful family, the Family Ginsburg (*pronounced* Du Pont), have come since I squeezed out that tiny steerage porthole and leaped from the bowels of the Mayflower into the cold waters of Portsmouth Harbor; giving the one-finger salute to my jealous tormentors at the railing. *Mieskeits!*—excuse my French—ugly things, who mocked my mammoth magical gifts, Hebronically engineered and genetically bestowed upon me from She Who Brings Forth Life, the Great Baleboosteh Ginsburg (*pronounced* Eleanor of Aquitaine).

Mein darling Cheryl, what did She Who Brings Forth Life, the Great Baleboosteh Ginsburg (*pronounced* Eleanor of Aquitaine) always tell us? *In indiscussum vita est non vitalis. (The unexamined life is not worth living.)* How full of wisdom she was, for it was my miraculous mounds that got me into the rave party those wicked little red devils in loin cloths were throwing—not to mention not having, for one humiliating second, to stand in line with that teased-up bridge-and-tunnel crowd.

If I tell you never have so many squeezed, my *two,* I would not be lying, *mein* darling Cheryl—I would not be lying. Bless those randy little injuns, as they squeezed and squeezed my triple Ds until the poor darlings grew so weary they fell asleep on beds of half-eaten magic mushrooms, but not before signing over the rights to their war-paint formula—which I sold to Revlon for what was then the gross national product of Sweden—and gave me, *in writing,* the sole use of the word "Indian," and all its uses for as long as the buffalo roam, which, unfortunately, didn't last quite as long as I had hoped, but long enough to produce enough wampum to buy me the controlling interest in the Southern Pacific Rail Lines.

However, the deal I am the most proud of, and the one your ancestors pooh-poohed the loudest, was the one where I got ten percent of the gross—not *net,* mind you—of any Hollywood movie using a white man playing an Indian.

Mein darling Cheryl, I know, I know, I should not dwell on the negative, but I am still *a shtyfer mogn*—excuse my French—constipated thanks to your blockhead of an ancestor, Younger the Elder by Three Ginsburg (*pronounced* Du Pont), better known as *"That Putz,"* who gave up the rights to collect, *in* perpetuity, a percentage of every Indian-Head Penny minted. *It's only pennies,* he is said to have whimpered.

Only pennies! That Putz! Excuse my French—that putz!

I blame myself for leaving that pussy pilgrim power of attorney while I went off on my mystical surgical tour to the sacred mountains of Mount Cedar, where I placed myself under the total care of the Finest Doctor, who those darling little Hittites called, "The *Macher* with the Mechanical Head," or something that sounded roughly like that.

Mein darling Cheryl, of course he was *meshugeh ahf toit*—excuse my French—off his rocker, but he was the *only doctor—finest or fanatic*—who could safely replenish organ-specific cells by using the embryonic stem cells of an extremely vulnerable female elephant.

What a brave doctor the Finest Doctor was, risking the wrath of the Cedar branch of PETA, who would have had him immediately drawn and quartered, not to mention nickel-and-dimed, had they had more meat in their diet.

Nevertheless, he courageously went ahead and performed the procedure that has allowed me not only the ability to grab peanuts from trays three tables away, but the genetic juice to live large these last 404 years (give or take), making me the oldest living driver in Palm Beach—despite what old man Standish says, because even though he spells Myles with a *Y,* he was *not* on the Mayflower. Come on—ask him where Pocahontas shopped for whale blubber and watch his eyes glaze over. *Putz!*—excuse my French—*another putz!*

Oh, I hear some of you out there muttering, *She's getting a little off message and maybe a little hostile, no?* Well, my loving family—as it so happens, I'm due for my thousand-mile tune-up, and I'm entitled to my womanly emotions. After all, *biology happens!*

Before I forget—which, for obvious reasons, is only an expression—I want to tell you that the *tsaloochesnik* Cousin Bea called. *A finstere cholem auf dein kopf und auf dein hent und fiss!*—excuse my French: A nightmare on your head, hands, and feet, you crazy, jealous bedbug, for spreading nasty rumors about Monroe beating out her Jakie for a Nobel Peace Prize. Ironic, yes—since Jakie discovered nuclear fusion, which if he hadn't, who would need a damn *peace prize* in the first place.

Another thing, if anyone should be jealous about not receiving the Nobel Peace Prize, it should be me; after all, didn't I name it in the first place? That's right, it was yours truly, Bubbeh Esther (*pronounced* Granny Smith Apples) who was with *Mr. Alfred Nobel* before the inaugural event. You should have seen Al, so nervous because he had no idea what to name his precious prize. So, like the good person I am, I relieved his anxiety with *three* out-of-this-world *mekheyes*—excuse my French—out-of-this-world orgasmic delights, causing Al to scream, "You win the Nobel Piece-Of-Ass Prize!"

What a hullabaloo, I tell you. Those words set such a storm of misinterpretation initiated by those nosey-parker paparazzi hovering four stories below, who greeted the cries of joy with such cheering that Al baby strode onto the balcony to take a bow, naked as a jaybird, but proud as an uncircumcised peacock. *Putz!*—excuse my French—*yet another putz!*

As I was talking, Cousin Bea is *meshugeh ahf toi,* and she proved it once again when that spiteful loony-tune bedbug tried to choke the air out of my lungs. And why?—because I told her she should sue Sleepy's for stealing her line.

Let's call a spade a spade, shall we? If anyone should be called a "mattress professional," it should be that Angelina-like, lip-puckering impostor!

And, while I'm at the register in Gap! And, with steel wire from a Brillo Pad, yet!!!

For this, I risked life and drop-dead wonders when I jumped off the Mayflower? *Iz brent mir ahfen hartz!*—excuse my French—*I have such heartburn it feels like someone stuck a blowtorch down my throat!*

Whoa, Silver . . . whoa. Down, boy . . . Close your eyes. Take deep breaths through your nose. See and feel your center.

As *grande dame* of the Family Ginsburg (*pronounced* Du Pont), I must hold myself to a higher standard, but when one of *us* strays off the reservation with a piece of steel wool ... *Ich vel dir geben a khamalye!*—excuse my French—I'll give you such a smack, because this elephant's trunk was made for swinging!

To all *mein* Ginsburgs (*pronounced* Du Ponts) . . . and especially to you, *mein* darling Cheryl . . . *mein* pretty one . . . let us lift our D-cups and pray they continue to runneth over and to shout, Halleluiah! Halleluiah!

A Happy and Healthy New Year to you all!

I love you all as only a Bubbch *(pronounced* Granny) can!

Bubbeh Esther (*pronounced* Granny Smith Apples)

From: Lulu-LuCrawford@PleasureIsWhereYouFindIt.org
Date: Sunday, January 2, 2005, 5:23 p.m.
To: Bubbeh.E@Ourmail.us
Subject: Miss Lulu-Lu Crawford (*pronounced* the way it looks)

Dear Bubbeh Esther (*pronounced* Granny Smith Apples),

You people are, like, so cool. I mean, first off, no one in my family has ever been, like, married, so unless you can, like, google up bastards outta Alabama on the Internet, I got no idea who my kin is, 'cept a course, when I go back to Hogs Breath and look for anyone with, like, one green left eye and one brown right one. Anywho, I liked your emails 'cause you, like, don't take no dog's doo from no one. I mean—startin' off with just a pair of bodacious ta-tas in a strange land with all 'em red-face injuns 'round, wow, that is soooo, soooo brave, B. E. You don't mind me callin' you that, do ya, B. E.?

And look at you, at your age, still runnin' things—man alive, B. E., I should be, like, so lucky!

Anywho, I'll be cool with it if you don't have the time to, like, write me back 'cause of your busy schedule and all. But, like Oprah—I love that gal—said on her show, you get nothin' unless you ask for it—or, somethin' like that—soooo—I'm gonna come right and, like, ask you this one big favor.

Oh, how rude of me, not introducin' myself first. I should, like, you know, know better, bein' from, like, the South and all, don't you think? I'm Miss Lulu-Lu Crawford (*pronounced* the way it looks) from Hogs Breath, Alabama. And no, I don't want you to have a titty reduction and donate your excess to me, 'cause I like mine just fine, thank you very much. Oh, sure I get tired of men callin' me boy, or askin' me to, like, turn 'round so they can see my chest. Like, who the fuck do they think I am—that Linda Blair bitch from *The Exorcist?*

Gee, this is, like, harder than I figured, 'cause I never actually met anyone who could make my dreams come true. But see, after readin' your emails and all, and, like, hearin' about the Finest Doctor of yours, it was like Oprah—I love that gal—was comin' right out of the TV sayin', *you go, girl, you ask for what you want, 'cause this B. E. come cross your path for a reason*, or somethin' like that.

OK, OK—like, here it is . . . I want a mechanical head! There, I said it! Whew! Lemme settle down some and, like, maybe get me some of that Grey Goose, with a beer back, Bermuda is always puttin' down.

OK, B. E., I'm here again and do I feel right smart. Man, like, I been carryin' this burden around like a big old stone strapped to my back since the good Lord made the hedgehog and the dog guys to catch 'em.

So, B. E., 'cause I feel, like, so much better about myself as a person, I'd 'preciate it much if you would, like, contact the Finest Doctor of yours and, like, set up a meetin' with 'im. B. E., like, I was also thinkin', so it don't come outta a left field and by way of warmin' 'im up to me, you could, like, tell 'im how I'm his biggest fan, and how I tell all my clients what a great man he is. I mean, B. E.—like, look what he did for you! Thinkin' on it, B. E., I can't count the times when I was a little bitty thin' and, like, I'd be in the movies and coulda used a elephant's trunk to grab me some corn from someone two rows down 'cause I was, like, too broke to buy me some on my own.

B. E., I reckon I got to be truthful and tell you I don't know how much a mechanical head costs since the doc likely don't take Medicaid. Like, that's kinda shitty and unfair, don't you think? Not like I got health insurance in the first place, 'cause you don't get that kinda benefits doin' what I'm doin'.

See, B. E.—well—I'm, like, turnin' tricks with Bermuda up here on the fancy East Side of New York City, where I, like, get to meet men who wears ties and have teeth. I also gotta say your granddaughter makes a whole lot more dough-ray-me than me, 'cause, B. E., like, when she shows off the Ginsburg (*pronounced* Du Pont) bodacious tatas, guys' eyeballs explode and max out their credit cards in, like, a New York minute. You know what I mean?

Men are so cute, aren't they? Like when they suck on your headlights and pretend they're babies again . . . like whaddya mean *again*—they're always babies, don't you think?

Anywho, like I was sayin', Bermuda makes more money than me, but I do OK, what with my Southern accent an' all, and the funny little thing I do with my tongue on their balls.

Oh, B. E., before I forget! I have, like, letters I wrote, startin' way back when I was, like, an itsy-bitsy baby to, like, Santa and God, askin' for, you know, a mechanical head. See I just wanna make sure the Finest Doctor don't think I'm some Johnny-come-lately who, like, wants a mechanical head just to be cool.

I swear, I'm not one for keepin' up with the Joneses neither, but keepin' a jones up is, like, my job, if you get my meanin'—ha, ha, ha.

B. E., Bermuda, she's different from me 'cause she's gotta have the latest whatever, 'specially when it comes to, like, whips and chains. Goddamn B. E., that gal's got, like, a collection that'll make me just blush every time I use 'em.

Well, B. E., I gotta scoot now, but, like, I just wanna say, this is, like, *so meant to be*, which is what Oprah—I love that gal—always says, and what Bermuda said the night she picked me up at that sassy little bar in Chelsea. Otherwise, B. E., I wouldn't be in the life: sharin' her bed, reading her emails, gettin' the mechanical head I've dreamed about—in color, don't you know?

Anywho, B. E., like, if you want to email me at LuLu-LuCrawford@PleasureIsWhereYouFindIt.org, that'll be just grand.

Oh, B. E., like, one last thing. Tell the Finest Doctor as far as payment goes—I'm up for, like, some swappin', and it'll be more than spit, if you know what I mean?

Respectfully and HAPPY NEW YEAR, Y'ALL!

Miss Lulu-Lu Crawford (*pronounced* the way it looks)

From: Sylvia.G@Ourmail.us
Date: Sunday, January 2, 2005, 7:23 p.m.
To: Bermuda.G@Ourmail.us
Cc: US@Ourmail.us
Subject: Mother will take care of everything

Bermuda, baby, I have just been on the phone with dear, sweet Uncle Clayboy. He told me he is in the process of contacting the authorities, who, he assured me, can properly chase down that Lulu-Lu Crawford *person*—if that's her name, which I doubt, because Lulu-Lu is such a sweet name, and the *thing* who sent that ugly, full-of-lies email that Bubbeh Esther (*pronounced* Granny Smith Apples) forwarded, is certainly not that.

Thank Goddess for dear, sweet Uncle Clayboy, who has always been there for us, and who I consider the *man* in the family, while your father is *you know where.* Dr. Peck says I should face things as they are, which, as you know, *is never what they seem*, especially when you're highly medicated. If I choose to believe your father is off on a *spiritual journey* and not on the lam in East Asia—the reason being the avoidance of extradition back here to the good old US of A, where he most certainly would face that trumped-up smuggling *thing* some gung-ho DA wants to make his bones on—well then, that's my business, don't you think?

I need a ciggie and a pee, but listen, baby: if I don't come back, it was because I had a stroke and *not* because I fell asleep with a cigarette in my hand again—a life-altering experience that taught me to never let my homeowner's insurance lapse. Another nice thing that came out of it: I no longer require a cleaning person who can't speak a word of English, because there's nothing to dust. Unfortunately, the echo can drive you crazy, especially when I hear those voices I told you about. OK, I'm off!

I'm back!

And not a single singe mark to be seen. Where was I? OK, I've got it! As I'm sure I've acknowledged, I have known Uncle Clayboy for roughly my entire adult life. I was seventeen when Caroline Peck—*oh my Goddess, oh my Goddess*, I wonder if she's related to my shrink? Bermuda, would you be a dear and remind me to ask him?

Wouldn't that be something? Six degrees of separation, isn't that what they say? Sometimes, I think it's six degrees of *desperation* when you look at my wrinkles.

Oh, well, before I ask the doorman to come up for a pity party and some Gran Patrón Platinum I had him stash in his locker, let me continue. Golly Jeez baby, I hope I'm not interrupting your studies. If so, turn off your computer and do your schoolwork.

Now, what I'm about to narrate, you must keep hush-hush, because I'm supposed to notify ATF if Daddy tries to contact me. (Well—*he has*, and wants me to remind you to separate the bills stained with the dye pack from those in blood before you pay your tuition bill.) Baby, you know, of course, how very proud I am you're back in school after that hit-and-run *thing* you were so, *so* falsely accused of causing. By Goddess, you did your time, not like some weak sons of bitches who run and hide in East Asia. By the way, are you still getting death threats from the brother of the girl you were *accused* of running over? I use the word *accused* because I still believe you're innocent. Sure, you confessed, but I know you did that to get a TV in your cell. Where was I? Oh right, meeting Uncle Clayboy. I was seventeen when Caroline Peck asked me to go on a blind double-date with her. She called our dates *two gorgeous hunks,* and were they ever. My Goddess, heaven help me if I didn't nearly faint when they walked in. Two blond Greek gods, that's what they were, in their blue blazers, white pants, and white bucks. Oh yes, and you know what else I remember? They both had on pink *Lacoste polo shirts and matching, pink socks.* Oh, so dashing! They reminded me of Van Johnson, who, as it turned out, they knew, and who came to our wedding. Poor Uncle Clayboy (Newport Road Island Yacht Club was his full name, but Clayboy was his pet name)—he was so brave the day of our wedding, even though he'd just lost this super hush-hush secret love of his and was so, *so* broken-hearted. Your father tried to cheer him up, even inviting him to join us on our honeymoon, but nothing would console the poor fellow. Little did I know *how* broken-hearted he *really* was, until we got the telegram notifying us that Uncle Clayboy had *slit his wrists.* Why, he simply didn't take barbiturates like your grandmother always did and spare us the gore is beyond me. Naturally, we returned immediately—even though it was only our second day in Bermuda. Your father said, so romantically, that our whole life would be a honeymoon. Well—that turned out to be a bag of empty promises, didn't it? Oh, baby, if I had known then what I know now, I would have run away with Delroy (*pronounced* John Rolfe), the hotel barman with those love-pool eyes and honeyed English accent. Believe you me when I say he couldn't take his eyes off of us while we were sunbathing. I never confessed this, but I once saw him in back of a cabana accepting money from your father after they shared a tearful embrace that lasted a little too long for my taste. I'm certain the money was to keep him from kidnapping me. I was *so young, so impressionable.* (I must find those honeymoon photos. I really, *really* looked good.) How could I say no to your father when he pleaded with me to return with him to New York? *After all,* he sobbed, *in times of travail we must embrace those who most need our help.* I had never seen a man cry before that, and trust me, nobody could shed a tear like your father. You can bet I'll never fall for that crock of crocodiles again. I need a drinkie and another ciggie.

I'm back, baby.

Are you OK? If this is too difficult for you, you just shut down your computer and go buy yourself a Judith Leiber bag. Oh, in case you're wondering, I blew out the black candles that that darling Haitian woman, Angelique d'Morte, sent me. Not that it matters—there's nothing here except the Hammacher Schlemmer porch chair and matching Louis Vuitton steamer trunks—and I had *them* fireproofed. You remember Angelique? Turn Your Husbands into Zombies chat room? Aunt Cheryl did the IPO.

Damn it, where was I? Sometimes, I think I've lost it. You ever get that feeling? Of course you don't. You're perfect, aren't you, baby?

OK—I got it! Your father and I rushed back to New York. I didn't learn all the details right away, but over the next twenty years I pieced it all together. Newport Road Island Yacht Club, soon to be known as Clayboy, came to New York to study Jazzercise, and immediately met your father, who was already a franchisee. Book 'em, Dano (the male progenies of the Family Ginsburg (*pronounced* Carnegie-Mellon) branch always had dashing and virile names, and your father, no exception—I won't fall for that one anymore, either), was also a water sign, having been raised in Hawaii at the Pearl Harbor Yacht Club. Before you start accusing me of getting what I deserved for marrying inside my own gene marina, when I met your father the IRS had just confiscated our boat and we no longer docked at the 79th Street Boat Basin. As I was saying, besides both being water boys, Uncle Clayboy and your father had a lot of moves in common, so they became roommates. First, they lived in a tiny walk-up on Jane Street, then, when I came on the scene, a charming little apartment on Gay Street—*don't even go there*! Uncle Clayboy and your father were inseparable, so the three of us did everything together. If only I had seen *Jules and Jim!*

Then, there were those scandalous Cole Porter parties. "In olden days a glimpse of stocking was looked on as something shocking but now, God knows, anything goes!"

You could have hit me over the head with a copy of *Redbook* as they fed me more martinis than Betty Bacall had during her lifetime with Bogie. That's why it never bothered me when, on the last Friday of every month ending in ER, your brothers celebrated Lobsterfest by dressing up as Iris Adrian. No—it wasn't because it was then that I started self-medicating in a serious way. You probably don't remember because that was your anorexia period. Now that I think about it, you *must* remember, because wasn't that when you got your Super 8 camera? My Goddess, it *was you* with the camera! I have to tell Dr. Peck, because during our last hypnosis session, I wasn't sure if the cause of my self-mutilation was real or imaginary. I need another ciggie.

OK, back again!

You know, baby, it's a damn shame your teachers didn't screen it. Don't they know anything about publicity over at Tisch? Nowadays, what with all the reality shows, what's the big deal about hiding cameras in a Boy Scout tent, or the rectory where your brother got dressed (undressed is more like it), or that disgusting roach motel near the Brooklyn Navy Yard? Baby, don't you agree, it was on the waterfront where you so poignantly illustrated the Italian neo-realist influence of De Sica—as well as your expert use of a dolly in the gang-rape scene. I see a little Fassbinder in the whipping sequences, don't you? Well, the DA wasn't afraid to show your film to the grand jury, was he? I think he loved the action sequences best, because he picked out that poetically *Private Ryanesque* scene of your father, knee-deep in surf, hauling in those huge crates to show them. If memory serves, the seaplane that dropped the crates belonged to Billy Joel's pool man. My Goddess, you were right there on top of the action, weren't you, baby? Tracking the operation right onto the beach, where your father—and believe me, no one was more surprised than I, except maybe the members of the jury—broke open the crates, raised that machine gun high over his head like Marlon did in *Viva Zapata*, and then—*Wham, bam, thank you, ma'am*—you jumped-cut from a close-up of his eyes to a medium-wide, revealing Daddy, in manacles, outside the Men's House of Detention. Wow—what *cinema verité!* I still don't see how you got out of the way when your father tried to smash your camera with a crowbar. Too bad you weren't as lucky when some of his pals came by and kneecapped you with a lead pipe. *But, you survived, didn't you?* And, baby, you started a new career—giving up filmmaking for beauty school, which is so, *so* smart, because now you don't have candy distributors standing in the way of showing off your creativity. Life is all about choices, the *right* choices. You know that. That's why I know in my heart of hearts that what that ugly Lulu-Lu thing said about meeting you *in that you-know-what kind of a bar* can't be true. You're well endowed with the best we Family Ginsburg (*pronounced* Du Pont) Girls have, and best of all, you know who your daddy is, don't you? Why else would you speak with a honeyed English accent, and each night, as I do, sing in delirium—"Bermuda, Bermuda, Bermuda shorts, Bermuda, Bermuda, Bermuda shorts—hey baby, hey-yay dig them shorts . . ."

   Love,

   Sylvia, your mother

   P.S. I need a ciggie and pee . . .

From: Bermuda.G@Ourmail.us
Date: Sunday, January 2, 2005, 9:00 p.m.
To: Sylvia.G@Ourmail.us
Cc: US@Ourmail.us
Subject: Bermuda's not a child anymore

Oh, Mama, quit your worrying and stop being influenced by such foolishness. You're a Ginsburg (*pronounced* Du Pont) Girl, and made of sterner stuff. So, take a few deep breaths, lean back in your porch chair, and think back to those holiday times when I was simply an innocent little girl.

Remember how I loved to get the Family Ginsburg (*pronounced* Du Pont) Holiday Newsletters? There wasn't an Internet back then, so, just before Christmas, they'd begin to come by regular mail. I see it all so vividly. I'm sitting watching the burning log on TV, thinking how lucky we are, living in the Village instead of Rego Park, where you couldn't find an all-night adult video store if your life depended on it.

Oh, Mama, what a treat it was to climb up on your knee as you sat serenely in front of the burning log (before your pyro days) and to point my Kodak Super 8 across the room as Uncle Clayboy and Daddy did their Jazzercise routine to "Let's Fall In Love," then to pan over to the brothers Hill and Dale, dressed up in their Iris Adrian outfits, hugging and kissing their lobsters the way only brothers do when dressed up as Hollywood hookers.

You can't imagine the impression those newsletters made on an undeveloped girl of five, especially the Holiday Gift Issue, where I fantasized about having a pair of those legendary D-cups that would enable me to finally get expensive jewelry from older men.

Then, three winters later, it came to pass, and my brothers did a Passion play to commemorate their outing, and all the wonderful support garments that came with my new gifts (that they could borrow, in the ER months, of course).

Even though it meant I couldn't go topless unless I got nipple rings, it was as if Robyn Bird came to Grover's Corners and filled my heart with prurient delights. Not that looking out onto Christopher Street wasn't special, but I could do that anytime. No, Mama, this was something transformative, because now, not only could I deeply inhale the intoxicating aroma of our traditional racy ricotta cheesecake, but like you, was now able to bend over and gently rub my perky peaks up against the robust chocolate boys that so gloriously decorated the rim of the cake.

I remember running up to my room, ripping off my chocolate-smeared Erotic Bakery T-shirt and staring wide-eyed at my tiny pink nipples that seemed to take on a life of their own as I tweaked and tweaked them. I don't recall if it was the memory of those chocolate boys in their compromising positions that made me moisten my fingers and rub the saliva over those nascent nubs and ask myself, *Was I really related to Sammy Davis Jr?* I know, *I know,* what a childish, silly thing! As if Sammy was the Pied Piper, and you simply followed his seductive tune to his bedroom suite in Vegas.

Now—Wilt Chamberlain—I can see *him* being my father. I read his book, and he was always bragging about how many pairs of "Bermuda shorts" he had. Why, sometimes, he changed "shorts" five, six times a day. Don't deny it, Mama, you loved going to those Knicks-Philly games at the Garden.

Oh, don't freak out! Since the moment I acquired my first set of Crayolas I recognized my skin tone was two shades darker than anyone else in the family.

I left you in the sun too long . . .

That worked until I learned to speak and in my honeyed English accent called the cop who stood outside the school a "Bobby." Of course, I heard you tell my teachers it was because—oh, I love this one—"*During my pregnancy I just loved watching Upstairs, Downstairs.*"

Finally, and one I just couldn't wrap my brain around until I had three Bermuda Rum Swizzles, there's that tune I kept hearing in my head—"Bermuda, Bermuda, Bermuda shorts, Bermuda, Bermuda,

Bermuda shorts—hey baby, hey-yay dig them shorts . . ."

How did you put it? *"A tragic result psychosomatically induced by the Royal Caribbean brochures you ate when you were two months old."*

Come on—don't go breaking my heart with any more guilt trips. Didn't that duck-back-into-the-alley Haitian Hex Lady make you forget about hotel bar men when you drank the blood of a chicken she had you sacrifice on your terrace? (By the way, I think that was so, *so* courageous—I mean, who actually uses their terrace in Manhattan?)

Anywho, I am getting another one of my nosebleeds. You said I would outgrow them—but then, nothing you ever told me was the truth, was it

Nowadays, the only truth I get is when I service my Bentley, and Jerry (*pronounced* Lord Sherwood Forest) tells me I'm more curvaceous than a Continental GT. (Incidentally, he likes it straight up, with the occasional spanking.)

I'm going to open a pint of Healthy Choice Brownie Bliss, pour in some rum, nuke the bad boy for a sec, pop in a flexible straw, and re-read a couple of Holiday Newsletters. I know, *I know,* I'll lean back, so I do not bleed all over the papers.

To quote She Who Brings Forth Life, the Great Baleboosteh Ginsburg's (*pronounced* Eleanor of Aquitaine's) famous holiday cheer—"*Biistis, dulces caricae.*" (You're finished, sweet figs . . .)

Love ya,
Bermuda

From: Laverne.G@Ourmail.us
Date: Monday, January 3, 2005, 9:00 a.m.
To: US@Ourmail.us
Subject: News and New Year's Greetings from Cousin Laverne

Happy New Year, all!

Well, here's news from the down-under branch of the Family Ginsburg (*pronounced* Du Pont) Clan. No, we didn't move to Australia—we've just been buried under so much shit, piss, and corruption we've got to look down to look up. I'm feeling so overwhelmed by misery, it's six to five I stab myself before I finish this email. Listen to me, *six to five I stab myself*. What do I know about odds? If I knew something about gambling, I wouldn't be spending a deuce a week on Scratch and Lose. I tried to quit, but when they put the game on the sides of the Dunkin' Donuts coffee cups, I was dead meat.

Speaking of dead meat, Jack's dead. You guessed it. Marie finally found a way to kill him and still get the insurance money on the trailer. It's rough losing a brother, even if he did try to take my hubby away from me.

It's going on eighty-five days now that Willie's barricaded himself in his room with only a case of Dr. Pepper and two boxes of assorted Krispy Kremes. As far as the hostages go, he released five, kept one, and one disappeared on him. I don't know why the papers are making fun of Willie for that. Tiny Evan lost so much weight during the first forty days, how could Willie be expected to notice him sliding under the doorjamb? They got the little fella in something like a bell jar up at the local hospital. Doc Martens says he's got a great chance he can live in a shoe, so things will turn out okey-dokey.

Clara Barton has turned into a real demon child and is making Willie's life a living hell. She's won every game of Chutes and Ladders, and to my mind, only making the negotiations for her release that much harder, because anyone who knows Willie for more than ten seconds knows he's not a good loser.

Did you watch Larry last night? Didn't he have on such cute

suspenders? Well, if you watched, you saw how his guest, our own Pastor Lawyer, made the case, right? I mean—it's crystal clear that Willie's classmates violated the school board's directive against teaching the theory of Unintelligent Design when they sent away for the DVD of the Beau Bridges-Jessica Lang 1976 remake of *King Kong*. My William had no choice but to kidnap the entire class and lock them in his room until they confessed all science is fiction, then sign a blood oath swearing they were each brought to Earth by the stork. The fact that *thirteen* out of fifteen signed proved his point, don't you think?

Well, at least I don't have to worry about Willie talking to some damn pervert, because the first thing the Feds did when they surrounded the house was cut off his Internet. I just couldn't handle seeing another one of my kids' faces on a milk carton because our government can't protect them from being lured to some out-of-state motel by a man dressed as a koala bear. Kids are so vulnerable nowadays, don't you think?

Sure, it's a damn shame he can't go to his chat room. Who'd have imagined a site called DarwinAintYourDaddy.com would draw so many pistol-packing friendlies? Not me, I'll tell you.

Speaking of good things coming outta bad—Conrad won the election for Student Class President. Yes, he did! Isn't that terrific!

Some—and I ain't naming names—would have you believe what really put my boy in the president's seat was him leading the search party. OK, Connie was front and center, but he didn't pay Glenn Beck and his camera crew to come with him. Heck, it was the night before the election and, take it from me, Connie would have rather been at home practicing his acceptance speech.

You know, this isn't anything new. Every year, it's the same thing. If it's not someone he's running against, it's someone trying out for the same team. It doesn't matter. Without so much as a hello or how-you-do, Conrad goes right into the woods after them missing kids. Now, don't you tell me it's his fault for not finding anyone. You bury a body in those woods, well, you know how fast a bear can eat a kid, don't you?

Hilda's dead, too. Yep, you guessed it: Murray finally figured a way of killing Mommy. I guess blowing up trailers and outsmarting insurance companies just runs in the family.

Here's some breaking news: everyone's been allowed back over by where Uncle Morty lives. Of course, Uncle Morty never left, so I'm sure the gas got him. I mean, all you have to do is look out his window and you can just about touch the spot where the train flipped over. If you count the fact that Uncle Morty never misses "Jerry Springer," and reckon he always keeps his windows open even if it's fifty below, you know he's a goner.

Hold on—I know what you're thinking, and you're wrong! Just because it's a known fact Daddy tried to kill Uncle Morty with a cordless power saw after catching his brother with Mommy in the men's room over at Home Depot don't prove Daddy intended for that train to catch fire after it rolled down the embankment.

If I have to blame anyone for half the population's being dead, it's the Railroad, 'cause they ought to have known better than to be sending trains filled with dangerous chemicals roaring through towns where people like to kill their spouses by tying 'em to the railroad tracks. Come on, like, what does the goddamn Railroad need to see—a billboard with the running totals that, counting Mommy, is up to ten dead for the year?

Face it, if we had bridges 'round here you'd see people dumping family over the side, but since we don't—you make do with what you have.

Radio says there's still a poison cloud hanging over town that could be moving our way, depending upon whether or not a wind kicks up. Personally, I think the cloud thing is just a government plot to get William to release Clara, and then come out and surrender. I know for a fact that Willie's not going to fall for that FBI bull. Didn't he toss out that note saying he just received a message from Goddess saying he should ask for more assorted Krispy Kremes? Why would Goddess do that, if she were fixing to poison us?

Speaking of Goddess herself, Jerry's still paralyzed from whatever's in the drinking water. My poor ole hubby, he just can't catch a break, can he? Pastor Lawyer got someone from the church, Sister Lawyer's her name, working up a class action lawsuit that oughta make things right.

Do you know there are nearly two hundred cases like Jerry's? That's a fact. See, the explosion up at the copper mine caused the toxic mudslide that ran into the wells that supply the entire town's drinking water.

I guess we should be thankful for the blessings we do receive, because if Jerry wasn't paralyzed, he'd been sitting right up next to Morty on the couch watching "Jerry Springer" instead of at home on his hospital bed.

Of course, if the Feds are right about the poison cloud, he'll be a goner anyway. I don't see his Bubbeh Marge (*pronounced* Grandma Moses) taking the time to push that bed out into the street, load it onto the back of their pickup, and get the hell out of Dodge. First off, she don't have a pickup, and second, I heard the lawsuit's worth more if he's dead. But listen, I'm the last one to be spreading rumors—you know that, right?

Since the copper mine closed tighter than a flea's ass over a rain barrel, the unemployment rate is nearly 110 percent, counting kids that'll be born this month. Come mid-February the only food left will be whatever pets you got, which ain't but a handful, judging by the numbers hitching train rides out of town. Too bad the reporters from *Boys' Life* don't do anything but tie knots, because I hear they're big spenders; but come sundown, they're on a helicopter to Las Cruces just like the rest of the media.

Speaking of going outta town—you can live in a town all your life and still not know that, on average, there's an alien abduction every week. Well, the *Boys' Life* article is going to change all that. We just put up signs leading into town saying, THE ALIEN ABDUCTION CAPITAL OF THE WORLD. That's a fact.

Judith Ann's already made a list of the people she doesn't see anymore. Firstborn Ginsburgs (*pronounced* Du Ponts) are so clever, don't you think? Connie's got his own list. I only hope my name's not on it, 'cause who wants to be eaten by a bear?

Oh, did I mention, Connie and Judith Ann are writing a movie treatment for a video game called *Abduct Someone Today.* Our dear Pastor Lawyer's brother, Pastor Agent Hollywood, thinks the kids have a good shot at a development deal.

Willie's really the one who thinks outside the Xbox, but until he actually gets out of his own box, he's resident genius—*trapped.*

I know what you're thinking. Besides blowing up trailers, we're good at kidnapping, but Judith Ann always said it was aliens who took those kids into the woods and not her brother Connie or anyone else in our family. She backs that up by saying that despite the fact Connie's palms still bleed every December 25th, he doesn't realize these missing kids were the same ones that nailed him to the cross, as part of the kindergarten Christmas Passion play—what, fifteen years ago?—and therefore, has no motive.

Everybody says Judith Ann looks like me, but then, when I look at Willie, I see Conrad. Of course, everybody thinks Connie is my brother instead of my son. My brother, my son, my brother—when I told Judith Ann, she said the aliens aren't interested in a remake of *Chinatown,* unless Jack contacts them via Shirley MacLaine and promises to invite them to sit courtside with him at Lakers games.

I received the money Uncle Jules sent, so after this kidnapping situation gets resolved, he wants us all to come live with him in Soho and help him design a new line of jewelry for his hip-hoppers.

Now—I'll be the first to admit I know zip about bling-bling except that Judith Ann says aliens won't abduct anyone wearing it. I told Uncle Jules that, but Uncle Jules said space invaders weren't his target market, but when they are, he's confident I could design something they would dig. He went on to say the jewelry I produced for the Sabrina Fair Road Kill Festival showed a real flare for the gaudy. I think what really got him and everyone at my trailer park excited was my mixing of homegrown materials. I don't mean to bang my own drum, but collage *is my* collateral, so it was only natural that I was the first one to conceive of the organic connection between chicken feathers, copper sludge, and Dr Pepper bottle caps.

Unfortunately, I have to say *no* to Uncle Jules. (Sorry, Uncle Jules!!!) It's not that I don't want to get away from here after the kidnapping situation is favorably resolved, (because who wants to get death threats the rest of your life?); and it's not that I wouldn't want to further my artistic career and branch out into hip-hop jewelry, (because Uncle Jules, as you predict, aliens may dig it)—but, and this is a *mighty big but*—I got too many relatives in the neighborhood need burying, and a few more need killing. So, until that day I've got to stay clear of the turpentine and keep sharp objects away from my eyes.

A healthy and a happy . . .

My everlasting love,

Cousin Laverne

From: TenderlyThroughMySupremeBanker@MySupremeBanker.him
Date: Monday, January 3, 2005, 9:00 a.m.
To: US@Ourmail.us
Subject: Hello and Happy Holidays to my loving family!

To my dear, wonderful family,

May My Supreme Banker, known by many names and different faces, bring you all love, peace, and harmony, and remind you—we are all connected by credit card debt.

Before I forget, the web site for the flu medicine is PharmaKarma.com/getsome.htm.

They are wonderful and kindly folk who are fluent in all foreign tongues, so they *will understand it when you call them bitch-bastards*. They accept all credit cards and are always running specials. There is also free shipping for orders of $50.00 and up, plus coupons for vitamins, herbal creams, and some fabulous laxatives. *Wowee!*

I should let you know there's been a run on cholera and diphtheria meds, so act now. Remember, you snooze, you lose, and the headstones prove it.

I've got extra supplies of both, so contact me should you have an emergency. In addition, I have a good supply of malaria pills you must take immediately. Why? Well—listen to this. Yesterday, I dropped off my next-door neighbor's three daughters at the local Indian movie theater (they were going to see *Bend It Like Beckham*). It's about a teenaged Indian girl who plays soccer in England. Maybe you saw the English version?

So, what happened? Out front, ushers were handing out malaria pills and soft-drink coupons. Thanks to My Supreme Banker, I already had all my shots for the subcontinent, but foolishly didn't think I needed malaria pills in Connecticut until spring, the usual time I take them.

You know what My Supreme Banker always says: "There's no such thing as coincidence in soccer." Well, this is a perfect example!

So, as soon as I could, I stopped the Humvee and thoroughly washed my hands two times with Boric Acid soap (I always have my Boric with me, and you should, too). Then, I thoroughly wiped down the interior (the girls had their balls with them so they could kick'em up and down the aisles when someone scored a goal on screen). Bless My Supreme Banker for extending his line of credit to Home Depot's Farm Equipment Car Wash on Route 100. They're the only ones near me with tracks wide enough for the M997. I put the big gal through three times (interior steam cleaning was only ten dollars extra), and while that was happening, used my Blackberry to go online to the CDC web site.

Dear Family Ginsburg (*pronounced* Du Pont), because I know there is no such thing as coincidence in soccer, I recognized these balls had come into my life for a reason—and guess what, right there at the top of the CDC web site was proof that there is a link between malaria and unwashed soccer balls.

Does My Supreme Banker know how to bring it on, or what?

I said a silent prayer to My Supreme Banker, and without delay emailed PharmaKarma.com. By this morning, I had my malaria pills!

Don't you just love the digital world, even though it's infested with worms and viruses?

(FYI— when you go to PharmaKarma.com, there's a wonderful review of the M997 by their Vehicle Swami.) As you know, I have the ambulance version, but the M997 can be outfitted in a number of ways. I quote, "The HMMWV (High-Mobility Multipurpose Wheeled Vehicle) is a light, highly mobile, diesel-powered, four-wheel-drive vehicle equipped with an automatic transmission. Based on the M998 chassis, using common components and kits, the HMMWV can be configured to become a troop carrier, armament carrier, S250 shelter carrier, ambulance [that's the one I have], TOW missile carrier, and a Scout vehicle."

Because these are grey-market babies, I had to go to Estonia to pick it up—so make sure you have your passports in order.

By the way, I saw *Bend It Like Beckham* last night and recommend it highly. I do want to make it clear that even though you're fully protected, if an unwashed soccer ball goes sailing into the seats, don't try to catch it.

Tonight I'm off to see *Kung Fu Hustle,* and again, thanks to My Supreme Banker, I'm so, *so* protected from anything I see on the screen, or that may be stuck to my shoes.

Another alert! Be watchful of chocolates out of Peru. Today, the CDC warned that certain confectionary delights could cause quite a different "high," as well as land you in jail. Apparently, someone wasn't using their thesaurus and mistook *coca* for *cacao*.

Speaking of chocolates, remember when we were kids, and Bubbeh Esther (*pronounced* Granny Smith Apples) brought us candy, and even though someone else opened the box, and they weren't individually wrapped, we'd eat them anyway? The chances we took! It's amazing we survived, isn't it?

Now where did she buy them? Blooms? No, that wasn't it. Oh, this is going to kill me! I'm going to take an extra dose of fish oil, two baby aspirins, do the *Times* crossword, teach myself Mandarin, and by tonight grow enough new brain cells to remember.

I keep telling you how great the CDC web site is—*and it is!* That's why every Ginsburg (*pronounced* Du Pont) should go there at least once an hour to discover what new infections and diseases are going around. Why—just a few minutes ago they posted breaking news about almonds, and that Wagner ate handfuls while composing *Götterdämmerung ,* and how eating them could help you stay awake while watching it.

(FYI—Don't eat any fruit or vegetables unless you wash off them with a mixture of raw lemons and Wild Turkey.)

A neighbor of mine just came down with lupus, and her personal shopper told her it's West African Lemur Season, and it's going around. The source—fake designer bags. Over the fence gossip backs this up as I heard that several of my neighbors are hooked on the hot fudge sundaes at Serendipity's, and because there's always a long wait, end up buying at least one bogus bag each from vendors parked in front.

Of course, when I heard this, I didn't tell them, but I bet a blood test would reveal they're all living on borrowed time. (FYI—if you know someone who's bragged about getting a Birkin for $50.00, make sure the house is burned to the ground before you put a bid on the property.)

Another thing to watch out for is any person who received a West African Lemur from FedEx in the last year. That could be anyone, but I'd look for women with a matching coat, bag, and shoes who is buying unusual amounts of chop meat and chives, which, as we know from Julia Child's wonderful cookbook, *Cooking Animals the French Way,* is the West African Lemur's favorite snack food. Once you spot a carrier, call Homeland Security. Of course, you still have to keep a vigil on the local pet stores.

Speaking of pets, did you happen to catch the segment on "60 Minutes" about people who dump alligators into local creeks simply because these undernourished creatures ate a family member? Wasn't that woman who had opened a shelter for these unwanted man-eaters such a wonderful inspiration to us all! And who would have thought that alligators loved Jacuzzis?

(FYI—what you won't hear on "60 Minutes," but you will hear on "Lou Dobbs" is about the fatal diseases you'll get from creatures that swim, crawl, or fly across our unguarded borders every single day. The Ancients knew how dangerous they were, and that's why they made virgin sacrifices so popular. Pestilence coming across our unguarded boarders is a serious subject. You should join me in writing the CDC and asking them to post a list of these creatures and the kinds of diseases they spawn. The Minute Men are doing a great job to keep these creatures out, but until they can get their Star Wars missile guidance system fully armed, they have to rely on automatic weapons, land mines, and hand-to-hand combat; and we all know that alone won't keep this country safe.

Trust me on this one, once you start seeing stories on the Six O'clock news about pestilence coming across our borders, we won't have much more time to live.)

Another of the reasons I'm taking up Mandarin is that China is home to the deadliest diseases of the last century. Once I learn the language, I intend to join the Chinese branch of WebMD, where like-minded people share insights and spread rumors.

Don't worry, as soon as I know, you'll know. (FYI—if you haven't already, send me your cell phone numbers so I can reach you when you're away from the computer.)

Whatever you do, don't buy any live creatures at Walmart. All their exotics are raised on chicken farms. In fact, I don't buy anything at Walmart for that very reason. Let's face it—one person with the Avian flu puts together a Hot Wheels, next thing you know every kid in America doesn't want to go to school.

(FYI the Avian Flu and chicken nuggets—the deep-fried crust will not protect you. *I repeat—the deep-fried crust will not protect you!*)

Live creatures from Home Depot scare me, too, but I was talking with one of the guys who work there, and on the QT and very hush-hush, he assured me everything was raised in Kansas. He said they put foreign labels on their stuff just to make customers think they couldn't get it cheaper anywhere else.

One thing I will not buy at Home Depot is plastic fish-tank plants. I don't care what they say—I know what made-in-America plastic tastes like!

Back-tracking a bit, don't be embarrassed to put on your cloth face masks. I know, at first it's hard to handle the looks, especially from people at work. Most companies strictly forbid it, unless you get a note from your doctor saying you've got a respiratory illness. Of course, that'll create issues, and you'll get the boot because no employer wants the Black Death hanging around the water cooler—that's been my experience.

Don't cry for me, Argentina—which reminds me, stay away from any and all beef products, because Mad Cow Disease is here—plain and simple.

I believe My Supreme Banker put me here on Earth to be his messenger, so please heed my warnings.

Happy and most importantly, a *healthy* New Year!

Love from My Supreme Banker Through Cousin, Tenderly

P.S. If anyone is planning to marry a Canadian, let me know. N95 masks are essential, and because someone's always ripping one off your face you'll need a constant supply. I have a list of the usual suspects, but prices are going through the roof.

From: SisterChanelSize8@SistersOfTheRuinedFeet.com
Date: Monday, January 3, 2005, 11:00 a.m.
To: US@Ourmail.us
Subject: Time to set the record straight!

(FYI, THIS EMAIL WAS WRITTEN WITHOUT TAKING A BREATH! FOR BEST READING RESULTS I SUGGEST YOU DO THE SAME.)

I was shaken and appalled by Bubbeh Esther's (*pronounced* Granny Smith Apples's) virulent and unwarranted attacks upon my person. To even suggest that I would attempt to garrote someone with a Brillo Pad wire while standing on the checkout line at the Gap because someone called me a woman of questionable morals is almost laughable, were it not so pathetically grotesque. I simply ask you to remember who in this family has all their clothes custom-made in Paris and would not be caught dead in a dry-goods establishment named after the space between someone's front teeth. Furthermore, to accuse me of posing as Angelina Jolie and going around *puckering my lips* for the expressed purpose of giving the aging Amish a thrill is not only patently false, but also grossly insulting to my true calling. I only ask you to spot-check your memories, and recall who sucked the chrome off of Don Miguel Gomez-Ginsburg's (*pronounced* Gomez-Du Pont's) Chevy pickup (earning her/me the reputation as the greatest "mouth flutist" of my generation) to realize Angelina could learn a thing or more from me. If you want to discover the origins of this monstrous mendacity, look no further than the person who was Don Miguel Gomez-Ginsburg's wife (*pronounced* Gomez-Du Pont) when I went *chrome*—none other than our mammoth matriarch, Bubbeh Esther (*pronounced* Granny Smith Apples). The fact that I am, and always will remain, a lady prevents me from even addressing these baseless insults so jealously hurled upon me by this remorseless elephantine. Perhaps, if Mater had been able to hold onto husband number twelve (and third cousin twice removed) she would not be so vindictive, but even with her trunk wrapped around his member (fondly remembered by all who knew it as the Sephardic Sausage), he slipped from her grasp and came to me.

Normally, all I would say is, Shame, *shame* on her—but I have recently come upon a scientific study that details the horrible side effects accompanying the treatments Bubbeh Esther (*pronounced* Granny Smith Apples) underwent at the hands of the antichrist. Sister Manolo Size 6, one of my sister-sisters at the sacred retreat of the Sisters of the Ruined Feet Sanctuary, secretly stole this pioneering work from the Finest Doctor's laboratory. After months of painstakingly translating the ancient Aramaic text into html (a labor of love causing three of us to go temporarily blind), we now have incontrovertible evidence that those revolutionary stem cell transplants, while extending life to lengths even Methuselah would envy, have dire fashion consequences. No, not the genetic screw-up that created Mater's monthly mammoth proboscises that thankfully never appeared in our transplants, but something much more sinister—something the Sisters of the Ruined Feet Sanctuary have suspected all along. If you may recall, it was the blessed soul Sole Sister Susan Bennis Size 6, the spiritual heeler who founded our order, who forecast this real-life health risk in her 1924 letter to *Better Homes and Gardens* entitled "Estrogen or Manolos: The Real Reason Why High Heels Made Me a Cripple." The fact that it was rejected because they never read the works of Philip K. Dick is why I refuse to open a copy, even though the personals are really hot.

I have to go to afternoon vespers now, but you can be sure that even though I have taken a vow of silence, *I will be heard*.

May Goddess bless you and make your arches strong in this New Year,

Sister Chanel Size 8, Formerly Known as the Aunt Named Bea

P.S. If you think My Supreme Banker would choose Tenderly to be His messenger you better check your shoe size to make sure you're getting enough oxygen to your brain.

From: Maxie.Ruthie.4Ever@Ourmail.us
Date: Monday, January 3, 2005. 11:00 a.m.
To: US@Ourmail.us
Subject: Maxie in Florida

Hello and Happy New Year!

I'm doing great! I run four miles a day and bench press 150 pounds without breaking a sweat. Can you imagine? *Emes!* No bullshit!

I'm a little down because Jerry and Johnny just died—may they both rest in peace, *aleichem sholom*. Ruthie, my wife of thirty-five years—may she rest in peace, *aleichem sholom*—used to say Johnny—may he rest in peace, *aleichem sholom*—was the only guy she got into bed with at night besides yours truly. Can you imagine? *Emes!* No bullshit!

Too bad Carson—may he rest in peace, *aleichem sholom*—wasn't on during the daytime, otherwise, Larry—the son of a bitch, bitch-bastard *mamzer*, may he rest in peace, *aleichem sholom*—would still be delivering mail. Can you imagine? *Emes!* No bullshit!

He rang only once, but I can tell you, he never came again after I stabbed him in the ass with Ruthie's mother's kosher six-inch carving knife—may she rest in peace, *aleichem sholom*. Can you imagine? *Emes!* No bullshit!

That was thirty-five years ago, March 17th. You know how I remember? It was Saint Paddy's Day. Too bad Larry—the son of a bitch, bitch-bastard *mamzer*, may he rest in peace, *aleichem sholom*—wasn't Irish, maybe if he had been, the luck of the Irish would have been with him, and I would never have left my wallet at home in the first place, but the son of a bitch, bitch-bastard *mamzer* was Italian and didn't have any four-leaf clover to protect him when I found him and Ruthie in *flagrante delicto*. Can you imagine? *Emes!* No bullshit.

It took thirty-five years for the chicken fat to make Ruthie sink like a stone in the bathtub—may she rest in peace, *aleichem sholom*. It was those goddamn breath mints. Sure, now you got "CSI"—but back then, who knew? All you had was your gut, and my gut said if chicken fat could turn white bread into a brick, why not Ruthie—may she rest in peace, *aleichem sholom*. Can you imagine? *Emes!* No bullshit!

"CSI"—that's where I heard it, you know . . . Certs—combined with lipids—prolong life. Naturally, that got me thinking—*Maxie—if you had to do it all over again, would you still use chicken fat?* I bet you think I wouldn't, right? *Ah ha!* See—you'd be wrong! It's not the length of time—*it's the quality*. Making the sandwiches, watching her wolf 'em down for breakfast, lunch, and during Johnny; smoking her ciggies; chewing her mints—*quality time*. What's more—it gave me something to live for, knowing each day I spread a schmear of schmaltz on her Tasty Bread brought Ruthie—that bitch-bastard, may she rest in peace, *aleichem sholom*—one day closer to sinking like a stone.

The trouble with young married people today—they're off doing their own thing and got no quality time together. Can you imagine? *Emes!* No bullshit!

Let me tell you another thing. It wasn't easy for me. How long you think you could last listening to a woman who sounds like a Jewish seagull . . . *hocking* you to death . . . over and over . . . day in and day out . . . over every tiny mistake? You couldn't—that's what. Nobody could, but me—Uncle Maxie—because I'm strong. I got stamina!

Twice a week I play handball with a twenty-five-year-old, and I beat his Yugoslavian ass. Then I go to the health club and run ten miles on the treadmill. You should see the women. When they sweat you can see their nipples. Can you imagine? *Emes!* No bullshit!

After the club I have freshly squeezed orange juice, vegetable cream on an everything bagel, and two cups of coffee, decaf, with three sugars at Benny's New York Style Deli over on Hollywood Blvd.

Around eleven, I watch the women coming in from their doubles game—they're all sweaty and you can see their nipples. During the holidays you see their grandkids, get to look at their tattoos and butt cracks. Can you imagine? *Emes!* No bullshit!

I'm on the twenty-fifth floor, facing east, and from my terrace I can see all the way over to Bebe Rebozo's place on Key Biscayne—may he rest in peace, *aleichem sholom.*

I read the papers out there, except when the wind gets crazy. There's nothing in 'em except murders, robberies, and carjackings, so I just read the sports section.

I still see Joe Robbie—may he rest in peace, *aleichem sholom*—every so often when I'm reading about the Dolphins, and he thanks me for selling him the land for his stadium. He's always standing in the same place, like up in a cloud, over the ocean, right there, maybe a hundred yards out and a hundred yards up. He still looks good. Can you imagine? *Emes!* No bullshit!

I go into South Beach every night for dinner. You should see the women! Most of the time they walk around half-naked! Can you imagine? *Emes!* No bullshit!

I own six properties down there. I bought'em for a song, and now they're worth a fortune. And let me tell you, there's nothing wrong with the way I shit and pee.

Yesterday, I just picked up my new Mercedes SL500. It's black! Everybody says it's very sexy.

You know, black cars are hard to keep clean, but I got two guys who come by every Friday morning, and they wash 'em up nice. Mercedes got a fancy name for the color—Black Metallic—that way, those bitch-bastards can charge more for it.

Ruthie—may she rest in peace, *aleichem sholom*—always hated black cars. We had a black Caddy back in the Seventies. She said it reminded her of a hearse, so I told her, don't ride in it. She never liked to go anywhere, anyway. But come Friday, when she wanted to go get her hair done, she was off like a bat outta hell, and it didn't matter if the car was purple—which, as a matter of fact, was the color of her sister Pearl's piece-of-shit Buick . . . may she rest in peace, *aleichem sholom,* that bitch-bastard.

You wanna hear something great? I got a silver car cover free. If you lease a new car for five years in a row, you get the fifth cover for nothing. Great deal, huh? And you know what else . . . it's washable!

All you gotta do is stick it into the machine, then put it in the dryer. Can you imagine? *Emes!* No bullshit!

I got my own washing machine and dryer, did I tell you? They're in a room all by themselves off the kitchen. It's called the laundry room. Can you imagine? *Emes!* No bullshit!

I keep all my cleaning stuff there. I got, what, eight rooms—but that's counting the laundry room and the powder room, which I never use. I was thinking of putting Ruthie—may she rest in peace, *aleichem sholom*—in the laundry room closet when company comes, and putting the cleaning stuff under the sink—but right now I just park her in the walk-in closet.

What I do is roll her in on this collapsible stretcher I found in the garbage room after Joe Abrams died—may he rest in peace, *aleichem sholom*. It sounds easy, but Ruthie—may she rest in peace, *aleichem sholom*—weighs a ton. Goddess forbid she'd roll off, fall through the floor, and kill Ida and Vic, if they're not dead already. Can you imagine? *Emes!* No bullshit!

Lenny—Jerry—I mean Jerry—Jerry Orbach's death hit me real hard—may he rest in peace *aleichem sholom.* Just like Johnny's, I still can't get over it. Sometimes, I just sit there and stare at the TV and just shake my head. Or, I'm in the bathroom doing you-know-what and I hear that *dun-dun* sound and I start crying.

Or, in the middle of the night, I wake up and I hear Lenny—I mean Jerry—Jerry Orbach—may he rest in peace, *aleichem sholom*—say, "What, were you expecting a visit from the tooth fairy?" Can you imagine? *Emes!* No bullshit!

Right this minute it's on, and I'm OK. You remember the one where everyone's a murderer? The first time I saw it I said to Ruthie—may she rest in peace, *aleichem sholom*—this is not "Law & Order." She told me, and I quote, to "just shut the fuck up and watch." End of quote. Later, I gave her a double *schmear* for that. Can you imagine? *Emes!* No bullshit!

Tell me the truth, is it tough for you to watch "Law & Order" and look at Lenny—I mean, Jerry—Jerry Orbach—may he rest in peace, *aleichem sholom*. He looks so good I think he's still alive. I think to myself that maybe I'll see him again at Joe's Stone Crab down in Miami. I love that place. I used to see him come in all the time.

Then I look at Ruthie—may she rest in peace, *aleichem sholom*—lying over on the bed with a pillowcase over her head, and I thank Goddess she hasn't moved in at least a month, because I'd throw myself over the terrace if I saw *her* walk into Joe's. Can you imagine? *Emes!* No bullshit!

I read all your emails, and they were very nice. I print them out, in color. I have a new Dell with a Pentium processor and an HP LaserJet printer, top of the line. I got'em free from this cement contractor I know, the bitch-bastard *mamzer*. I give him plenty of business, and he knows if I mention I need something, he gets it; otherwise, the next building I build, he gets *bupkis*. Can you imagine? *Emes!* No bullshit!

Like they say, "You don't get unless you give,"— right?

I like to read your emails down at the pool. Don't worry, I put them in a waterproof plastic folder and that keeps them dry, because there's lots of humidity. It's an Olympic-size pool with a *cockamamie* waterfall at the deep end. I swim in it twice a week. A hundred laps, each way. Everybody watches. Every Wednesday, from two to three, I race the lifeguards and I beat 'em every time. That's how I got Leslie Dickstein to sleep with me, that bitch-bastard. Can you imagine? *Emes!* No bullshit!

I was talking to Pearlstein, the president of the condo board—the bitch-bastard *mamzer*—and I told him, who needs a *cockamamie* waterfall in a pool? He said it's a great selling point because the grandchildren love it. Screw the grandkids. They just pee in the pool and scream so fuckin' loud you wanna kill'em. Can you imagine? *Emes!* No bullshit!

That reminds me of a joke I just heard. Melvin Schwartz is called up before the president of the condo board. The president says, "Mel, we can't let you go in the swimming pool because you pee in the pool." Mel says, "Why? Kids pee in it all day." And the president says, "But not from the diving board!"

Get it . . . *but not from the diving board!* Funny, right?

Did I tell you I speed walk over at the health club? On the treadmill, twenty miles a day. Then I use the machines for an hour. You gotta wear a belt. I see kids in there without a belt. I tell them, "Wear a belt, or you'll get a hernia the size of a grapefruit." You should see the women over there. When they sweat you can see their nipples. Can you imagine? *Emes!* No bullshit!

Pearlstein, the bitch-bastard *mamzer*, he's the one who pushed through the new elevators that are falling apart already—like I knew they would—the bitch-bastard *mamzer*. Anybody with eyes could see the glass would crack if you sneezed on it. He said, "If it's too thick, it'd be too much weight for the cars." What *farkakte* bullshit. I told him so. They threw me out of the meeting for cursing, but let me back in for coffee and cake.

I wanted my elevator guys to come in—you know the company that put in the two banks for the thirty-story condo I just built on Ocean Avenue in Boca? These guys are professionals and know what they're doing. I told the Board they'd come up with a good price, but the Board, those bitch-bastard *mamzers,* put up a stink. They said it would be a conflict of interest. Yeah, it would conflict with the kickbacks Pearlstein, the bitch-bastard *mamzer,* was getting from his son-in-law's company. Can you imagine? *Emes!* No bullshit!

What's with Bermuda? I told her, come down here if you want to put your cash to work, because those hair salons are making a fortune. I know, I got two in malls, and believe you me, they're cash cows. A Cuban guy and his wife run the one I got in Palm Beach. I hear they have five more. She drives a white, 2004, 600SL with the big engine. Her name's Matilda and she's got *some* tush. Can you imagine? *Emes!* No bullshit!

We got some Cubans who work in the condo, and they all got great asses. I never seen Matilda's husband. I heard he's in jail. I also heard he drives a black 2004 Mercedes 500S with tinted windows, probably bulletproof. Matilda's the one I see all the time and the one who writes the checks. I think she owns a couple of workout places, too. I'm always telling her, the next one she puts up, she should talk to me first because I have stores opening up in Wellington and Palm Coast—you know, in my condos.

The other place is over in my Coral Springs shopping mall. A Korean owns it. What a smart cookie, this girl. And nice. Always says, "Hello, Mr. Maxie. You're so handsome, Mr. Maxie." No tits, but a real nice ass. Not as round and firm as the Cuban's. Asians have everything small, but tight. I think she's younger than Matilda. Can't really tell with Asians. Her, I'd *shtup* in a Miami Heart Hospital moment, but I'm not getting mixed up with the Korean Mafia, those bitch-bastard *mamzers*. Can you imagine? *Emes!* No bullshit!

I told Bermuda, there's no money in these workout places, but hair salons are golden. Can you imagine? *Emes!* No bullshit!

Joe Greene and Herm Epstein saw Bermuda last month. I got them in, and now they want to run me for president of the condo board. I just might do it, just to see Pearlstein's face when he loses, the bitch-bastard *mamzer*. They can't do enough for me, the *hazas*. Neither can Saul Turpin, or Benny Ackerman, those bitch-bastard *mamzers*. Benny says he can get me Viagra for less than twenty cents a pill. Can you imagine? *Emes!* No bullshit!

Can you believe Bermuda's girls are booked solid for three months? You only got to wait a month at the new South Beach sushi joint everybody's talking about. I got two properties nearby, but they're residential.

Ruthie, may she rest in peace, *aleichem sholom*, used to have a thing for the Cuban super over there. I used to double her *schmear* whenever we went over. He thought Ruthie—may she rest in peace, *aleichem sholom*—was from Havana. It was the chicken fat. Everyone knows it gives us the "Cuban Look." Can you imagine? *Emes!* No bullshit!

Did I tell you, I have an extra bedroom? I face south, and you can see Key Biscayne. Anyone who wants to come down, you got a standing invitation—except *That Putz*, you bitch-bastard *mamzer.* Why I let you talk me out of Intel when it was at twenty, I don't know. I should have poisoned you instead of Ruthie—may she rest in peace, *aleichem sholom*. She may have been a bitch-bastard *mamzer* like you, but she never cost me $500,000. Can you imagine? *Emes!* No bullshit!

If you're coming, just let me know in advance so I have time to put Ruthie in the closet—may she rest in peace, *aleichem sholom*. And if anyone asks—and those bitch-bastards in her mahjong game will—just tell them what I tell them: she had plastic surgery and looks so bad she's afraid to come back to Florida. Can you imagine? *Emes!* No bullshit!

Love,
Uncle Maxie
P.S. *Remember, no peeing in the pool.*

From: Cheryl.G@Ourmail.us
Date: Monday, January 3, 2005, 12:06 p.m.
To: US@Ourmail.us
Subject: re *Bulletin de vacances* (Holiday Newsletter)

Bonjour encore! (Hello again!)

Only three days have passed since my end-of-the-year email, but since reading your correspondences, I feel it my obligation to share my latest good tidings with those less fortunate in the hope my blessings will be your blessings.

Oh, where to begin, where to begin!

Monroe's Nobel Peace Prize led him to a new position as President and CEO of ArmsAndAmmo.com. He's ecstatic because he felt this peace thing was making him stale, and he desperately needed new challenges to light his fire. Thankfully that will happen now, as the company he's joining makes this unbelievable napalm.

The day after Grant received his Academy Award, he took a meeting with Clint (Eastwood, who else?). So, listen to this—Clint wants him to star in all his movies, starting with the one about Clint's own life. It's only natural now that he's had face time with him. I mean—he'd have to be blind not to see the family resemblance. They could be twins! Of course, Grant's young enough to be Clint's son. (If you ever meet Clint, don't ever tell him I said that.)

I don't know why Grant still thinks he looks like Gregory Peck. Maybe there was a resemblance to when he was into wearing gray flannel, but certainly not in *The Boys from Brazil*. Of course, his *Duel in the Sun*-like standoff at Playland got our attention, didn't it?

Oh, listen to this—after Tyler got his Pulitzer, Tyler's agent (he's got five wire-tap convictions, so he's in the know) tore up the Random House contract and opened up the bidding for Grant's next opus at five million dollars.

Of course, what Tyler hoped for was the opportunity to direct Angelina Jolie in an adaptation of his award-winning book, *Karl Marx: The Man, the Myth, the Ballroom Dancer*. It certainly looked he would after he won the Pulitzer, but then suddenly Angelina's people told Tyler's people they weren't going to green-light the project. It wasn't that she didn't want to play Karl, because as you know, Tyler's portrait of Karl's teenage years (when he went through his loan-sharking phase), though obscure to most scholars, could be updated to present-day LA; and with some car chases (Nick Cage playing Lenin), Angelina's got her *Gone in 60 Seconds* fan base coming back for more.

And don't think for a moment Angelina was afraid of playing a teenage boy who only spoke Russian and had a full beard at fifteen. (She saw *Boys Don't Cry* and knows a star-turn role when she sees one.)

No, of course, it was Aunt Bea who messed things up. It happened down in Jacksonville at the Super Bowl. With just under two minutes to play before the half (and the Eagles moving the ball real well), a group of aging Amishers, now fully recovered from open-heart surgery, forced their way into the box where Angelina and the manufacturer of Botox were sitting, and demanded she *pucker up*. (You should have seen the faces drop on the boys from Botox when they realized she wasn't going to show off her newly chemically injected folds on national television.) It took all of halftime to get things straightened out, but then late in the quarter (with the Eagles again looking to score), one old bird had a stroke. The cast from "CSI" gets to working and suddenly there's talk of charging Angelina because the video replay shows he took the header out of the skybox while watching her suck down on a wide-mouth Pepsi. (Ironic, he met his maker in the lap of GE's CEO). *C'est la vie!* (That's life!)

Of course, you know that Washington's Medal of Honor got him a guest shot on "Oprah", where he confessed the female person he most wanted to emulate was Dinah Shore. (Talk about a mother's heartbreak.) If I knew how much he loved golf, I would have bought him a set of clubs instead of *Jane's Book of Nuclear Weapons*.

You're all probably dying to learn all about Madison's appointment to the Supreme Court of the United States. She'll miss those class actions, and who knows how that will change her relationship with

"Bingo" (that's the secret name she calls John Grisham, because that's what he did while she ghosted his books—played bingo).

Laverne, honey, I know you're upset Madison isn't going to take Jerry's case. She's won a ton of copper mine leakage litigations, and nobody's better when it comes to gouging mining corporations. In all fairness to Maddy, she crunched the numbers and didn't think it was billable. Needless to say, that's what makes my daughter a top-notch lawyer and an even better Justice of the Supreme Court of the United States.

Madison did promise that if the leakage spreads to the university's water supply, that would get her face time with Greta Van Susteren. I didn't think that would be an option, because when I get a college catalog, all the kids are carrying private-label waters. Well, Maddy wised me up. She said, to keep up with rising costs, colleges are rebottling tap water and making their label required drinking for all students. I didn't believe her, but then she told me to check my stock portfolio. There it was on every one of my fifty thousand shares of Well It's All The Same Water, Inc. I bet you're all laughing at me, right? Special thanks must go to Bubbeh Esther's (*pronounced* Granny Smith Apples's) prescient 1895 purchase of all U.S. and Canadian water rights. Sorry, Bubbeh Esther (*pronounced* Granny Smith Apples), I should have remembered.

Now, about Clinton's meeting with Goddess. What can I say?: after he brought down the additional, five commandments (plus a lovely CD), all of which will be aired on "60 Minutes", unless Barbara plays the Heston card and brings up *his* version of getting the commandments, a story he says can be backed-up by the special effects guy who set the burning bush on fire.

Clinton couldn't get over how good She looks. I wonder if She goes to the Finest Doctor. Then again, why in Her name does She need to get Her stem cells transplanted, unless She wants to be a He—something Tenderly, bless her demented soul, is always saying would be a great idea for an end-of-life video game.

As you all know from my holiday correspondence, I don't approve of that kind of medical mischief. I'm on record as declaring there's no point in living after your hand mirror cracks into a thousand pieces. Oh, I know what you're thinking. When big-talker Cousin Cheryl's time comes, she'll be begging Goddess to let her have just one more face lift, even if that means she won't be able to open her eyes again.

Did I tell you the Little Mister has laryngitis? They say it's common amongst two-year-olds who gargle red wine out of the same glass as the Three Tenors. The cheap whore-secretary had to leave the tour and go into hiding because she had outstanding warrants in two out of the three states where Eisenhower is performing. *Quelle surprise!* (What a surprise!) As it turns out, the cheap whore-secretary's crack-fiend husband (posing as her brother—what a laugh—ha!) has a midget sister who immediately bonded with the Little Mister and concocted her own home-brew remedy that quickly cured his throat problems.

We girls of the D.O.D. (a.k.a., Daughters of Darkness, a.k.a., Anne Rice Stake and Ale Investment Club) are making our annual pilgrimage to visit Lestat's burial ground, and figure we'll be in New Orleans when the Little Mister performs. I think he's thinking of doing some John Lee Hooker lieder for his solo encore. It'll be the first time since the Little Mister's been born that his daddy (the polo-playing low-life) and I have been in the same state without either of us being up on a domestic violence charge.

Speaking of the D.O.D. (a.k.a., Daughters of Darkness, a.k.a., the Anne Rice Stake and Ale Investment Club), these wonderful ladies of the night have helped me come to terms with my anger toward the little bastard—*excusez-moi,* excuse me . . . I meant the Little Mister—by teaching me to throw a pot.

The girls say I'm a natural around a kiln. I think I've finally found my voice. What really gives my latest vase its magic is the decorative use of finger gestures to tell my life story which, according to *American Art and Hand Creams,* "Is a motif that was just waiting for the right vessel."

Sure, I still get the urge to toss the little so-and-so into the fire, but then I think of Reagan—my exquisitely scented candle that will always light up the darkest and most demented corners of my brain; the bell that will always chime the most harmonious one-note melodies; the little girl-child who Goddess, in her infinite wisdom, didn't want me to have ... (Although, it's been two heartbreaking years since I received that smeared and mangled postcard from Laos written in block letters with that horrible smudgy purple lipstick: MET A NICE WARLORD—LEARNING TO USE A MACHETE—COME VISIT ANYTIME. I'll kill her if she lost her Mont Blanc.) *Juste badinant.* (Just kidding.)

Not much more to add about Carter's record-breaking flight across the Atlantic on the back of a paper airplane (except I think he's going to try a paper clip next), Jefferson's reincarnation, Lincoln's coronation, Kennedy's abdication, and of course, Ford's sainthood ... (Aren't children born out of wedlock special?)

I just want to end by saying I have a lot of real feelings for you all, including Sister Born Again, formerly known as Aunt Bea, who the Amish have not forgotten and will raise like a barn when she steps out of the convent to go to the *Manolo Walks With Goddess* Retrospective at The Fetish in Philly.

Of course, as always, with love that won't go away either ...

Jusqu'à l'année prochaine! (Until next year!)

Cousin Cheryl, A Very Proud Mom!

P.S. I thought Tenderly was in a medically induced coma?

P.P.S. Remember... *El amor nos guardará juntos. (Love will keep us together.)*

SING IT LOUD! SING IT PROUD! SING IT NOW!

From: YoungerTheElder23@Ourmail.us
Date: Monday, January 3, 2005, 10:56 p.m.
To: US@Ourmail.us
Subject: Update from Your Humble Servant

Dear Members of the Family Ginsburg (*pronounced* Du Pont),

It's almost 11:00 p.m., and I'm still at the office, working on the family portfolio. You know I am saying this not just to blow my own horn. I am only the faithful and most humble servant of the Family Ginsburg (*pronounced* Du Pont), as was my father, his father, and his father before him, all the way back to Younger by Elder by One Ginsburg (*pronounced* Du Pont), may they all be inscribed in *The History of the World, Book of Ratings,* Chapter 11, The Great CPAs of History.

I want to take this opportunity to remind everyone you must sign and return your year-end statements before the 15th of January, as I leave the following day for my usual two-week holiday. We do not want a repeat of last year's unfortunate episode, when many of you thought I'd fled the country and in a panic, called the IRS Tip Hotline. It was our good fortune they had no Yiddish speakers on duty that evening, or else, well—why entertain such painful scenarios when we don't have to—isn't that so?

Mr. Nicholas Graham will, of course, handle all business affairs while I am away. Last week, Mr. Graham received several death threats, and while the callers never identified themselves, the frequent use of "bitch-bastard" leads me to believe there may be a connection to the calls made to the IRS. I want to use this occasion to again caution you that using the telephone lines to issue threats of this nature is a federal offense, and although I have chosen to let peace reign in providence, any such repetition will be met with severe legal consequences.

No one is more conscious of the rumors swirling around concerning the missing money than I, but I can assure you, until all the facts are in, there is no reason to either point fingers at Mr. Nicholas Graham, nor believe he paid for his floor-through apartment in the Trump World Towers, one floor below that of Mr. Bill Gates, with any ill-gotten Family Ginsburg (*pronounced* Du Pont) funds. When I hired Mr. Nicholas Graham, I was told he was a lucky fellow and could expect him to suddenly and without any explanation, come up with serious amounts of cash.

I also knew of the stolen jewelry affair and the counterfeit painting charges. In talking with Bubbeh Esther (*pronounced* Granny Smith Apples), I was assured he was never her boy toy, nor did he, on any occasion, show the slightest intentions of stealing her ruby-and-diamond, elephant-ear-shaped pin and matching earrings; her gold tusk-shaped broach; or any of the other twenty pieces of museum-quality elephant-inspired jewelry that are on the list I sent you when the burglary was first discovered.

Regarding the five-hundred-thousand-dollar reward the insurance company is offering, let me make this perfectly clear—it is not open to any family member, nor anyone who has been awarded a reward in the last six months. I know this has been a bone of contention with family members, but as the First District Appellate Court in the State of New York held and I quote, "One family member cannot, for the sake of his or her own personal gain, anonymously pay another member of the family to commit a felony against an additional member and then pursue the collection of said reward by turning said family member in." I also want to take issue with the notion that anyone who says they got this idea from *The Thomas Crown Affair* just doesn't know their movies and is a disgrace to the family name. I can't tell you how hopping mad that made me.

Regarding the other issue—the counterfeit paintings were only a practical joke on Nick's part, and I for one was amused he could sell the same Dali to twenty-five different celebrity collectors. His explanation that the whole thing was a pilot for a reality show was backed up by the fact none of the twenty-five pressed charges, and further confirmed when all but one agreed to appear on the show.

Donald Trump is the only one to say no, but there was no way Nick was going to change the name of the show from "The Forger" to "The Forger's Apprentice," or let the Donald play him. Nick spent too many years mastering his technique to be taken over by a less-skilled "paint-over artist." If you have ever seen The Donald's work you would know, in an instant, he hasn't a true understanding of Dali's brushwork, nor is he able to accept the fact that one can't sign Dali's name in huge gold block letters.

You know, since the Enron business, it is against my policy to go into any detail about our twenty-five thousand (give or take) shell corporations. Be that as it may, if you have seen the newspapers, you already know that the price of a single share of any one of these twenty-five thousand (give or take) shell corporations is second only to Berkshire Hathaway. However, if you look at what a single share of stock from any of these twenty-five thousand (give or take), shell corporations cost back in 1975 and match that against Mr. Warren Buffett's numbers, you must take into account what a dollar of undeclared money could buy then, as to what it can purchase now. Now, isn't this is an accomplishment worthy of a *Wall Street Journal* centerfold!

I want to thank those of you who attended the Younger the Elder by Eight Ginsburg (*pronounced* Du Pont) Memorial Service, may he be inscribed in *The History of the World: Book Of Ratings,* Chapter 11, the Great CPAs of History, honoring the 125th anniversary of the day he so gallantly died at the Battle of Trenton. The reenactment again made me ask myself—what if? *What if the battlefield surgery had been successful?* Not only would it have saved Younger the Elder by Eight's life, may he be inscribed in *The History of the World: Book Of Ratings,* Chapter 11, The Great CPAs of History, but it would have made stomach stapling as popular as breast augmentation, thereby, preventing the obesity crisis that is threatening our nation today.

I know some of you question the relationship I have with high-ranking members of the Bush administration, as well as key officials in several "axis of evil" nations. It has also come to my attention some of you were bothered by Michael Moore's revelations. More worrisome was the momentary slippage in stock prices as a result of the film going to DVD. Let me reiterate what I said on the "60 Minutes" segment, "The Haves and The Have Nots"—I am not Younger the Elder by Three (may he be inscribed in *The History of the World: Book Of Ratings,* Chapter 11, The Great CPAs of History), and I would never have sold the rights to the name *Indian* in the Indian Head Penny.

Happy New Year, and as always, your humble servant,
Younger the Elder by Twenty-Three

From: Clarice.G@Ourmail.com
Date: Tuesday, January 4, 2005, 3:25 a.m.
To: US@Ourmail.us
Subject: Cousin Clarice has something to say . . .

It's Christmas Eve, and I just evicted myself from my domicile because I was playing the same song on my stereo for three days straight. But, you all know how important family is to me, and I believe it is my Goddess-given right as a Family Ginsburg (*pronounced* Du Pont) Girl to play "We Are Family," or whatever it was, as long as I f-ing please if that's what it takes to make me feel part of this f-ing family, which I am not feeling right this f-ing holiday minute; nor have I felt that way since that f-ing film came out, and someone in our f-ing family started calling and doing their piss-poor imitation of Anthony f-ing Hopkins. *Clarice . . . Clarice . . . wash your mouth out with soap . . . Clarice . . .* And just because it's in f-ing Yiddish, don't think I don't f-ing understand you!

Before you all start popping your anti-depressants, I just want to say two things: It's not f-ing Christmas Eve anymore, and *I really wasn't f-ing evicted.* How can someone throw themselves out of *their own* f-ing townhouse when there are no locks on the door?

I just wanted to get your f-ing attention.

Poor, pitiful Clarice. All her money and she's still not happy. Well, f-you! Just because I didn't want f-ing Chinese on f-ing Christmas doesn't make me a loser. Double f-you, and get used to the fact sushi is the new takeout—let the wasabi kick in!

Speaking of kicking in, that's what the Fiornals are doing. I can go just so long trying to see out of just one f-ing eye.

I did decide to get out for Christmas Eve, so I took a suite at the Plaza. I'm facing east. I'm not high enough to see the Luby Chevrolet showroom on Queens Boulevard, but it's good enough to remind me of the first time I boosted an Impala. That'll be in my tell-all—but more on that later.

The f-ing hotel is packed with f-ing designer labels on the make—and

I don't mean the kind down in Cancun—*the* place south of the border to find a guy who wants to make love inside his own MRI machine. I'm strictly a banker's broad now. I did seriously consider a landlord, but I'm not living in an f-ing church, even if it is across from Saks—not when his holy father owns the St. Regis, the St. Moritz, and anything else with a "St." in front of it. I'm better off with either Morgan or Stanley, or if I played the deuce card, both of them.

I'm happy for Monroe, because it's not every day your favorite nephew wins the f-ing Nobel Peace Prize, but when I asked him to be the keynote speaker at Amnesty for Perdue Oven Roasters, he blew me off. What—his "amnesty" is better than mine? And not for nothing, aren't we all Goddess's f-ing creatures?

Sure, he's got this new gig and he's too busy—but, you know what, when I asked him for a case of f-ing assault rifles, he told me to call Uncle Book 'em Dano because *he's* the arms dealer in the family. Well, f-you, Monroe! Book 'em Dano's selling out of some Asian sneaker factory, and your company is right here on Park Avenue.

It would go a long way to making things right with Amnesty for Perdue Oven Roasters if we could arm our members, storm Frank's ad agency, and haul 'em all to the World Court.

But, it's holiday time, and I'm listening to "We Are Family," or whatever, and let's talk about more pleasant things.

For one, I'm not surprised Grant's in with *Dirty Harry*. I mean, didn't I always tell you how much my nephew looked like Mr. Rawhide? And here he is, going to play him in the movies. I feel especially proud because I was the one who bought Grant the f-ing Polaroid camera so he could take pictures of himself dressed up like f-ing Gregory Peck in *The Man in the Gray Flannel* Suit. He was only ten, but even then he knew he wanted to act—*had to act*.

I know—I had the same grease paint surging through my veins, but I was in my Jane Fonda phase and insisted that everybody refer to me as "Hanoi Clarice"—something old daddy thought was a career-stopper.

I told daddy (when old Honest Abe wasn't suing anyone and would listen to me for more than a minute), once you got your Dr. Pearlswine passport picture, you'd think you were Ingrid Bergman and turn on us. Remember, Miss High-and-Mighty Cheryl, how you stayed in your room all day saying you were Anastasia—writing those mushy letters to Misha, the head waiter at the Russian Tea Room, begging him to interview you so you could prove you were the last of the Romanovs?

Then you got bored, discarded that role, and started telling me Rick was going to give you those stolen letters of transit so you and Victor could leave f'ing Casablanca.

I never told a living soul—so why couldn't you do me a solid and stop your daughter from sending me up the river?

I remember Bubbeh Esther (*pronounced* Granny Smith Apples) taking me into the park across from the court house and explaining that if a city judge (that means *Madison,* Cheryl) wanted a federal appointment they had to send a relative to jail, especially an aunt (that means *me,* Cheryl) who breast-fed her because Madison's own mother (that means *you,* Cheryl) locked yourself into your room and refused to come out because she/you got it into your dumb f-ing head she/you had turned into Dana Wynter. *Invasion of the Body Snatchers*—for Christ's sake, what city apartment has closet space for f'ing pods?

Going to jail wouldn't have been so terrible if Grant used his connections and showed my screenplay to his buddies at AA. Oh yes, I know the only higher power he was seeking was an agent at William f'ing Morris.

I'm not jealous or anything, but compared to what's on Pay-Per-View, my screenplay, *The Five Ginsburgs (pronounced Du Ponts) I Don't Ever Want to Meet in Heaven,* has more sex, drugs, and rock and roll than the junk that's out there now.

The warden up at the prison read it and immediately saw how influenced I was by poltergeist eroticism in a way that was honest and clean, yet didn't pull any punches like most other family confessionals. His compliments meant a lot to me, because he's written several screenplays. As far as I know, none have been produced, but rumor has it *he* and *not f-ing* Stephen King wrote *The Shawshank Redemption,* but, because he's still warden and bound by the Official Secrets

Act, he can't claim his rightful authorship.

The double vision's gone, so I'll be able to find the mini bar. Then, as is our tradition, I will stare into the burning Yule Log until I can put it out using mind control.

Happy New Year,

Cousin Clarice

P.S. My tell-all book will describe, in detail, at age five, Uncle Maxie giving me a quarter at the Carnegie Deli when I correctly identified the leanest pastrami.

P.P.S. Kitty Kelley says it will be a f'ing masterpiece!

P.P.P.S. More book news to come!

From: Bubbeh.E@Ourmail.us
Date: Tuesday, January 4, 2005, 2:45 p.m.
To: Clarice.G@Ourmail.com
Cc: US@Ourmail.us
Subject: You go girl go!

Take it to the limit, Clarice girl! Tell it like it is!

Bubbeh Esther (*pronounced* Granny Smith Apples)

P.S. Maxie—at your *bris,* I should have cut you off after your third pastrami sandwich!

From: Sylvia.G@Ourmail.us
Date: Tuesday, January 4, 2005, 9:00 p.m.
To: Cheryl.G@Ourmail.us
Subject: Taking care of your sister

I've just gotten off the phone with Uncle Clayboy and he assures me you are well within your legal rights to declare your sister, Clarice, insane. I know you're a little gun shy around the legal system, but the arson charges have been dropped, so I say go for it. I wouldn't tell your kids because they've always preferred their aunt to you. The last thing we want is for *them* to declare *you* insane. *That Putz* will go along with whatever we decide because putting away Clarice will give him power of attorney and a chance to grab up her estate. I hear Clarice got at least five million from the last two divorces, plus another three from her last hubby's Homeland Security IPO. *And*—I know for a fact, she's got another five mil in real estate when you count Ellis Island, the Hudson River Tunnel, and the three-real estate trusts her first husband, the one who owned Rio's entire beach-front property, signed over to her before he went into his coma. Obviously, this is in addition to her Ginsburg (*pronounced* Du Pont) holdings that must be examined, line item after line item, to determine if they can be seized upon her being institutionalized. I also wouldn't breathe a word of this to Bubbeh Esther (*pronounced* Granny Smith Apples) because, as you know, Clarice was her favorite until you cleverly convinced her it was Clarice and *not you,* who sent that forged love letter to the Elephant Man. I still can't believe you got away with that, since everybody knew about the five counts of forgery and how you even forged your way out of *that situation.* Bubbeh Esther (*pronounced* Granny Smith Apples) may have an elephant's trunk, but *you* certainly got its balls.

Goddess only knows why Bubbeh Esther (*pronounced* Granny Smith Apples) liked Clarice so much in the first place—you and I have bigger gifts. I need a ciggie and a pee.

OK, I'm back.

You realize you can't treat this thing lightly. If Bubbeh Esther (*pronounced* Granny Smith Apples) ever gets wind of what you're up to, she wouldn't give a second thought to strangling you with her trunk, so my advice to you is to go black ops on this one.

I recognize that it's holiday time, and we should be of good cheer and have compassion for the less fortunate, but I'm worried about what a loose cannon Clarice is turning out to be. If the Carnegie Deli incident is any indication, she can remember back to when she was a young child, and I don't have to spell out *what that means*. After I spoke to Uncle Clayboy, I phoned Bermuda and left a message with her service. I asked her to look through her Rolodex. After all—what good is washing a person's hair unless they can help you wash away your troubles? That goes double for those she met in prison.

Just thought of something—can anyone get to Kitty Kelly? Don't get me wrong, Cheryl, I'm not advocating violence. The last thing I would want is for your sister to end up with Jimmy Hoffa. I simply cannot have the family's name splattered across the front pages, especially now, when there is a very good chance we can get Book 'em Dano home in time for the Super Bowl Sunday. Of course, everything hinges on whether or not Book 'em Dano drops a dime. If he does, he'll have to go into the witness protection program. I've already told him I'd go with him, but I'm not sure Uncle Clayboy wants to leave the West Village—unless, of course, they relocate us to San Francisco. Cheryl, darling, I can't thank your kids enough for making this happen for Book 'em Dano. If Madison hadn't pulled strings on the Federal level, the First Lady wouldn't have brokered the deal. It also goes without saying, Monroe had a heart-to-heart with the Ballet Russe before he became the First Lady's snitch. The last thing anyone wants is WMDs showing up at the Brooklyn Academy of Music and going BAM. Although Monroe didn't come out and say it, if everything goes according to plan, not only will the records of this sordid affair go away, but Book 'em Dano's juvie record would also disappear down a dark hole. So, you can see why

Clarice has to be stopped. I was thinking, maybe you could run the whole thing by Madison? Better still, why not pow-wow with the entire clan? We could have a videoconference. I think you can rent space at Costco.

Love,

Cousin Sylvia

P.S. After we take care of Clarice, we'll go after Tenderly.

I need a ciggie and a pee.

From: LawyerUp@AbeSues4You.edu
Date: Wednesday, January 5, 2005, 6:45 a.m.
To: US@Ourmail.us
Subject: Uncle Abe's GM case

Hello and Happy New Year!

Uncle Abe wants to let everyone who has been following Uncle Abe's GM case to know Uncle Abe's attorneys have just informed Uncle Abe that the Supreme Court Justices of the United States are cutting short their Christmas vacations so they can deal with Uncle Abe's sexual harassment suit. This will be Uncle Abe's very first case before the highest court in the land, and Uncle Abe couldn't have done it without you, Uncle Abe's loving family.

Uncle Abe now wants to take the opportunity to formally thank everyone who wrote Hannity and Colmes, Rush Limbaugh, and *The Riley Report*. Uncle Abe also wants to thank those of you who sent money to the Bush and Cheney campaigns and to Senator Tom DeLay's Travel Fund.

Kudos also has to go Brad Pitt. As you know, Brad went to Barbara Walters with Uncle Abe's story, and she immediately put him on her show. For those of you who didn't tape or TiVo it, Uncle Abe can make you a copy. If you go to Uncle Abe's web site, AbeSues4You.edu, you can see excerpts that include the segment where Brad confessed that he, too, was groped by an exotic-car salesman.

Uncle Abe did a little editing and freeze-framed the very moment Barbara broke down in tears, as Brad describes in gruesome detail how this predatory car salesman put his arm around him after Brad selected his Porsche G3.

Uncle Abe knows the media has come down on Brad for not bringing the salesman up on charges, but what they don't take into account is how that kind of negative publicity can ruin an actor (and of course, prevent him from ever receiving another free Porsche). Nevertheless, Uncle Abe thinks Brad's one hell of a hero for coming forward now (especially after his latest picture was rated P.G.), to take up Uncle

Abe's plight (and the plight of countless others who have purchased exotic cars), only to then have their hands shaken too vigorously, their Black Card squeezed too long, or be subject to other personal boundary violations.

Up on Uncle Abe's web site, Uncle Able also has the clip of Barbara showing the video of Uncle Abe buying Uncle Abe's Revlon-red Eldorado with a beige top (so everyone could see the salesmen putting his arm around Uncle Abe as Uncle Abe filmed them standing next to his purchase).

Uncle Abe also has the clip of Brad telling everyone how brave Uncle Abe was for taking on GM, and then directing viewers to Uncle Abe's web site so they could contribute to Uncle Abe's heroic cause.

Sure, Uncle Abe understands that for the purposes of full disclosure Barbara had to mention Uncle Abe has over seven hundred lawsuits pending and has been called "a sue-happy money grubber," "psychopathic attention-getter," and "just another litigious lowlife."

Uncle Abe was a little pissed off that she brought up the crap about how Uncle Abe has a brother suspected of killing his wife by derailing a trainload of chemicals over her body, thereby creating a poisonous cloud that wiped out an entire town.

If that didn't drive the stake deep enough into Uncle Abe's heart, she followed it up by telling the world Uncle Abe has another brother who makes jewelry that forces the wearer to form a posse and kill rival entertainers.

To prove her point, Barbara showed cell phone photos of Angelina Jolie wearing Jules's nose rings at the Super Bowl peering over the side of her box at the moment the Amish guy sailed off (who, as it turned out, *wasn't* the drag queen Angelina suspected was doing her at the Venetian in Las Vegas).

Thank Goddess ABC News broke in with a Laci Peterson update, or else, Angelina's lawyers would have had national face time and put *another* nail in Uncle Abe's coffin.

The Goddess must have been looking out for Uncle Abe, because after the show, fifty death-row inmates contacted Uncle Abe asking Uncle Abe to see *who they could sue.*

Uncle Abe's lawsuit against Sara Lee is stuck in the Lower Courts. They're making a big deal over the fact that Uncle Abe had diabetes *before* Uncle Abe ever ate their cakes.

Uncle Abe put them in their place when he showed a video of Uncle Abe being regressed. In this video it's clear to anyone who doesn't have a sugar addiction that in various past lives (including the ones where Uncle Abe was a farm animal), Uncle Abe was addicted to Sara Lee apple pies and that addiction carried over into this life—and gave Uncle Abe diabetes.

Uncle Abe also thinks the judge was certainly swayed when it was demonstrated that Uncle Abe was once a woman who was married to the judge's great grandmother. Uncle Able thinks that was icing on the cake—no pun intended.

Next week, Uncle Abe we'll in the Big Apple for Uncle Abe's case against Mr. Softee. Who would have thought hearing the Mr. Softie ice-cream-truck jingle could cause Uncle Abe to become impotent? Uncle Abe's shrink suggested Uncle Abe take Viagra, but that only caused Uncle Abe more grief. He did warn Uncle Abe about seeing flashes of colors, but he never said anything about Uncle Abe's *shvantz* turning to match the colors of the day on the Empire State Building—something Uncle Abe could have lived with if it had stopped there, but when it took the shape of New York's tallest building, Uncle Abe really got worried.

The only person who didn't seem to give a damn was Marlene. She kept calling it the Starship Enterprise because "it went where no man ever went before."

Now, Uncle Abe's got the whole mahjong group calling Uncle Abe up for dates. It's even worse when Uncle Abe sees one of these women in the lobby or by the pool. They begin to lick their lips at Uncle Abe and hum, "Somewhere Over the Rainbow." The really raunchy ones keep asking Uncle Abe to "Beam them up."

Everyone at the hospital said they never saw an erection take that shape before. As far as the duration, one nurse did say she had a guy come in and stay hard for twelve hours, but there was no antenna.

The doctors tried numbing it with a topical painkiller, but when that didn't work they wanted to stick it with a needle. Nobody was going to stick needles into Uncle Abe's *shvantz* as long as Uncle Abe could take a breath. Finally, they gave Uncle Abe an IV that caused a rash on Uncle Abe's arm that still hasn't cleared up.

Uncle Abe's lawyer in Miami has a claim against Viagra, Uncle Abe's personal physician, the hospital (except for the nurses Uncle Abe still sees socially), and the manufacturer of the IV Drip.

Uncle Abe's trying to figure out how to attach it to the Mr. Softee claim, but Uncle Abe's not so sure Uncle Abe's New York attorney wants to share his contingency fee.

Get this for coincidence: both attorneys are friends, because they were part of a class action suit against the State of Montana and the Big Sky Ranch. If you remember, that was the case where people at the ranch were getting dizzy looking up at the sky because the clouds were moving so fast it caused them to get on the first plane back to New York where, thankfully, they cannot see any sky.

It's similar, but not the same, as the case Uncle Abe has against the United States Weather Bureau and An Act of Goddess.

You know, Uncle Abe still can't look up at the sky when it's raining without seeing Mercedes-Benz cars flying through the air. Uncle Abe already has ten insurance companies testifying that the four hurricanes were an Act of Goddess, justifying the case against Goddess.

In response, the National Weather Service outsourced the service to the country of Bangladesh, leaving Uncle Abe with no one with deep pockets to go after, unless Uncle Abe goes after Goddess directly—and Uncle Abe, being Uncle Abe, knows that isn't smart.

Uncle Abe was happy to see that Uncle Abe's brother, Uncle Maxie, is inviting everyone down to his place. It's a palace, and he should live and be well. Uncle Abe just wouldn't go into the pool when the kids are in there. The fact that Uncle Maxie doesn't sue is a testament to his generosity. Of course, Uncle Maxie might reconsider when he sees the information Tenderly got off the CDC web site warning of the possible relationship between pool peeing and pellagra.

Uncle Abe

From: Jules@JewelerToTheStars.us
Date: Wednesday, January 5, 2005, 10:00 a.m.
To: Laverne.G@Ourmail.us
Cc: US@Ourmail.us
Subject: A chance of a lifetime!

Laverne, sweetheart, I beg you, get away from that mobile backwater home of yours and come up here where your true genius will take root and flourish. If you don't believe me, look at the attached photos of the two rings I recently designed, both inspired by your line of Laverne's Dr. Pepper Arty Bottle Cap Rings. Of course, I had to make a few subtle changes based on my clients' special needs, but after you carefully look at the craftsmanship, I know you'll agree that substituting diamonds for the chicken feathers and gold for the copper sludge hasn't diminished the integrity of the pieces. All my patrons are screaming for one. Beyoncé brought in a cap from her favorite bottle of Evian and intends to decorate it with rubies and sapphires. Ice Cube is ordering five Johnny Walker Black Labels with diamonds for one hand and five Reds with sapphires for the other. Clint sent me a Coors cap from a bottle he gulped down on the set of *The Unforgiven* and wants it encrusted in green and blue topaz. I even have royalty clamoring for them. Both Queen Elizabeth and Prince Phillip want matching Diet Ice Tea Snapple rings, and get this—they sent their own Crown Jewels from the Tower of London. Apparently, they've given up drinking English teas, but that's just between you and me.

I've made up my mind, so don't argue—you're going to get twenty percent of all sales. No—don't argue with me! I want you to use the money to set up a defense fund for Willie, or at the very least, keep the little fella in Dr Pepper and Krispy Kremes.

There's another reason I want you up here: it's my new Transplant U Collection. For my first creation, I took a client's eye out and replaced it with a ruby. I wasn't ready for all the buzz, which led to a rush on more ocular removals, as well as requests to swap fingers and toes for gold, silver, and precious stones. I can't tell you how many of my best consumers have made appointments to have their entire arms and legs replaced. It's all the rage, especially with my rapper trade. For patrons who are less ostentatious (thank Goddess they're in the minority) and don't want their transplants to show, I'm experimenting with non-essential gland and organ replacements, starting with thyroids and appendices.

Did I tell you I've been approached by the Brooklyn Museum? Isn't that wild? They want to mount a show of my work, and you know, they are a take-no-prisoners kind of museum that understands how to get the biggest bang for their publicity buck. If you recall, they created a real brouhaha a few years back with *The Weeping Madonna of the Mercurochrome,* an exhibition that really raked in the bucks for them. Camera Ferrari, Curator of New Exhibits, called me personally and invited me for Starbucks at the museum. Camera believes my work can potentially be more exciting than *Mercurochrome,* but only if it meets their criteria. The Brooklyn has a list of targets of opportunity they would like to offend (churches, minorities, children, elected officials, etc.), and before they commit, they want me to document how and to what extent my work meets their desired goals.

I have a special client, Monsignor Def Rev, who joins me every Thursday evening at Peter Lugers for dinner and a chat. Def Rev has very refined tastes and the bling to back it up. One of the pieces I made for him is a magnificent gold crucifix encrusted in diamonds that I embedded into his groin area. When you get up here I'm sure Def would love to show it to you. Last Thursday evening, after mulling over my problem over a dry, aged, thirty-eight-ounce Porterhouse and more than a couple of Jack and Cokes, he gave me a few hints on how I could beef up my proposal (no pun intended). I could directly blaspheme Jesus, or I could go after Mary. Both are terrific targets of opportunity and would rile religious folks around the world, but he did not hold out much hope for those options because he regards my work as, while "spiritually challenging," certainly not sacrilegious. However, his next suggestion hit the mark! "Do something funky with the fetus, no matter how tasteful, and there would be no stopping the hue and cry on the Fox News Network."

You know—I just thought of something! Def Rev is extremely influential in the world of extreme religious music, owing to his popular daily talk show, *Def-Jamming with the Rev,* that goes out over a thousand radio stations and into all the mega-churches in the U.S. and Asia. (FYI: Def's connections to extreme religion music come from his Pentagon pals who he met when he served as a chaplain at General Dynamics.)

What I'm going to do is call Def and explain your situation. I'm willing to bet he will be sympathetic to William's cause. I cannot see why he would not use his show to gather up support for William. Why, I would even wager he would raise up such a stink, the school would immediately vote to remove *King Kong* and any other "ape date" movies from the required video list. That would give William his victory, and then he would let his hostage go. William could come out of the house and become a hero in the Right-To-Kidnap Movement. It's stories like this that make for blockbuster video games with never-ending sequels, don't you agree?

It just hit me! I could make Willie a great piece of jewelry! A solid gold kid (Willie) standing on top of a platinum Empire State Building, holding a Dr. Pepper in one hand and an onyx ape in the other. I could design it so William could wear it as a pin signifying his victory. We could manufacture plastic knock-offs and make a fortune. What a great idea! Hon, don't you worry. I am going to take care of everything.

A happy and healthy New Year!
Love,
Uncle Jules

MARCH 21st, THE FIRST DAY OF SPRING

From: Cheryl.G@Ourmail.us
Date: Monday, March 21, 2005, 7:35 a.m.
To: US@Ourmail.us
Subject: *Sorpresa, sorpresa!* (Surprise, surprise!)

Hi, everyone! No, it's not the New Year. So why, you ask, is Cousin Cheryl sending you her Holiday Newsletter? I'll tell you in *un momento* (one moment).

It all started when I went to see the movie *Spring, Summer, Fall, Winter . . . and Spring*. I was putting it off, not because Grant passed on doing the lead, which he swears was not because he has anything against foreign directors (he did tell me a lot gets lost in translation when they can use only hand signals), but because they didn't want Clint playing the Zen Master.

Can you imagine anyone saying, *I don't want Clint Eastwood in my film because he can't lip read?* And all the while I thought Koreans understood the needs of the movie-going public, didn't you? (Why, everyone I know is addicted to manicures, pedicures, and those incredibly delicious neck and back rubs one simply cannot live without.)

Of course, you all know Grant is such a loyal friend, and since he's teamed up with Clint (a partnership you can read about in this month's issue of *Germ Warfare*), he won't do anything to injure that relationship.

Naturally, I didn't let my misgivings stop me from renting the movie at Blockbuster. I know, *I know,* I should have used Netflix, but those well-built young bucks at Blockbuster are so hands-on, I felt I owed it to them to go in there at least once a day and rent a movie, or at the very least, buy some sucking candy. (You can see where my boy Grant gets his loyalty from, can't you?)

Anyway, even though I pictured Grant and Clint in every scene and kept thinking how they would have been *so, so* much better than trying to follow all those fluttering hand signals, it suddenly came to me like an epiphany—there was no earthly reason why *I* should have to wait an entire year before I wrote my traditional Holiday Newsletter, or why *you* should have wait an entire year, before *you* heard the wonderful things that happened in my life. *Non accosentite?* (Don't you agree?)

I said to myself, *Cheryl, what I'm going to do is write four family updates—one at the beginning of each season—because this is an opportunity to renew my Ginsburg-ness (pronounced Du Pont-ness) just as nature renews itself. Brillante, huh?* (Brilliant, huh?)

Of course, the recent attack on my life, WHICH LEFT THE RIGHT SIDE OF MY BODY LOOKING LIKE IT WAS SOAKED IN BOTOX FOR A LIFETIME, makes typing with two hands impossible. So, it's hunt and peck until they dig the bullets out of my spine and regenerate the nerves, which will then return movement and feeling to the half of me THAT IS NOW AS USEFUL AS A FUCKING PIN CUSHION!

I don't want to start off this newsletter on a downer (I hold no grudge or bitterness toward the bitch-bastards who nearly turned me into a vegetable—may they rot in hell), especially on a beautiful day like today, when healthy people are out and about, WHILE I'M HALF-PARALYZED, FUCKED THREE WAYS TO SUNDAY, FEELING NO LOVE OR HOPE TOWARD ANY LIVING CREATURE. I find comfort by saying to myself, *Cheryl, you are one lucky SOB, because how many people in your similar position have the money to hire sadistic torturers and pay them to search to the end of days, if necessary, until they FIND THE BITCH-BASTARDS WHO DID THIS TO YOU AND DO TO THEM AND THEIR POLITICAL REPRESENTATIVES TWICE WHAT THEY DID TO YOU!*

Of course, that profound understanding, my brothers and sisters, is the one thing guaranteed to put a smile on the half of my face not frozen in stone, and that gives me the hope tomorrow will be a brighter and better day.

Once and for all, I want to put to rest the rumor that it was Aunt Bea, that bitch-bastard, who shot me. I've watched every episode of "Law & Order: Criminal Intent" to know that someone who likes to kill at close range with a garrote isn't likely to change their M.O. (See

September's "America's Funniest Chain-Store Videos" Gap segment and watch Aunt Bea choke Bubbeh Esther [*pronounced* Granny Smith Apples] with a Brillo Pad wire.)

The person who shot me with a bolt-action Mauser 86 as I was entering Shirley's Sister's Ex-Mother-in-Law's Market, is not the same kind of up close and personal bitch-bastard who likes to whisper in your ear as you gurgle down your last throaty breaths, *You should have drowned in Portsmouth Harbor.*

The worst part is, I keep hearing over and over in my head . . . *Shirley! Shirley, Shirley bo Birley, Bonana fanna fo Firley, Fee fy mo Mirley, Shirley!*

To get back to Aunt Bea, the bitch-bastard—in addition to having the wrong M.O., when you add the twenty sworn statements extracted under oath from Bea's shoe-sisters (from the same people who brought you *The Manchurian Candidate,* I might add) swearing to the fact Aunt Bea was in monastery lockdown for the attempted garroting of an initiate (who she swears was trying to steal her 80s pair of Susan Bennis platforms), well, you have a non-starter. *Quello è il senso che il biscotto si sbriciola* . . . (That's the way the cookie crumbles . . .)

Of course, I also want to go on record as saying I'm not ruling out her involvement in the failed attempt of a week ago when someone sneaked up behind me at Shirley's Sister's Ex-Mother-in-Law's Market (yes, I went back—*the wild Atlantic salmon was on sale*) and put a Walther PPK up against my spine and screamed, *Die, bitch-bastard, die!* (The ninja hood muffled the voice, but I've seen enough Bruce Lee films to recognize *Die, bitch-bastard, die* when I hear it.)

Shirley! Shirley, Shirley bo Birley, Bonana fanna fo Firley, Fee fy mo Mirley, Shirley!

Thank Goddess she didn't remember that the manual safety had to be turned *up,* not *down,* which is usual for most weapons of this type. (Obviously, she was a fan of the older Bond movies, because, in his most recent ones, he's using a P99.)

How do I know I'm not just making it up? *Because* an undercover *News 5* camera man captured the entire incident on tape—*that's how!* (He was there filming a segment for "Shame On You" exposing how easy it is, to pass off chicken fillets for wild Alaskan salmon. Of course, Shirley's Sister's Ex-Mother-in Law's Market blamed the distributor, who blamed the fishermen, who say lots of salmon fishermen name their boats *Chicken of the Sea*.)

Shirley! Shirley, Shirley bo Birley, Bonana fanna fo Firley, Fee fy mo Mirley, Shirley!

I'm also going on record and saying I'm not ruling out the possibility Aunt Bea was the one who ordered the hit (because she knows how much I mean to Bubbeh Esther [*pronounced* Granny Smith Apples] and this is a way to get at her), but for now, Aunt Bea, the bitch-bastard, is not a suspect.

This is a good thing, because I no longer have dreams ABOUT SLOWLY PULLING OUT HER FINGERNAILS WITH A PAIR OF PLIERS AND TURNING THOSE STUMPY FINGERS INTO BLOODY, EVEN STUMPIER PULPS.

Shirley! Shirley, Shirley bo Birley, Bonana fanna fo Firley, Fee fy mo Mirley, Shirley!

Well, enough about the cripple. Let me tell you about Eisenhower, the Little Mister. After the attempt on my life (by the way, the reward for any information leading to the finding and mutilation of the perpetrators is up to $100,000), my little darling immediately flew home to be with me, even though he was still in the studio with the Three Tenors laying down tracks for their new album featuring blues tunes from their Red State Tour.

Of course, I immediately ordered him to return because I didn't want that good-looking blind boy, Andrea Bocelli, to overdub my little boy's voice. (Blind people can be very pushy, especially when they want you to help them cross the street, which is something I CAN'T EVEN FUCKING DO ANYMORE unless I want to hurl the left side of my body toward the opposite side of the street, which only causes me to immediately crash to the ground and smash my head open LIKE A FUCKING WATERMELON!)

Did I hear anyone ask where Skirt Chaser #6 was during any of this? You guessed it—with his cheap whore-secretary and the whore's crack-fiend husband (posing as her brother—what a laugh—ha!) who, I now understand, is dealing Ambien at Ambient Light festivals. I checked out the fucker's alibi, as well as the cheap whore-secretary's, and that of the crack-fiend husband (posing as her brother—what a laugh—ha!). They were all attending the Pataki is a Pistol NRA Shootout just outside Syracuse. (Not that I want him here until I install window guards and Nanny Cams in every room. I'm not going to end up being picked up with a sponge and declared a suicidal nut job when there are people to mutilate.)

I've got news about my darling daughter Reagan, the sunshine of my life. Of course, like me, you all over-medicated when Reagan's photo was plastered on TV and she was wrongly fingered as one of four suspects wanted in connection with the hateful London bombings. What she was doing in England in the first place is beyond me, because as you remember, the last we heard she was in Laos learning how to use a machete. *Triste, ma allinearer.* (Sad, but true.)

Sure, it *was* Reagan jumping the turnstile, but that doesn't make her a terrorist. All they had to do was ask me, and I would have told the authorities that from the time Reagan jumped out of my womb, she was always jumping *something*. My Goddess, do you remember when she won the gold in the high-jump event in Barcelona? *Era magnifica!* (She was magnificent!)

Looking back on it, I think she was most proud of the fact she jumped into bed with every member of the Dream Team, which if you've seen *Mandingo,* is every white girl's dream. (Oh, those were the days when I could take care of myself five times in a row while listening to Casey Kasem roll out "America's Top 40." Talk about a voice that could get you hot . . .)

Of course, the British authorities finally did take her picture off Sky News—thank Goddess. (The angle was her least flattering. It made her chin look weak, which it isn't, and shortened her face, making her look so butch, which she most certainly isn't.)

Everyone knows those surveillance cameras are programmed for the royals, who want their faces shortened. What—you don't believe me? Let's be real! You look at the wives of Henry The VIII and the first thing you want to do is lead them around a racetrack. *Se non lo credete, chiedere ai francesi.* (If you don't believe me, ask the French.)

The London cops (over there they're called bobbies) said they just got the pictures mixed up, because the real terrorist was also jumping a turnstile. You tell me how you can mistake my darling blonde-haired Reagan, who was totally in the nude and had no wires sticking out of any orifice, with that wired-up and fully-clothed *man* with a backpack bulging with dynamite?

Of course, there's no fucking way you'll buy that load of anti-feminist bullshit. (Don't worry, neither will a jury.)

Reagan called me right after her picture hit Sky News to tell me she hired a lawyer (only over there they call them "barristers") on a contingency fee and will be suing the cops, Sky News, the BBC, and any other station that carried the live feed.

Naturally, Reagan immediately got in touch with her grandfather and found out Abe had already initiated a lawsuit on behalf of *la famiglia* (the family) against the Fox News Network, because, as you may remember, it was their London affiliate's feed that maliciously slandered my darling daughter's gender when their reporter (that English snot) made the totally outrageous and libelous accusation that Reagan was Osama bin Laden's realtor for his place in Kabul *before* she actually got her real-estate license, which as you know, would mean she'd have to repeat the course. In addition, we're suing any program that maligned Reagan, including the Animal Channel, which devoted an entire show to comparing her jumping style to canine and equine champions.

My Goddess, you saw that photo! Were those Ginsburg (*pronounced* Du Pont) D-cups standing at attention, or what? And I didn't see any swinging dick there, either. *Riposo la mia cassa . . .* (I rest my case . . .)

I knew the whole thing was bogus from the start, and I'll tell you how. The London Chapter of the D.O.D. (a.k.a., Daughters of Darkness, a.k.a., the Anne Rice Stake and Ale Investment Club) has several members on the Metro Police Force. One in particular (Pricilla's her name*)*, just so happens to monitor all of London's CCTV cameras. This is a particularly valuable position, because the D.O.D. (a.k.a., Daughters of Darkness, a.k.a., the Anne Rice Stake and Ale Investment Club), as you'll read in Anne's next book, is in the final stages of capturing Lestat (who has been stalking Elton John in hopes of collaborating on a new musical blood type). (FYI—we've had Elton under surveillance for years—how smart are we?)

As soon as I heard from Pricilla, I called Abe, who immediately filled me in on the media lawsuits, as well as the one he made on behalf of me, the entire Family Ginsburg (*pronounced* Du Pont), and all our domestics, naming everyone in England as slanderous co-conspirators in a plot to denigrate American women who choose to go naked in the subways. (They call their subways "the Tube" or "the Underground.")

Meanwhile, the girls at the national chapter of the D.O.D. (a.k.a., Daughters of Darkness, a.k.a., the Anne Rice Stake and Ale Investment Club) took up a defense fund. The first thing they did was to take the false fangs Tom Cruise wore in *Interview with a Vampire* and put them up on eBay. Would you believe in the first twenty minutes the bidding reached $10,000 and in the auction's last minutes, the Risky Business Fan Club (the Women in Politics Chapter) won with a bid of $34,750? *Che eccitamento!* (What excitement!)

You can just imagine how touched I was by this extraordinary gesture, because, as you know, those fangs are amongst the D.O.D.'s (a.k.a., Daughters of Darkness, a.k.a., the Anne Rice Stake and Ale Investment Club) most valued possessions.

(FYI—it was Ms. Rice herself who gave them to us!) Why, Anne even showed us where Tom bit her when they were on set together, and how the fangs fit exactly into her scarred flesh. I think that awe-inspiring moment equaled the time we broke bread and drank lamb's blood with Anne and then drove a stake into the heart of the West Hampton Vampire who Rents. *Ché notte!* (What a night!)

There had been some debate as to whether we should have

disinfected the fangs, but I made it known that washing off Tom saliva would diminish their value, and surely, who in their right mind doesn't want to be bitten by the acting bug?

Shirley! Shirley, Shirley bo Birley, Bonana fanna fo Firley, Fee fy mo Mirley, Shirley.

Sorry . . . I JUST CAN'T CONTROL MYSELF! But *please,* I'm not looking for pity. Remember—out of crisis comes change, and since THE FUCKING ASSASSINATION ATTEMPT ON MY LIFE BY THAT DIRTY YELLOW RAT BITCH-BASTARD . . . *Breathe— breathe—breathe . . .*

As you know, I have learned to RELAX by throwing pots. What you don't know is that recently I have been only using my *left hand,* and this has made it possible for me to produce some even more remarkable work. *American Art and Hand Creams* called my new work "A must-see . . . and . . . heartbreakingly sensitive." *Non era quello piacevole?* (Wasn't that nice?)

To be more explicit, I have created a series of ceramic bird feeders in which I depict the Twelve Stages of Torture Facing the Person or Persons Who Attempted to Assassinate Me. Set against redolent garlands of real grapes, the figures in the series of friezes wind their way around the U-shaped feeder until they disappear into a mound of unrecognizable flesh, yet still remain incredibly lifelike—even as their limbs are hacked off and their skin is torn away from their bones.

Speaking purely as an *artiste* (artist), I can't tell you how pleased I am to have finally mastered the art of freeze-drying grapes, because, ever since my first Passover Seder, the pictures of grapes on the Mogen David wine bottles have had an unexplainable hold on me. *È vero.* (It's true.)

I have so much more to report, my loving Ginsburgs (*pronounced* Du Ponts), but the doctors tell me I shouldn't overdo it because any sudden movement could dislodge the bullets, causing fragments to work their way into my spinal fluid and eventually get sucked up into my brain, and then—I'D REALLY BE FUCKED.

Not to worry. I'm a Ginsburg (*pronounced* Du Pont) Girl, and we

G (*pronounced* D) Girls are survivors. *A vaffunculo!* (Fucking A!)

Fino alla stagione prossima I, miei dears! (Until next season, my dears!)

Cousin Cheryl, A Very Proud Mom!

P.S. Abe and I are also suing Shirley's Sister's Ex-Mother-in-Law's Market over the bogus wild Atlantic salmon (a.k.a., whatever) sale.

Shirley! Shirley, Shirley bo Birley, Bonana fanna fo Firley, Fee fy mo Mirley, Shirley!

P.S. Remember… *El amor nos guardará juntos.* (Love will keep us together.)

SING IT LOUD! SING IT PROUD! SING IT NOW!

From: Laverne.G@Ourmail.us
Date: Monday, March 21, 2005, 8:40 a.m.
To: Cheryl.G@Ourmail.us
Cc: US@Ourmail.us
Subject: Cousin Laverne's here for you

Oh, Cheryl honey, I feel your pain. And I just want to say that as soon as I resolve my issues with the Feds, I'm on a jet to New York City. For reasons that will become all too obvious, I can't disclose my whereabouts except to say it's a spitting image of Sammy's Roadside Upchuck Lunch Wagon, and there ain't no little pink houses anyplace I can see.

I'm in trouble with the FBI because they think I was the one who helped Willie escape, right from under the nose of their Assistant Director, don't you know. You remember I'm sure, William barricaded himself inside his bedroom to show the world Darwin ain't our daddy? Well, Uncle Jules got his monsignor friend, Def Rev, to interview me on his radio show, and don't you know, the very next day the Daughters of Adam and Eve along with five hundred of their sisters showed up at our house and staged a 24-hour vigil that—well—lasted up until the escape, which I guess is three months, right?

Willie was such big news that, will you believe, "60 Minutes" called and said they wanted to interview me as part of the story they were doing on the relationship between Kids Who Barricade and prenatal beer bingeing!

I said that would be just fine, but they had to interview William. I figured I could disguise myself as somebody from the show and once into the house I could find a way to get him outta there. The sheriff, who is president of the local Franz Kafka Book Club, said OK, as long as "60 Minutes" let him explain why David Duchovny is a cockroach. Naturally, the Feebs wanted their time, and not with just their local guys, but with some head honcho from Washington. Of course, "60 Minutes" agreed on that one, too, because all their producers are ex-agents.

The guy the Feds sends down is this hunk of an Assistant Director who I'd do in a New York *Minuto*. "60 Minutes" sends down Leslie Stahl, who, by the way, is really, really hot, and has wrists that are almost as thin as mine, even though I've been living the life of a Trailer Park Mama here in Unintelligent Design County for Goddess knows how long.

Anyway, while the TV crew is setting up in William's room, the Spielberg wannabe says William and his hostage looked a little sickly. He comes out of the house and tells me this. "No shit, Sherlock," I say, and you can quote me. But instead of offering them a decent meal, the moron wants them ASAP in the makeup trailer for some sprucing up.

Now, if anyone knows about trailers it's Marie, who, as everyone who doesn't have a finger up their you-know-what knows, has a thing for torching mobile homes for the insurance money. Incidentally, guess who now owns a Mary K Distributorship?

So, Marie, thinking she can make it up to me for toasting my brother Jack to a crisp, says she knows a way to help Willie escape. Well, I figure her idea may be better than me dressing up as Leslie Stahl, so I say *yes* to Marie. Well, she must have read my future mind because she pulls out a blueprint of the trailer. Does this psycho pyro come prepared, or what?

Marie goes on to say how easy it'll be for her to rig explosives in the overhead light fixtures, causing one hell of a diversion so nobody will notice us going up through a floorboard hatch and getting Willie out.

I'm thinking, what about Clara, the hostage? Then I think, what do I care about a demon child who won't let my son win a game of Chutes and Ladders?

Marie must be reading my future mind again, because she tells me she wants to take Clara, in case we need a hostage for later. Besides, she's sure the kids have a little something going on and doesn't want to deprive William of his—to use Marie's own words—"punch doll."

Well, the next thing I know, Marie's in and out of the makeup trailer before the makeup people bring the kids out. You should have heard the Daughters of Adam and Eve. They were chanting, "Free Willie, Free Willie, Free Willie!"

Once the kids were in the makeup trailer, the Daughters of Adam and Eve began launching green fig-leafed balloons with COME TO THE GARDEN on 'em. Then, someone goes and attaches their iPod to their car speakers and starts blasting "The Loco Motion" by Little Eva. The Daughters of Adam and Eve began ripping off their clothes and dancing naked under the balloons that start exploding as they boogie. Let me tell you, it was so very cool.

Well, instead of waiting for the light fixtures to explode as the diversion, Marie and me decided to use the dancing to our advantage and went right ahead up through the floor hatch and grabbed the kids.

We had no problem getting out of the trailer and over to Marie's car, what with all the Feds busy using their cell phones to take pictures of the Daughters of Adam and Eve dancing around in only the clothes Goddess gave 'em.

I had nothing to do with the violence that was brought upon the hair-and-makeup girl. It was Marie who knocked her out with the blow-dryer to the head. Thank the Goddess the stylist was blown free when the trailer exploded.

The biggest surprise of all is that William *is* really doing Clara, and that they want to go to Vegas. I told them they were underage and I could go to jail for helping them. You know what they said to me? *"What happens in Vegas stays in Vegas."* Kids!

Marie sees how happy I am I have my little one back, so she takes me aside and confesses: *not only did she murder my brother Jack, but she also helped my dad kill my mom by teaching him how to blow up their trailer to make it look like a propane accident.* OK, saving my boy may have squared the accounts, but you can bet I'll never step inside another trailer as long as Marie's around.

I've been in contact with my other kids, and while they've been supportive, I found out Conrad's back in the soup. Yep, you guessed it. Another one of his classmates went missing and the cops are blaming him. What a surprise! This kid Connie hardly knew, even though there was talk about the both of them competing for the last spot on the varsity basketball team. The stink's really on Connie's shit this time, being the kid's father's brother is some hotshot writer for "CSI," so naturally, the whole cast is out there investigating the case.

Judith Ann's dealt with these Hollywood types, so she set Connie straight. Before he answered any questions, or let them take a DNA swab, she found him an agent, who got him right into SAG. Not only is Connie getting a speaking part, but also he'll have union benefits. What we're all hoping for is a two-part episode.

I was praying they would also spot Judith Ann's talents. My Goddess, she's got a double portion of the Ginsburg (*pronounced* Du Pont) gifts, but when she met with "CSI" she was wearing a shroud. She told me the aliens wouldn't consider her unless they get "first look." I told her passing up "CSI" for "going alien" was so, *so* brave—but would you expect less from a Ginsburg (*pronounced* Du Pont)?

Judith Ann says the aliens have put up an invisible shield around her and Conrad so the poison gas cloud won't kill them, but she doesn't hold out much hope for anyone else in town. I guess I caught the 3:10 to Yuma just in time.

To show you how big-hearted I am, I told Jerry I'd get him out, wheelchair and all, but he told me to go fuck myself. He swears *I* was the one who poisoned the water and made the whole thing up about the copper mines and mud slides. He says everyone in my family is a murderer, and that his only salvation is through the magic of crystal meth. Can you please tell me why I married that man?

He wants me to go to his web site, Kill.Laverne.com and see pictures of him in various tries at standing without a hoist. Then he tells me that until the day comes he can walk up to me on his own two feet and put a bullet right between my eyes, he ain't leaving.

Jerry also says he's getting the crystal meth from the FEMA people, who he brags are first cousins he hasn't seen since they disappeared twenty-years ago when they went on a school trip to Washington, D.C.

He says his cousins' mission is to get relatives to get in touch with their inner self and then give them enough crystal meth until the End of Days, or when incest becomes legal, which to some is the same.

At least Jerry's not staying for that little bitch-bastard hussy, who slings hash and hauls your ashes at June's on Juniper. She's a short, flat-chested bitch-bastard hussy who doesn't mind sitting on Jerry's face and playing Guess my Weight.

Cheryl, honey, don't you worry, I'm monitoring the situation, and if there's anything to this magical cure I'll have the local Rapture Chapter of FEMA at your bedside before you can call CVS for some Sudafed. Ooops, Sammy caught the kids shoplifting. Gotta run!

Love to all!

Cousin Laverne

P.S. Love this seasonal shit.

P.P.S. If you want to contact me, use Ginsburg (*pronounced* Du Pont) email address.

From: Bubbeh.E@Ourmail.us
Date: Monday, March 21, 2005, 8:50 a.m.
To: Cheryl.G@Ourmail.us
Cc: US@Ourmail.us
Subject: A *choleryeh* on them!

Mein darling Cheryl,
Oi vai iz mir!—excuse my French—woe is me!
I have not lived large for 404 years (give or take) and gone through the agony of throwing away clothes only to see them come back into style twenty seasons later to now have tragedy like this happen to one of my own. Who but someone so jealous of our genetics would do such a nasty thing? *A choleryeh ahf dir!*—excuse my French—a plague on you!

I only wish you had gone with me to see the Finest Doctor and let him put eyes in back of your head, the way he did for me. Then you would see the world as I see it. But no, your father wouldn't let me take you to Mount Cedar. You were only a little girl then, and even though the Finest Doctor said that was the best time to do the operation, the *chadrool* was afraid of the psychological side effects. Numbskull!

I can't tell you how many times those extra pair of eyes saved my hide. You could have been like Donna Troy with her Enhanced Vision.

You know, *mein* darling Cheryl, the concept of a magically created "Duplicate" started with She Who Brings Forth Life, the Great Baleboosteh Ginsburg (*pronounced* Eleanor of Aquitaine), who, you should also know, was the real-life inspiration for Wonder Woman. Check out the latest issue. Look at the way she manhandles men, knows every discount outlet, loves gossip, and gets her jokes right out of the Talmud. If that's not proof enough, look at that profile. If that's not a Dr. Pearlswine passport, I'll give up eating peanuts. She's got She Who Brings Forth Life, the Great Baleboosteh Ginsburg (*pronounced* Eleanor of Aquitaine) written all over her face, but this is all hush-hush, top-secret, because there's enough anti-Wonder

Womanism in the world already.

There's so, so much about our family that's historic, and yes, so much is nicely documented in those cave paintings (oh, how thin I was), Egyptian tombs (colorful), the Dead Sea Scrolls (I could have used some lipstick), and of course, the Bible (all versions); and we mustn't forget those nice Greek boys, who wrote such sweet things about us, especially Homer, but *az och un vai,* alas, the really good stuff hasn't been declassified. *Mein tsatskeleh der mamehs,* momma's little pet, I would like to impart this one piece of our history that you may or may not be familiar with.

In 1941, I was a little past the halfway point (give or take), of my fourth century. I had seen enough of life to know the Huns and the Nips were going to try and clean our clocks, so I was itching to take it to those *vantzen.* And let me tell you, I could have really made a difference. You see, *mein* darling Cheryl, not only did I have my magical ovaries that bestowed upon me elephantine powers, and thanks to the eyes in back of my head, my Surround Vision 360, but I had other little things done to me over the years.

Oh, yes! Wonderful, magical things were bestowed upon me. For instance, when somebody said. "Read my mind," I *could do it.* Or, "Put yourself in my place." *I could do that, too!* Imagine what a secret weapon I would have made!

Alas, it was not to be. How could it? I was the richest woman in America. I had my face on the covers of *Look* and *Life,* and after Little Orphan Annie, yours truly—*your Bubbeh Esther (pronounced Granny Smith Apples)*—was the woman boys under ten most wanted to marry, so, naturally, *Boys Life* picked me as their Camp Girl of the Year.

I know what some of you are out there thinking. *How could Bubbeh Esther (pronounced Granny Smith Apples) be a pinup girl when she had a trunk?* Easy peasy—I only had the trunk during the time I had *my friend* with me. And, let me tell you something else—having a trunk is a lot better than PMS, which used to made me so unhinged that during the American Revolution I had to twice sacrifice chickens just to keep my sanity—and let me tell you, just trying to find a kosher butcher in a Hessian neighborhood could make you crazy. *Emes*—true, it's true, it's true.

Speaking of sanity, maybe a little animal sacrifice here and there might save your poor sister, Tenderly. Of course, chickens are out, but as far as I know, there's no sheep flu.

As I was talking—the trunk only came out during my period, so naturally, during that time I just stayed out of sight. Thanks to She Who Brings Forth Life, the Great Baleboosteh Ginsburg (*pronounced* Eleanor of Aquitaine), I was regular, so I could set my calendar. Things are a lot different now thanks to that lovely man who did the make-up for *Mrs. Doubtfire*.

Anyway, *mein* darling Cheryl, as I was talking, I—me—your Bubbeh Esther (*pronounced* Granny Smith Apples) was becoming so popular with the boys, suddenly, those fools in Washington were afraid to send me off to war and risk me being killed. So, they had the bright idea to parade me around the country like a trained elephant, no pun intended, selling war bonds with draft-dodging movie stars like John Wayne. *A nahr bleibt a nahr*—excuse my French—a fool remains a fool.

Naturally, being a Ginsburg (*pronounced* Du Pont) Girl, I wanted to fight like Robert Ryan, or Lee Marvin. These were real celebrity heroes. Ted Williams was another. Did I ever tell you Teddy had such great eye-hand coordination he'd keep dry in a thunderstorm just by swatting away the raindrops? I could too, but I had an advantage. I had a trunk!

I never stopped badgering those fools in Washington, and was about to take things into my own hands when my luck changed!

I have to thank my darling A. E. for recognizing my true talents and for helping me to achieve my finest hour. Of course, I helped A. E. achieve *his* finest hour more times that he could count, but that's all relative, pun intended, and you know I'm not one for splitting hairs when I was splitting atoms.

Yes—you guessed it, *$E = MC^2$ was mine!* Like all great breakthroughs, it was part inspiration, part perspiration. During a quantum mechanics orgy I was showing A. E. how much energy leaves the *shvantz,* and how the *shvantz* shrinks in proportion to the energy that leaves it, when suddenly it came to me! (Pun intended.)

People think A. E. was so smart, but I can't tell you how many times I had to get him off before he finally agreed with me.

I remember when they dropped the Atomic Bomb over Japan. A. E. and I were in a movie theater, watching the newsreels, when he took my hand, put it on his *shvantz* and said, "*Liebschen,* I'm going to leave my wife for you."

Du kannst nicht auf meinem rucken pishen unt mir sagen class es regen ist—excuse my French—you can't pee on my back and tell me that it's rain! Not when I can read minds! I just played with the *putz* and smiled.

You know, don't you, later on A. E. gave me a nice portion of grade-A plutonium for Hanukkah that I quickly flipped and sold to the State of Israel, for which I was inscribed in *The Book of Their Life,* by no less a figure than Ben-Gurion, who not had only nice hair, but was quite the stud bagel.

Oh, the stories I could tell, and I'm not even talking about what's going on now with Mr. Big Shot Homeland Security, who, my darling, is on your case. In fact, right this minute he has his people questioning former contestants of "Survivor" because he suspects wild salmon poaching is the motive behind the assassination attempts on your life.

I know what you're thinking, and I told him those young boys don't steal salmon, they fondle D-cuppers. Unfortunately, I've learned from years of doing wet work for the Company, once a spook gets a bug up his *toches*—*er drayt sich arum vie a fortz in russel*—excuse my French—he wanders around like a fart in a barrel.

Don't forget to eat your chicken soup; you need to be strong for the plane ride. I'm having the Second Avenue Deli cater, so don't you worry about not having enough *kishka.*

I'm thinking of having some little things done, but this trip is all about you, *mein* darling, Cheryl. When I last talked to the Finest Doctor he had just viewed your x-rays, and told me to tell you to keep smoking that special something he sent you, and that he'd see you in two weeks. He also said to tell you not to do any walking when you're smoking. He didn't mention your weapons training, so I assume the assault weapons mounted on your bed aren't a problem.

I was also thinking that after Mount Cedar, we could go to the Caymans and do a little spear fishing and some money laundering. I just wish *That Putz* wouldn't be so soft with those cement companies of mine, but I think that little stretch in Lewisburg really turned him into "somebody's punch"—so there it is.

Remember, *mein* darling Cheryl, if you think sunshine can be found behind a cloudy sky filled with gunpowder and dope, follow your instincts, let your hair down and cry out: *I'm a Family Ginsburg (pronounced Du Pont) Girl!*

It works for me, *mein* darling Cheryl, it works for me.
I love you all as only a Bubbeh (pronounced Granny) can!
Bubbeh Esther (*pronounced* Granny Smith Apples)

From: Maxie.Ruthie.4Ever@Ourmail.com
Date: Monday, March 1, 2005, 9:02 a.m.
To: US@Ourmail.us
Subject: Maxie in Florida

I'm doing great! I run thirty miles a day on the treadmill and then I do the machines for two hours. Ivan, my personal trainer, says after him, I'm the strongest guy he's ever seen. Can you imagine? *Emes!* No bullshit!

You should see the women! When they get sweaty you can see their nipples. Can you imagine? *Emes!* No bullshit!

I'm not afraid of the *farkakte* hurricane season, so stop calling and asking if I'm all right! And stop with the emails, already. I've been coming here longer than you've been blacking out on painkillers, so I know a thing or two about hurricanes. That Andrew was a bitch-bastard and a half, but my condo stood up to it like Briscoe and Green stand up to crime, so stop with the worrying.

Ruthie—may she rest in peace, *aleichem sholom*—is on her side of the bed, which is away from the window. Can you imagine? *Emes!* No bullshit!

That *mamzer* Malek, the bitch-bastard, says he's gonna come up and fix the leaks in the bedroom windows, but the condo's got him moving everyone's porch furniture inside. Just in case a hurricane does hit, I got Ruthie—may she rest in peace, *aleichem sholom*—nicely wrapped up in that green raincoat she bought at B. Altman. It was the day before they went out of business, so she got a great deal, plus she walked away with an extra set of buttons. That's one good thing I can say about Ruthie—may she rest in peace, *aleichem sholom*—she always knew how to get an extra set of buttons. Too bad she didn't know when to button her pants, huh?

That reminds me, I got to go to Walmart and get room freshener before they're sold out. That's what happens when people hear there's a hurricane coming—the goddamn bitch-bastards clean off the shelves before you can get up and pee. Can you imagine? *Emes!* No bullshit!

It's those goddamn sissy-boy weathermen like that Dr. Bob on Channel 66. So, big deal, he won the America's Cup and sailed solo around Cape Horn. You should see his wife. Another Cuban, only this one has blue eyes and a Greek father. I'd also do her in a Miami Heart Hospital *minuto*. Can you imagine? *Emes!* No bullshit!

I've bribed insurance adjusters longer than Dr. Bob's been *shtupping* female traffic reporters, so I know something about hurricanes. You know, he owns three clothing stores. That's the only reason he's always wearing Brioni, the bitch-bastard *mamzer.* His South Beach store's in one of my properties, so I go. I was there on Tuesday, but I didn't see Bob. He's never there when there's a sale. I bought three suits—Brioni, naturally. I'm not going to let some weatherman look better than me. I also bought a couple sports jackets, also Brioni, also marked down. Between you and me and nobody you know, they threw in a few pairs of silk socks because I told them I'd do something about the leak in the toilet and because I paid cash. Like they say, "Cash talks, nobody walks."

Ruthie—may she rest in peace, *aleichem sholom*—knew all about Dr. Bob from Gianni, her sissy-boy hairdresser—may he rest in peace, *aleichem sholom.* Get this one: Gianni—may he rest in peace, *aleichem sholom*—told her that Dr. Bob secretly married a telephone repairman from Coconut Grove. You could have hit me with a nine iron. I said to Ruthie, "How can he be a *faygeleh*? He's got a wife." She told me, and I quote, "I was a stupid fuck for not keeping up with the latest news." End of quote. She showed me the paper where it said, "The city says people on TV can now marry one person from both sexes as long as their mates are really great looking." The next day I tripled her *schmear.* Can you imagine? *Emes!* No bullshit!

She then goes on to tell me that Gianni—may he rest in peace, *aleichem sholom*—told her he did everybody's hair for the reception dinner and the wedding. And get this—*everyone wore hair extensions*. Can you imagine? *Emes!* No bullshit!

I said to Ruthie—may she rest in peace, *aleichem sholom*—what the hell is a hair extension? She said, and I quote, I was "an ignorant fuck," and she didn't know why she "ever married me." End of quote. Then she said it was like a wig. I said, so why not call it a wig? She said, and I quote, "It's really not a wig, it's extra hair they attach to the regular hair. That's why they call it hair extensions." End of quote. She called them something else—*dreadlox!* I almost threw her off the terrace, the smart-alecky, bitch-bastard *mamzer.* Can you imagine? *Emes!* No bullshit!

Making fun of my favorite fish! Can you imagine? *Emes!* No bullshit!

I've been eating novie-and-veggie cream cheese every day of my life, so I know for a fact there is no such lox.

And how about this—the next morning I was having my novie-and-veggie cream on an everything bagel at Maury's over on Sunrise, when don't you know it, the whole Dolphin team comes in, and I see everybody's got hair, like in braids. Can you imagine? *Emes!* No bullshit!

I only went to Maury's because Ruthie—may she rest in peace, *aleichem sholom*—likes their fruit cocktail. I think she had a yen for Maury, that overcharging bitch-bastard *mamzer* behind the counter, sucking on his Makers Mark Torpedo like it was a chicken wing. Maury's one of those Sephardic Jews from Spain, and he thought Ruthie—may she rest in peace, *aleichem sholom*—was one, too. He was always talking Spanish to her. He was real dark skinned, but Ruthie—may she rest in peace, *aleichem sholom*—was even darker. That's how much chicken fat she had in her. Can you imagine? *Emes!* No bullshit!

You know a small black coffee in there was over two dollars? And that was before Starbucks, those bitch-bastard *mamzers,* ever opened a place. I always quadrupled her *schmear* after we had coffee there. Can you imagine? *Emes!* No bullshit!

I nearly choked when Ruthie—may she rest in peace, *aleichem sholom*—opens her mouth and says to the football players, "Nice dreads." I thought they would drag me out to my car and turn it over with me in it. I was driving a red 55 SCL at the time, with the top down, naturally. Can you imagine? *Emes!* No bullshit!

I could see them eying my key ring, which was lying next to my novie-and-everything bagel, so I knew—they knew—I knew someone was going to have to call the paramedics.

In the car, Ruthie—may she rest in peace, *aleichem sholom*—spells it out; and we had quite a laugh. Can you imagine? *Emes!* No bullshit!

Ruthie—may she rest in peace, *aleichem sholom*—could make me laugh when she wanted. Too bad she couldn't come up with the funny stuff when I killed Larry the *mamzer* postman—may he rest in peace, *aleichem sholom*. Can you imagine? *Emes!* No bullshit!

You know what was funny, too? When I got into the parking lot there must have been twenty other cars like mine, so all my worrying was for nothing. Can you imagine? *Emes!* No bullshit!

Benny Ackerman and Saul Turpin say they heard on the Weather Channel we're gonna get twenty-one hurricanes this season. They're like sissy boys, the way they run out to the pool and tell everyone, the bitch-bastard *faygelehs*. Can you imagine? *Emes!* No bullshit!

You know how nuts they are? They wanted to invite some know-it-all called Hurricane Tracker Man to our monthly condo board meeting. And listen to this: For twenty-five dollars plus dinner, this bitch-bastard *gantse kener* is gonna show us pictures of hurricanes and tell us how we can protect the condo so it won't wash away into the ocean. Can you imagine? *Emes!* No bullshit!

That's all we need to do—spend twenty-five bucks plus dinner on this *putz* and you know what happens: the *snowbirds*, those crazy bitch-bastards *mamzers,* who already complain we spend too much on *farkakte* cleaning products, will be pulling the fire alarms, and setting off smoke detectors like they did the last winter. Can you imagine? *Emes!* No bullshit!

I almost pulled Blanche Friedman's arm out of her goddamn socket when I caught her pulling the alarm on my floor. The bitch-bastard *mamzer!* I would have done it, too, but she'd have called the cops, and then I'd have to hide Ruthie's body in the powder room—may she rest in peace, *aleichem sholom*—a major problem, because when I invite women over, I love to show them the powder room. I got gold faucets in the shapes of swans. It's beautiful. Can you imagine? *Emes!* No bullshit!

Turpin still owes me thirty-five bucks from the other night, the *mamzer*. Benny, another *mamzer*, tells me he won't play with me because he says I don't remember whose turn it is and I don't know the rules. I've been playing poker longer than they've been playing with themselves, the bitch-bastard *mamzers*. Can you imagine? *Emes!* No bullshit!

This is the same Benny Ackerman who was on his hands and knees kissing my *toches* after I gave him Bermuda's number. This is the same Benny Ackerman who sold me a thousand after-market Viagras and screwed me on the price. I bought 'em anyway because I happen to know for a fact that he lost his shirt with those phony baloney stocks his no-good bitch-bastard son-in-law's always talking up.

See what happens when you do somebody a favor—they stick it right back up your *toches*. Can you imagine? *Emes!* No bullshit!

Tenderly said she's got a place on the Internet that sells Viagra for ten cents a shot. It's the place where you can get the snake venom kit that I don't need, and I told her so. It's nice that at least one of my daughter's is looking out for her old man.

Hey, Sylvia, your husband still *shtup es in toches*? *Um-be-shrien!*

You know, if I eat four pounds of almonds in a day, I can't shit? Can you imagine? *Emes!* No bullshit!

I can thank Publix for putting them on sale. That reminds me, I got to call Abe to see where that lawsuit is going.

Listen to this, Benny and Saul told me I was a *schmuck* for not storing my car inland. That's what they did, the bitch-bastard *mamzers*. They lease white Jags. Only *faygelehs,* who wear white loafers without socks, and women who play mahjong drive white Jags.

My Mercedes dealer, the bitch-bastard *mamzer,* told me he wouldn't take the responsibility. Jake Shapiro. He pronounces it—*Sha-pie-row.* What a *gantse macher* this one. His father used to own the Chevy dealership in Ozone Park. Back then it was called *Shapiro*, not *Sha-pie-row.* Can you imagine? *Emes!* No bullshit!

Melvin—may he rest in peace, *aleichem sholom*—was a *mentsch* and wouldn't think twice about storing my car. This *mamzer* son of a bitch is giving me the shaft because he's pissed I got the free cover. I know this because Michele Stein, another bitch-bastard *mamzer*—you know, the one who gave the clap to Benny—she's storing her leased SL 600, list price $140,000 with everything, and says, Jake told her he never liked the idea of giving away free covers. Can you imagine? *Emes!* No bullshit!

I told Benny she was trouble, but he wouldn't listen. She's also got a Silver Seraph, two-tone, cream and brown. A lot of good it'll do when he can't sit still for even two seconds without scratching his balls. Can you imagine? *Emes!* No bullshit!

I hear through the grapevine she's storing it in the Rolls Royce Miami Beach showroom on NW 2nd Avenue. Benny tells me the place looks like Fort Knox and is *one-hundred-percent hurricane proof.* I own the property across the street, the one with the Aston Martin dealership in it. That's where I got my new Vanquish S. It's in the goddamn shop because Pearlstein, that bitch-bastard *mamzer*, clipped my fender. Twenty-five hundred and fifty bucks to remove the yellow paint! Can you imagine? *Emes!* No bullshit!

I know it's him, because when I was looking at the GT2, the salesman, the bitch-bastard *mamzer*, showed me one in that same ugly yellow. I told him I wouldn't take it even if he gave it to me, and not just because the *putz* Pearlstein's got one, but because that car only looks good in Seal-Gray Metallic. The bitch-bastard agreed with me, too.

I know Pearlstein hates me because he heard the boys want me to run for president of the condo board. If I didn't like Porsches so much, I would have slashed his tires, or maybe keyed the driver's side. Can you imagine? *Emes!* No bullshit!

I got a good mind to tell the board Benny got the clap from Michele Stein. The trouble is, I know for a fact she got it from Malek, the bitch-bastard *mamzer.* And, I also know for a fact Malek carries a machete; and forget about him fixing my leak. Can you imagine? *Emes!* No bullshit!

Did I tell you I'm thinking of dating Miriam Klein? She's got a white 2005 Corniche. Very sporty, with white seats trimmed in red. On her it looks good. And, I know for a fact, she's clean. Ruthie—may she rest in peace, *aleichem sholom*—told me Miriam hadn't had sex since her husband, Hymie—may he rest in peace, *aleichem sholom*—got the prostate operation. The next time I saw him I gave him some Viagra. Ruthie—may she rest in peace, *aleichem sholom*—told me, and I quote, I was "just a fucking insensitive, uneducated slob." End of quote. Can you imagine? *Emes!* No bullshit!

I gave her an extra *schmear* of *schmaltz* for a week after that one.

How's this for a coincidence? Ruthie died the same day as Hymie—may they both rest in peace, *aleichem sholom*. Can you imagine? *Emes!* No bullshit!

Since the funeral I could see Miriam had an itch for me. I could always tell these things.

I'm also thinking of marrying my Cuban maid.

Did I tell you I run fifty miles a day on the treadmill? Can you imagine? *Emes!* No bullshit!

Love,
Uncle Maxie

From: Clarice.G@Ourmail.us
Date: Monday, March 1, 2005, 9:20 a.m.
To: Maxie.Ruthie.4Ever@Ourmail.us
Cc: US@Ourmail.us
Subject: Clearing the air!

If everyone didn't hate Ruthie so much, we would have informed on you so f-ing fast, maybe we could have saved the old witch.

Do you know Tenderly has to fly all the way out to f-ing Oregon to find a f-ing deli that doesn't serve chicken-fat sandwiches?

And just think of what you did to Sylvia, your other daughter. Do you have any idea how many hours of aromatherapy she needed to overcome her fear of white bread?

Now that I have my Fiorinals down to a manageable dosage and I'm not seeing Williams-Sonoma stores blowing up whenever I turn off my lights, I know it's you calling.

Clarice... Clarice... wash your mouth out with soap... Clarice...

What's more, don't you ever, *ever* mention f-ing Jerry Orbach's name again. He was a great f-ing actor and never drove cars that were too f-ing young for him.

And—enough with this *"aleichem sholom"* business. If you want someone to rest in peace, maybe you shouldn't have killed 'em in the first f-ing place.

Hey, Pops—I'm after you, too. You don't put a restraining order on a five-year-old and expect there won't be repercussions. Not one of my nursery-school playmates came near me after that; and your offer of milk and cookies plus immunity from further TROs didn't work either, did it? It wasn't until I was twenty that I had my very own playdate, and I had to go to f-ing *Marrakech* for that—thank you very much.

Which reminds me, Honest Abe, what's up with the trial, huh? You said they'd be picking a jury next week, right? So, why haven't I heard from you? What kind of a f-ing father takes care of a stranger's lawsuit before his own daughter's?

Do you know how much f-ing pleasure I'm going to have when I watch you cross-examine that writer-dick; see him sweat, see him squirm as you take him apart, bit by bit, until he f-ing realizes he can't use my name in vain and get away with it?

And that f-ing Hopkins, he's going to pay through his actor's nose, too; you can bet the farm on that, Pops.

Let this be a lesson to anyone who wants to use someone's name in literature, or in the movies without asking their permission.

Don't think I'm gonna stop with f-ing celebs; there's more f-ing name-robbers out there destroying the lives of honest, hardworking Americans, and I'm going to get them, too.

I'd start with the United States Hurricane Bureau, one of *the* worst f-ing name-robbers on the planet. Imagine your name's *Andrew* and you live in f-ing Florida? Your world's a living nightmare. Everyone's always staring, thinking *you're* the cause of the most devastating hurricane in the history of the state, sending you emails, blaming *you* for their house being destroyed, or their unemployment because the f-ing building they worked in doesn't have a roof any more.

But first, Daddy Dearest, you win the case for your darling daughter. It won't make up for robbing me of my childhood playdates, and it won't save *this* Clarice and her name, but if we can confiscate every copy of *Silence of the Lambs* and put a restraining order on Hopkins's ass so he'll never again utter "*Clarice*" in an English pub, you'll have helped to wipe the slate clean, make it safe again to name a girl *Clarice*. A name that once upon a time, every little boy at Miss Wonderly's Dance School had on his lips until you forced them into bankruptcy with your too-much-wax-on-the-floor lawsuit.

Cousin Clarice

P.S. Sister Cheryl, I wish I could go with you and Bubbeh Esther (*pronounced* Granny Smith Apples) and lend you the moral support you need. The truth is—well—when I got my first crank phone call, I f-ed up and thought the Yiddish was actually *German*; and since the only German I know is the Finest Doctor—well—I thought it was *him* saying, you know ... *Clarice* ... *Clarice* ... *wash your mouth out with soap* ... *Clarice* ...

To get even, I called and pretended I was Diana Ross. Well—things got a little out of hand—and—every hour for the past six days—umm—we've been talking. Actually—umm—*I've been singing.*

Well—don't be so surprised; you were always jealous that I sounded like Diana. Of course, everybody at the karaoke bar said I looked like her, too, but I don't see the resemblance, except maybe when I wear my hair up.

The thing is—it's gotten serious, and he wants me to come to Mount Cedar and *marry him*. He says he's going to give me wings for a wedding present—*so I'll really be a songbird.* That's what he calls me, his "Little Songbird." You can see now why I can't come, can't you?

P.P.S. At Kitty's suggestion, I'm going make an entire chapter out of the time you, Uncle Maxie, and Uncle Jules took Cheryl and me to the f'ing pickle factory.

P.P.P.S. Kitty just wishes she could have borrowed some of it when she was writing about Frank.

From: Sylvia.G@Ourmail.us
Date: Monday, March 21, 2005, 9:23 a.m.
To: Cheryl.G@Ourmail.us
Subject: What a nice idea!

Dear Cousin Cheryl,

Now do you see that your sister is nuts and should be committed straight away? Uncle Clayboy has done all the necessary paperwork, and we're ready to grab her as soon as we find out where she is—and *that* I'm leaving to you. I've got some leads, but more on that later. What a nice idea to have us all communicate with each other like this, instead of that damn cell phone. Those dropped calls make me want to kill someone. Don't they just drive you crazy, too? And what about the calls that don't go through? I called my provider, and the imbeciles had the nerve to tell me the people blocking my calls *were the people I was calling*. Well, I know that's a damn lie, because I only use my cell to call family members. Of course, it could be the ATF. I need a ciggie and a pee.

OK, I'm back.

I can't remember, but have I asked if you're happy with your provider? If you are, I'll switch. Will they let me keep the same number? It's the one the fire department has on speed dial. Speaking of men with hoses, did I tell you the fire marshals would be coming at the end of the month? You remember those guys, don't you and that headline: "Hooter Lighting—Another Victoria's Secret Burns to the Ground." Of course, they couldn't prove a thing. After all, there were plenty of women besides you who were burning their bras and dressing up like Betty Freidan. Uncle Clayboy says it's my landlord and the insurance company, checking to see what I can torch. Not to worry. Just steamer trunks and porch furniture, and all fireproof. No 18th-century French this time. And, forget about the Aubussons. Oh sure, they were priceless, but I *now* know *it was their designs that triggered my hallucinations.* You know—if I hadn't gone out onto the terrace and passed out, I might have gone back for my ciggie, and that would have been the end of me, because the fireman said the rugs went up in minutes after I dropped it. Just the same, I am thinking of Crate and Barrel and their line of fire-retardant faux wood collection. I know, I know I like living without furniture, but it's getting harder and harder to deal with those multiple personalities echoing through the empty apartment repeating the same things *over and over and over again.* And when Dr. Peck said it was either doubling up on the Percodan, or puncturing my eardrums (a padded cell in Mount Sinai was not an option), Crate and Barrel looked better every day. Remember their Christmas party, last year? All those handsome Broadway Chorus Boys; and weren't *we* the hit of the party? I even recognized a few from Hill's Bar Mitzvah. Oh my Goddess, *that was over twenty years ago!* I remember it like it was yesterday—the day Hillary became a man, and the day *I first attempted suicide with a firearm.* I need a ciggie and a pee.

OK, I'm back.

I know you thought Hillary and Dale looked great on "Ellen" the other day, and I certainly was thrilled their design firm was chosen to decorate all the Budweiser Breweries in the style of Versailles, but I can't help being overprotective, and it has nothing to do with those hysterical outbursts I get when I watch Clydesdales pulling beer trucks. Cheryl, does your provider allow you to make free calls to anyone in your plan? Won't that be fun if we can talk to each other for free! I don't know why you paid to see that Korean movie when you know the box-office receipts go straight into Kim Dae Jung's pocket, and then he turns around and buys his cognac from Hennessy instead of from Courvoisier and *giving us the profit.* I'm not supposed to know this, but agents from the ATF told me Book 'em Dano's a regular in North Korea. I should have known that when he sent me those shawls reeking of machine oil. Why, anyone married to an arms dealer knows that smell! You can imagine my surprise, or shall I say *horror*, when I saw the exact shawl in Soho. Fifteen hundred and up, and that's Goddess's-honest truth. Bermuda was just as surprised. I told her Daddy should give up gunrunning and go into the rag trade. If Ralph can graduate from polo shirts to polo ponies, why can't Daddy go from shotguns to shawls? Maybe you've seen them? You're always shopping in Soho—I meant before the shooting. Cheryl, it's great news you're going to see the Finest Doctor next month, but in the meantime—I know I've said this a hundred times before—it's simply not healthy, you sitting around your place all day long planning those murders. You need some air. Take it from me, I know—and I know *you* know *I know*. It doesn't have to be a *wheelchair*. They have those wonderful motorized *scooters* that come in all different colors. They even have their own outlet, The Scooter Store. Isn't that fantastic! You see the commercials everywhere, and the people doing wheelies on them look so happy. Book 'em Dano had one in Honduras. You remember, while his legs were healing? It even had a rack for a rocket launcher. It was red and had a Nike logo, and *"Just do it"* on the windscreen. At his trial, the AFI guys showed me a picture. I'm sorry you weren't there, but I understand. I think the next time they'll have wheelchair—I mean, *scooter*—accessibility. Oh—what am I saying! By then, you'll be back on your feet again, won't you? Anyway, it'll all be on Court TV. It's not every day people get to see a trial held in absentia. Book 'em Dano had no choice, really. It was either that, or getting stomped to death. Then, of course, there was the possibility of jail time, but that was remote, considering he had all those names to trade. Did I tell you the bastard called Bermuda *last night*? He's in Moscow, can you believe? And, don't you know, he's working with the same people he was going to turn in. Book 'em Dano's always been the one to forgive when it had to do with business—*and forget* when it had to do with our wedding vows, or he had one of his own daughter's kneecaps broken. What really pisses me off is that he and Bermuda talk all the time. She's completely forgiven him. *Me* she treats like someone who can't be trusted with matches, but her father can do no wrong. She says he's a better listener. LISTEN TO THIS… I HATE THAT SON OF A BITCH! I need another ciggie and a pee.

OK, I'm back!

OK, *OK,* Cheryl, you were right. I should have taken you up on your offer to have your people *handle* Book 'em Dano after they get the sons of bitches that shot you. My Goddess, Cheryl, you're such a giving person. But, if you remember, I was having a QVC Moment and I couldn't focus on anything else but that to-die-for eighteen-carat onyx-and-jade panda-bear necklace with matching earrings that originally sold for $5,500.00, but was on special for $9.99, plus shipping and handling. Oh, there they are again, those voices in my head. Do you think it could be from the stool softeners? My Goddess, I'm sounding like Tenderly. Oh, where the fuck is the Crate and Barrel catalogue? I need another ciggie and a pee.

OK, I'm back!

You know, I can understand where Bermuda is coming from. Martyrdom was one of Book 'em Dano's most attractive traits. Uncle Clayboy's got it, too. Maybe it's a crucifixion thing? Did I tell you Monroe's with Book 'em Dano in Moscow? Bermuda told me to tell you Book 'em Dano said to tell you Monroe had to leave unexpectedly and couldn't call because of security reasons, but that he'll try and telephone you tonight. He said you would know where and when. Bermuda also said Book 'em Dano also said Monroe flew in on a stealth bomber, but he would be returning on the company jet. Bermuda also, *also* told me that Book 'em Dano also, also said they were discussing *a job opportunity*. Apparently, Monroe wants Arms and Ammo to get into space stations and thinks Book 'em Dano, owing to his expertise in thieving without borders, would be perfect for the job. I need another ciggie and a pee.

OK, I'm back!

Where was I? Oh yes—beautiful people just get a fucking free pass in this world, don't they? You and I have to work our D-cups till the nipples are raw, not to mention throw up after every meal, while all they have to do is show up in a pink Lacoste polo shirt, pink socks, white bucks, put a hand nonchalantly through their hair and everyone's on their knees praying to Nobu. Look at your son. Why do you think Monroe always looked up to Book 'em Dano? He was the good-looking father figure he never had. Why do you think he brought *him* and not *Lou, his own father,* to Parents Day? And why,

why when Monroe accepted the Nobel Peace Prize, did your son single out *my husband* as the one person in his life he most admired and sought to emulate? Monroe even dyed his hair strawberry blonde, put in those tacky blue contact lens, and started wearing pink Gucci socks. Remember? Book 'em Dano was supplying arms to the Khmer Rouge at the time, but I think he saw the ceremony on a satellite hookup. Can you imagine how that murdering band must have felt when they saw this blond Adonis-like creature walk into their jungle with a hundred cases of automatic weapons and twenty cases of Stinger missiles? Just think of the first time you saw Fabian and multiply that by a thousand.

No wonder I slept with the bastard the first chance I could, even with Uncle Clayboy in the bed with us. No wonder, I let Uncle Clayboy stroke my Book 'em Dano as I pleasured the Adonis's life giver. No wonder I let Uncle Clayboy munch on my lover's ear while my Adonis munched on me. But, like they say, "every dog has its day," and while Book 'em Dano's away—this pooch will play. Sure—I'm disappointed the testosterone injections haven't taken, but it's *my* ear Uncle Clayboy's nuzzling now. Why is it women are drawn to men who will hurt them? I need a ciggie and a pee.

OK, I'm back!

That was a good one. Where was I again? Moths drawn to flames and burned to ashes, wasn't that it? Cheryl, darling, have you ever felt that you're in a wheelchair—shit, I mean a *scooter*—because of your gifts? Oh sure, you were voted "*Penthouse* Disability Chick of The Year," but be honest, was it any fun getting your favorite Manolos all scratched up when they wheeled you down the red carpet? Do you think what Tenderly says could be true? Could it be karma? I know, *I know*, dinosaurs will walk the earth before Tenderly says something that make sense, but is it possible that in our past lives we Ginsburg (*pronounced* Du Pont) Girls misused our gifts, and as punishment, we have to come back *over and over and over* with even larger ones until we can work through it? I have to check my horoscope, see if it's true. I need another ciggie and a pee.

Love, Cousin Sylvia

From: Bermuda.G@Ourmail.us
Date: Monday, March 21, 2005, 10:00 a.m.
To: Sylvia.G@Ourmail.us
Cc: US@Ourmail.us
Subject: Remembrances of things past...

Oh, Mama, *Mama,* you are such a fraidy cat, jumping at every teensy-weensy thing. Why, Mama, I remember you were never like that when I was growing up. Remember the Purim party when brothers Hill and Dale surprised us all and *both* dressed up as Queen Esther? They were tired of drawing straws with the loser getting to play Queen Vashti, which was always a bummer, because she got herself killed right at the start.

Anyone else would have panicked, but not you, Mama—not you. You simply looked at the trays of hash *hamantaschen* each had baked, then calmly announced you'd throw one from each tray against the wall, and whoever's cookie stuck the longest could dress up like Julia Child at the school bake sale—however, they would also forfeit the opportunity to be Queen Esther. Wow, what King Solomon wisdom and strength of purpose!

As I recall, that was also the year you gave me fifty dollars so I would switch with you, so you could get to play Haman, and I would play Uncle Mordechai. Daddy played King Achashveyrosh, and was such a good sport he even went along with your plan to hang him in the final scene. Boy, weren't we lucky Brother Hill turned the lights on, and Dale cut Daddy down before he actually had his neck broken?

Mama, I think this is where I get my talent for building scaffolds, although I'm a little more careful than you with my nooses, no matter what the police reports say.

Mama, that was the same Purim party we invited Masters and Johnson to come to, remember? I remember it so well because during that party, I did something I had never done before—had sex with siblings *at the same time.*

You know why else I remember it so vividly? If you added our three ages together, you've got thirty-nine, and, if you subtract three from nine you've got six, which is my dress size. It's funny what the mind recalls, isn't it?

Mama, I can see it clear as if I were looking at a Polaroid—you taking your unfiltered Pall Mall cigarette and, when Daddy wasn't looking, putting the burning tip up against his golden paper crown. Brother Hill tried to put it out with his grape juice, but he always threw like a Mary and missed, which turned out to be really lucky for Daddy, because he and brother Dale weren't drinking grape juice, they were chugging Mogen David laced with Vodka. You never knew that, did you, Mama? You always thought they were such goody-two-shoes, but me—*you blamed me for everything*, even your dry skin that I also happen to know you've had since birth.

Why, Mama, why?

Oh shit, I'm getting one of my nosebleeds! Not to worry, I've been following your instructions and have my lucky quarter right here, next to my Grey Goose and some Healthy Choice Jumpin' Java.

Just hold on a minute, I don't want to bleed all over the computer, because that's harder to get off than coffee.

OK, none the worse for wear, and not a drop on my Mac. Pretty funny if I had, huh, Mama?—then my Apple *would really have been red*.

Mama, if I look at the next Polaroid of Leo Loeb, I can picture myself picking up one of those blue seltzer bottles he delivered every Monday morning. Leo always made a racket when he took away the empties. That was his signal for me to come out into the hallway and let him put his hand under my skirt. The first time brothers Hill and Dale watched, I thought Leo was going to get mad, but what did I know about what he really wanted? After all, *I was only fourteen, Mama*.

Oh damn, I'm dripping again...

Okey-dokey! All cleaned up. So—getting back to Daddy's burning paper crown. I must have really been so excited I didn't realize I had the nozzle pointed at *me,* and boy, did I spray myself good. Once my eyes stopped burning, I turned it around and gave Daddy a full blast, and the flaming crown just flew off his head along with some burned-off hair.

We were lucky, weren't we Mama, that it didn't hit the drapes and instead, landed on the floor where I gave it another real good dousing? Then brothers Hill and Dale stomped on it, whopping and hollering like wild Indians—the drunken sods.

You know, Mama, some smart writer once said, *You can never go home,* but between my videos and the Polaroids, I can visit anytime I want.

Mama, I can also remember how good you were at hiring people to take care of us when you, Daddy, and Uncle Clayboy went out of town "on business," or abandoned us for one of your month-long "retreats." You were really ahead of the curve to recognize how important it was for us to learn a foreign language, but Mama, you really have to believe me when I say I simply do not have the ear for it, like brothers Hill and Dale.

Looking back on it, I guess Maria from Nicaragua, who made the best *nacatamales,* was the easiest to understand because she learned a little English when she worked with the CIA. Of course, I could not practice my Spanish, even if I wanted to—those damn Dog Tooth peppers she got from her Sandinista buddies burned like a blowtorch, which by the way, was something she was really handy with, too. Not that she ever used hers on us, although I think she was tempted a few times.

I still remember the other tricks Maria learned in the jungle—for instance, how to knot a Somoza handkerchief around a guy's scrotum so he would confess to just about anything. I remember it like it was yesterday, maybe because *I used it yesterday.* What do you think, Mama? Is that the reason?

Actually, it makes for good business to have toys like that in your goody bag when you're entertaining a client who's homesick and wants to remember the good old times. We all know how that goes, don't we, Mama?

Brothers Hill and Dale were much better at tying knots because their fingers were longer and so much thinner than mine, but I possessed greater *chi*, and when I kicked a person in the head the way Wrong Girl Mary taught me, I could kill someone.

You remember Wrong Girl Mary? She came after—gee, I cannot remember who she came after.

Wrong Girl Mary didn't speak a word of English, even though she waited tables in that wonderful Chinese restaurant down on Mott Street when she wasn't caring for us, or teaching me the thousand ways to kill with my big toe.

Hung Low, I think that was the name. Remember, the place with the duck testicles in the window? We used to eat there every Sunday evening along with the rest of the congregation of Temple Beth-Sel (*pronounced* St John the Divine).

And, Mama, remember how Wrong Girl Mary used to give brothers Hill and Dale stuff from her makeup kit, so they could really look like Suzie Wong? Oh, she gave me red eyeliner once, to use when I couldn't take someone's eyes out with my toe.

Besides providing me awesome power and near invulnerability by cultivating and controlling my *chi* through the exercises of the internal martial arts styles she was taught as a child in Northern Shaolin, Wrong Girl Mary showed me how to order duck testicles with no MSG (the only thing she could say in English).

Remember, too, Mama, how you tried so hard to give up smoking and always left the table for a few hours, so you could get your acupuncture treatment while grabbing a few toots from that strange pipe Dr. Happy Child Chin had up in his office? I had a hard time getting any movies of that until I dressed up like a delivery boy from the Second Avenue Deli. You were a little out of it, so you didn't notice, but for a hundred-year-old guy, Dr. Happy Child Chin sure could put away the pastrami like one of the family.

We were so proud you finally cut down to a pack a day and didn't start any fires for three months, but then Dr. Happy Child Chin died, didn't he? I couldn't go to his funeral because it was back in China and his brother, Chairman Mao, thought serving us Happy Meals would bring his family bad luck in the afterlife.

The only reason you and Daddy were allowed was because it was the Year of The Elephant. You guys won for best costume, right? Bubbeh Esther (*pronounced* Granny Smith Apples) was the head, you the middle, Daddy the back—or was it the other way round?

I wish I'd gone, because none of your parade pictures came out, and you never took any when you played frisbee with Mao.

The only China memories I have come from Aunt Cheryl. You remember, you took her so she could learn to bind feet and eventually help my brothers portray Suzie more realistically in the school production of *The World Of Suzie Wong, The Early Years*.

"*Suzie gives me sanctuary. She's a place for me to hide. A place where we get high.*"

We used to sing that little verse day in day out; and, boy, were we out of our minds on ludes, otherwise, we couldn't have hit the high notes. Actually, that's not entirely true. Brothers Hill and Dale could always hit the high notes, even if they weren't high.

Oh, what? You thought your two little goodie-two-shoe Marys didn't do drugs, and it was only me? *Well—hello!*

Oh, heck —I gonna bleed again! No? OK!

I remember Aunt Cheryl showing me her scars, the only remnant of the feathers that once grew on her extremities as a result of the sickness she got while playing golf.

Crazy Cousin Tenderly called it the Birdie Flu, the existence of which had come to her in a dream, brought to her in living color by someone called My Supreme Banker.

Mama, remember how we all went around flapping our arms, hopping all around in your golf shoes and making chirping sounds. Well—it's not so funny now, is it?

Cousin Tenderly, I just want you to know, I always wear my End Of Days Last Alert Wristband and Heart Defibrillator, even in the shower; and, I will never call you crazy, or laugh at you, or My Supreme Banker.

Mama, I have to go now, but I wanna leave you with one piece of good news that I know will keep you strong. Remember you were voted Best Mother of the Building, ten years running? You forgot, I bet, didn't you? Anyway our old neighbors hadn't, so if you return to Christopher and Bleecker, you'll still see the sign 'Sylvia's Way' on the lamppost in front where our apartment house used to be (until you burned it down)—and where, thanks to the insurance money, our old neighbors live in a luxurious forty-story glass condo. Is that something to smile about, or what?

Love ya,
Bermuda

From: Cheryl.G@Ourmail.us
Date: Monday, March 21, 2005, 10:10 a.m.
To: US@Ourmail.us
Subject: *Tu amor me mantiene vivo!* (Your love keeps me alive!)

Mi familia estimada, cariñosa, (My dear, loving family)

Thank you all for that wonderful chain-prayer email. I know it will go a long way in influencing INS to return my passport. In the meantime, I'm hoping the Finest Doctor will return to the States and perform the operation. (Laverne, it was sweet of you to offer the Winnebago, but I am taking those meds you sent—what did you call them—Mexican Jumping Greenies?) *¿Eres listo retumbar?* (Are you ready to rumble?)

Oh and Laverne, honey, I did as you said and Googled the Daughters of Adam and Eve Out-Patient Surgical Centers, and you're a-hundred-percent correct. Even though the Center's mission is to get men to have their missing rib put back (soy ribs are available for vegetarians), by law they must allow the outsourcing of foreign physicians (regardless of board certification) to operate on women who are willing to pay any price. Not only that, but the Finest Doctor's foreign-status medical malpractice insurance deductible totally covers up any and all mistakes, including double billing, providing him full immunity in these centers. Talk about convenience! By the end of the month they'll be in every Dunkin' Donuts south of the Mason–Dixon Line. And, listen to this—you get to take home any drugs that aren't used. Unfortunately, the major obstacle to his stateside return is Judge Judy. That's right, you heard me—*Judge Judy,* my doubles partner and long-time soulmate, is the only one standing between my life and my death.

If I could laugh, *which I can't* (paralyzed facial muscles, you know), this would be a screamer. It seems clever "Miss Judy-Woody" (that's the secret name I call Judy) signed the Finest Doctor to an exclusive agreement stipulating that while here in America he can only perform surgery *on her* and *only her* during one of her Home Shopping Network shows.

Sure, I thought of getting another doubles partner, but she has a heart of gold and played with me when nobody else wanted to; and besides, the Finest Doctor would kill me. *¡Es verdad—es verdad!* (It's true—it's true!)

You see, they go back a long ways—not as far back as Bubbeh Esther (*pronounced* Granny Smith Apples) of course, but far enough.

If you recall, Miss Judy-Woody (Elisabeth Schwarzkopf back then) was the star of *Scar Tissue*, the Finest Doctor's first made-for-TV experimental-surgery show that put him on the map and got her a TV agent. The episode she starred in was called "The Skunk's Tail Implant." Ah, now you remember, don't you? In that show, after five failed attempts, the Finest Doctor successfully half-completes the Skunk's Tail Implant that, for the first time ever, allowed Miss Judy-Woody, or any woman who had a fetish for black robes, to give up yoga—*but* still have the flexible spine she craved. It made television history and won an Emmy for the Finest Doctor, Miss Judy-Woody, and Snickers the Skunk, who gave his tail and his life in the name of ratings. *¿Es un mundo pequeño, huh?* (It's a small world, huh?) Incidentally, the first six episodes are out on DVD and make a very nice hospital gift.

It's too bad Miss Judy-Woody's fur collection had a non-compete clause, because the use of a sable, or even mink, would have been the tail of the tape (it's called video now).

Also in the contract is the guarantee that Miss Judy-Woody will one day be able to sit on the bench without squirting. Unfortunately, that's a tad too late for those brave ladies of the Mount Vernon Drum and Bugle Marching Band who wished only to touch Miss Judy-Woody's spine (for luck) as she emerged from the hospital. (I understand they'll be in quarantine for another year and will lose any chance at a national championship.) *Es una lástima.* (Too bad.)

Clarice—Bubbeh Esther (*pronounced* Granny Smith Apples) tells me the Finest Doctor's fallen so madly in love with you that in addition to the pair of wings he's making for you, he intends to overdub your vocal cords so that when his "Little Songbird" flies, you'll sound like Diana Ross and the Supremes. *Cómo es romántico.* (How romantic.)

This is great news, but Bubbeh Esther's (*pronounced* Granny Smith Apples's) a smidge concerned that the Finest Doctor may take it the wrong way when he finally gets to meet you. She says he has quite the temper when things don't go his way, but it's short-lived, and he usually leaves it on the operating table. (We don't want to be his next patient, now do we?) *Apenas bromeando.* (Just joking.)

Listen—the Finest Doctor's been in Mount Cedar how many years? And, in all that time, has he ever been up close and personal with anything but a bootleg copy of one of Diana's performances? (You see where I'm going with this, right?) *¡Exactamente!* (Exactly my point here!)

My advice Clarice—when he gets off the plane, just give him one humongous hug, and then shove your tongue down his throat and act like nothing's the matter. Trust me, love is blind, especially with doctors who take as many drugs as they give their patients. However, if he should ask you to sing "Where Did Our Love Go," or "Nothing but Heartaches" (which he won't), you just belt out "See About Me."

And, Clarice, remember what Pope John II said in his book. *"Admit nothing, even if they have pictures."* (Or, in your case, a scratchy bootleg copy of the 45.)

Uncle Maxie—I'm so glad to hear you're enjoying yourself. I just wish you'd inspire Daddy, who doesn't seem to want to take advantage of all that South Beach has to offer.

Of course, you know Madison was thinking about running for governor of Florida and would have been a shoo-in considering all the redistricting she did during the last presidential election. But, instead she chose to heed her president's call and accept the Supreme Court nomination. (Personally, I would have taken the cash and an ambassadorial post to a super-shopping destination.)

Wearing black robes instead of Prada (see Miss Judy Woody) isn't my cup of tea, but Madison always had her eye on being the first woman president. So, I wouldn't be surprised if she's using the High Court as a way of courting the nomination. Since she refused to take the reward money the party offered for her redistricting job, I wondered if there'd be blowback, but then she said, *Where did you get the idea I wasn't going to take the money?*

I'm pleased to announce there was talk at the highest levels of government asking Washington to run—a wise move, since a Medal of Honor recipient can just about write his own ticket, especially in a state that has no gun control laws. *¡Qué gran país!* (What a great country!)

Speaking about Florida's weapons' program (which, as you all know, we wrote), that's another wonderful incentive to owning Noriega's old place. Where else can you get your own personal armory? Did I tell you the house has a Panamanian-size pool that will allow me to continue my pistol training while undergoing physical therapy?

Can you imagine—all those amenities *and* you're only a few steps from the beach? *¿Cómo afortunado soy?* (How lucky am I?)

I'm not going to ruin your day by complaining ABOUT HOW UNBEARABLE IT IS TO DRAG MY HALF-PARALYZED WHALE OF A BODY INTO THE SHALLOW END AND THEN HAVE TO USE MY ONE GOOD ARM AND MY ONE GOOD LEG TO MOVE A FRACTION OF AN AGONIZING INCH—OR, HOW I'D RATHER TAKE MY CHANCES TIED TO THE 500-FOOT ANCHOR OF THE FUCKING *QUEEN MARY*, but I'm going to suck it up, and you're not going to hear me complain—not on such a beautiful spring day WHEN EVERYONE BUT ME IS OUT FOR A WALK UNDER THEIR OWN POWER IN CENTRAL PARK! (NOT WHILE I STILL HAVE THREE ROUNDS LEFT!)

If you think shooting a Glock 33 using only your right hand without the recoil sending the barrel crashing into your front teeth is easy, why don't you come by some morning and try it? HUH, HUH!

I know my Disney reality-show deal won't go through unless I demonstrate the ability to kill with a machine pistol without shooting off my own leg. (FYI, Sylvia—the Pixar people bought me a fabulous motorized forty-mile-an-hour scooter, and fit both handles with machine pistols that can be fired by voice command. I don't think there's a better weapons company on the face of the planet.)

Did I tell you Disney finally decided what to call the show? "The Wonderful World of Getting Even." Isn't that to die for! They're guaranteeing me *two* full seasons. In the first, I hunt down and kill the people who tried to kill me. In season two, people write in about someone they'd like *me to kill*. I read the letters and choose the one who pisses me off the most, then hunt and kill the son of a bitch. Glenn Close is narrating. She left "The Shield" because of me ... can you imagine? ¡*Qué mujer*! (What a woman!)

(FYI, I just received my waiver of immunity from Hunters Without Borders, who, in partnership with the NRA, is sponsoring the show.) If the foreign-rights deal goes through, I'll be getting a waiver from The Hague. Until then, I can only hunt and kill people in the U.S. and its territories, including Guam.

Speaking of the NRA, they just asked Clinton if he wanted to be chairman, but since his meeting with Goddess, he has other plans. No, they don't include running for governor, which would be a gimme. Apparently, Goddess told Clinton he was *Her* only American son, and that she had *special plans* for him.

Naturally, if Clinton is *Her* American son, I'll attain *His American Virgin Mother* status.

(Everyone knows I would lie under a bullet train before I'd ask one of my kids to ask Goddess for a favor—BUT GODDAMN IT, WHO WANTS AN AMERICAN VIRGIN MOTHER WHO CAN'T DANCE?)

As far as sainthood, I'm certainly going to push for it while I'm alive. I wish I could give you more details, but Clinton couldn't divulge anything else except this: Goddess *didn't* ask him to build an ark, which goes to prove what I've been saying all along—*all that talk about hurricanes is way overblown.*

Did you hear that some people are blaming Ted Turner for this hurricane hype? Take it from me, "Really Big Boy" (that's the secret name I call Ted, who happens to be a darling man, and hung like a rhino) is not the one to blame. The real force behind this hurricane-watch bullshit is Really Big Boy's son, Wolf Blitzer, who makes me anxious just watching him shuffle papers.

"You're in the Situation Room." . . . THE SITUATION ROOM, MY HALF-PARALYZED ASS!

Don't get me started on the media after what the Brits tried to do to my lovely daughter. And, if you think inviting Reagan to that fucking wedding would make a difference, you've been smoking some of the Queen Mother's stash. Oh sure, Camilla was all hugs and kisses, but where were the royals when the cops were blaming Reagan for the subway bombings and plastering that ugly picture of her all over the BBC? You didn't hear Camilla ask the newspapers to print a retraction, did you? No, you didn't, because she was too fucking busy giving Charles mobile-phone sex. And making that King Lear reference showed her true chauvinistic colors—and, how bad a speller she was. (Obviously she never saw *Bedtime for Bonzo,* or else she'd have understood the real meaning of hero worship.)

Goddess bless Hillary—she went on "Larry King Live" to defend Reagan, and if you think it was because they both belong to the Chef Boyardee Fan Club, that's probably only half the story.

Of course, the Brits aren't buying that Camilla shit, either. They saw "Larry King Live," too. Besides, they all loved Princess Di, so they know the same disgusting people who plastered Reagan's horribly unflattering photo on the BBC also defamed Di and Dodi.

Uncle Maxie, it's so funny you love "JAG." Grant was up for the lead, but turned it down after he won his Academy Award. His people at William Morris decided Grant shouldn't go back to the small screen (at least not just yet). I think Clint had a hand in it. Since "Rawhide," do you see Clint anywhere on the boob tube? And then, there's George to think of. After "ER" you don't see him doing any TV either, do you? *¡Comprobarlo hacia fuera!* (Check it out!)

George is the only one in Hollywood who comes close to having Grant's box-office numbers. Grant and George both have the same agents, and Grant tells me George will be directing something in black-and-white about Ed Morrow. Remember Ed Morrow, Uncle Maxie? Come to think of it, didn't you used to play poker with him?

I think Daddy played, too, until he was indicted, and then he pretty much stayed away from everybody until the witnesses disappeared.

Grant had lunch with George at Spago, and that's when George offered him the part of Ed Morrow, but Grant said he didn't want to *play old*. Of course, Clint's got Grant on his multi-pic deal, and even if that weren't the case, this Clooney pic sounds like a small-market film without much broad appeal. After all, who knows who Ed Morrow is, much less cares about him? *¿No piensas?* (Don't you think?)

By the way, it was Madison, when she was the Judge Advocate General, who wrote the pilot for "JAG," and got it picked up when Bubbeh Esther (*pronounced* Granny Smith Apples) sold CBS back to whoever she was *dating* at the time—so get out those tapes (videos) and get ready to make some popcorn. (Don't forget the Dr. Brown's Cream Soda, either.)

Of course, my plans could change if Tyler wants me on the set. Now that everything's straightened out with Angelina, the cameras are ready to roll. They're shooting in Mt. Pisgah National Forest down in North Carolina. Tyler tells me there are parts of the forest that look exactly like the Prussian neighborhood where Marx grew up.

Did I mention that's where the whore-secretary, her crack-fiend husband (posing as her brother—what a laugh—ha!), and the midget-sister are from, and that you'll see me in hell before I set foot near that trailer park?

For those of you who loved *Legally Blonde,* you'll be happy to hear Reese Witherspoon has signed on to play Engels, and the writing of *The Communist Manifesto* is going to take place at Looking Glass Rock, which is the spitting image of a Brussels bathhouse. (FYI, Angelina and Reese are to be completely naked during the entire Writing Scene.)

Tyler says this scene will make film history because it will be the first time stem-cell researchers will win an Academy Award for body prosthesis in a period piece drama.

Tyler also says after the film is wrapped, he's going to bring me a prosthesis so I can have it for Judge Crater's Coming Out of the

Ground Chelsea Pier Halloween Bash.

Speaking of Halloween, Uncle Maxie, you were always such a fancy dresser and the combinations you wore were *tan estrallando* (so dashing). *¿Recuerdes?* (Remember?)

Clarice, do *you* remember the time Daddy went on trial for kidnapping, and Uncle Maxie took us over to the East Side for lunch at the Croydon Coffee Shop on Madison and 86th Street? Maria Callas was there and got so jealous when you began singing "Day-O."

Then, there was the time Mommy was drying out at Doctors Hospital and Uncle Maxie drove us to the Tip Top Inn for Sunday Brunch. Uncle Maxie even bought us new Mary Janes for the occasion. Remember? Yours were red, and mine were black. Then, when we got to the restaurant, we switched. That's when we saw Maria Callas again, and boy did she get pissed when you started singing "Day-O"—this time in Italian. *Ésos eran los días, mi amigo.* (Those were the days, my friend.)

Uncle Maxie was like a second father, while Auntie Ruthie never showed us the time of day. And that shit about the cars looking like they belonged to a funeral home was pretty fucking lame if you ask me.

Come on, Clarice, where in the world did you get the idea Tenderly had to fly all the way out to Oregon to find a deli that didn't serve chicken-fat sandwiches, or that Sylvia needed aromatherapy to overcome her fear of white bread?

Did you ever consider how these insinuations would hurt attendance of the Little Mister and the Three Tenors Oklahoma Tour sponsored by the Renderers Association of America? Or the blowback to Madison, who will be ruling on the Supreme Court case White v. Rye, over which should be the national bread? Oh, *oh*—what about poor Grant, whose third scheduled pic with Clint is a remake of *The Ten Commandments,* with Eastwood as *Moses*? (Can you imagine the movie without the Spreading of the Schmaltz scene?)

And Clinton's relationship with She Who Brings Forth Life, the Great Baleboosteh Ginsburg (*pronounced* Eleanor of Aquitaine), because no matter what Charlton Heston said in his memoirs, *Goddess loved fishing*. (See last week's History Channel show "The Biggest Catch.")

Clarice—do you supposed I could ever open a refrigerator again if Uncle Maxie had made me count the number of chicken-fat containers until my nipples got so hard they tore through my I Love Bobby Darin T-shirt?

Come on, Clarice, let me send you a "Baby" Glock 26 and get you started on some close-range shooting. IT'S THE ONLY THING THAT'S KEEPING ME SANE!

Love,

Cousin Cheryl

Buenas noches, mis queridos! (Goodnight, my darlings!)

P.S. Just for fun, I did a series of six headless male ceramic figurines. (Actually, they're not completely headless; several have heads hanging off by a teensy-weensy strand of freeze-dried grapes.) I have the figurines wearing darling Baby Gap baby T-shirts. (*Très chic*) Very chic.

The people from the MOMA were here taking photos for the brochure that accompanies my one-woman show. *Art and Hand Creams in America* came as well, and after having their in-house lawyers and shrink look at the photos and seeing how they captured my ex-bastard-husbands so remarkably well, this distinguished magazine called *Cut Off From Reality* (that's the name of my show), "Bursting at the seams with joy and happiness . . . Exactly what you'd expect when a genius with no range of motion gets her paralyzed mitts on clay . . . A must-feel-good experience."

I guess I should be excited but . . . *Shirley! Shirley, Shirley bo Birley, Bonana fanna fo Firley, Fee fy mo Mirley, Shirley.*

From: TenderlyThroughMySupremeBanker@MySupremeBanker.him
Date: Monday, March 21, 2005, 10:21 a.m.
To: US@Ourmail.us
Subject: Spring has sprung!

Hello, and happy spring to my loving family!

May My Supreme Banker, known by many names and different faces, bring you all love, peace and harmony, and remind you that we are all connected by credit-card debt.

I know that springtime turns a man's fancy to love, but bathing in unfiltered water can turn a man's fancy into an untouchable, so please, wear your body condoms, check partners' faucets on FilterFax.com and wash body parts five to six times a day with Simoniz Glasscoat. I wouldn't wish these diseases on my worst enemy (Bobby Fishman), who knows exactly what he gave that innocent thirteen-year-old (me) when he opened his pool on senior-prom night. For anyone out there who might be dating Bobby's male offspring, I urge you to go to PharmaKarma.com/badpools.htm.

I, for one, love to go to this nation's capital to see the cherry blossoms, however, I'm passing it up this year because of the latest warning posted on DeadCowsWalking.com. It seems that several senators from both sides of the aisle have been infected with Dead Cows Dementia. While they vehemently deny they are suffering from this deadly disease, their recent appearances on Comedy Central would suggest otherwise. Unfortunately, not enough brain matter could be obtained from the senators during their recent lobotomies, so whether they do in fact have this fatal brain-wasting disease, or not, will have to wait until we can see them on "Family Guy."

Fortunately, the cow, which died of complications while calving on the Senate floor as part of the beef-subsidy filibuster, poses no threat to the human food supply because it was raised specifically for lobbying events and did not enter the human or animal food chain. There is one bit of irony. The senators involved have the worst attendance records and were there only for a photo op with Maggie May.

(For those of us who love trivia, the CEO of the lobbying group [Beef for Me] owns the cow and, *and*—also happens to be the president of the Texas Chapter of The Rod Steward Fan Club—hence the name, *Maggie May*.)

The Sonoma Valley is another of my springtime destinations, especially the Gallo Winery. If you remember, this is where I first saw wine served out of a glass and not a paper bag. It was also the first time I had wine since Bobby Fishman's senior prom. The wine tasting tours are fun, and the guides at the wineries help you into and out of the vats for the naked grape-stomping festivities.

I checked the CDC web site and there are only a few airborne diseases to be concerned with in the Sonoma Valley this time of year. As long as you've had measles and or tuberculosis, there is no risk associated with being bitten by the *Aedes caspius inebriate*, better known as the Drunken Mosquito.

Any trip to the Sonoma Valley should be accompanied by a visit to San Francisco. Friends are asking me, will I get the Avian Flu if I go to San Francisco? While there is no definitive answer one way or another, I think there are enough quarantines in place to guarantee you a safe journey. So, my suggestion is to heed the warnings and stay away from Asians who are math geniuses and want to play poker, and whatever you do, don't go near the wharf area if you're foaming at the mouth. That said, I would add my own bit of advice and don't go anywhere without your N95 mask. In fact, I would keep it on during my entire stay and only remove it when I'm taking a shower, making sure to face away from bacteria-infested shower heads unless they act as a cell tower for you mobile phone.

Since my Christmas email, prices for these masks have come down to where it makes sense to order a dozen at a time. My new favorite place on the web to order the N95 is DeconByDesigns.com. They offer a nice selection of colors, fabrics, and interesting fashion shapes to choose from. They have all the necessary banking safeguards in place—VeriSign, NSA, and Satellite Surveillance—so they are completely trustworthy. That includes their promise not to sell info regarding your blood type to the Red Cross. As I have discussed previously, once that happens you might as well take your own life. The Red Cross will bleed you to death with low-interest offers on bankcards, home mortgages, extra minutes on your cell phone, free trips to blood-sausage factories, even free tickets to see "Regis and Kelly."

Just remember, watch what Internet sites you visit, accept no cookies, don't open any attachments, and always wear your N95 masks when logging on.

I know I have talked to some of you about ordering the N95 from TheLongStranger.com, but as of today, they are off the recommended list. I recently learned that using their chat rooms could lead to the Heartbreak of Psoriasis, so you can imagine what you may pick up from their masks. I've checked with the CDC, and while the two cases of carpal psoriasis have been confirmed, the CDC has not put the chat room on their Disease Chat Room Watch List. Personally, I think it's only a matter of time before that happens.

I understand the World Health Organization's Strike Team, in coordination with the government of Thailand, raided the offices and warehouses of TheLongStranger.com, so I would suggest checking with the WHO's web site for further info.

In the meantime, if you have purchased anything from TheLongStranger.com within the last year, I would immediately take it to your local toxic dump. Do not, under any circumstances, burn the masks, as they may contain harmful erectile-enhancing substances that immediately go airborne above 360 degrees Fahrenheit

I am also happy to say I quickly discontinued my TheLongStranger.com relationships when neither one of my cyberspace lovers would agree to meet me for coffee at Starbucks's newest location in the middle of The Dead Sea. This is an immediate tip-off that the man to whom, for nearly a year, you have been confiding your most secretive sexual fantasies would never buy Dr. Perricone's products for your birthday.

I recently met a very clean gentleman at Whole Foods. He had his own pan of distilled water for washing down the produce before squeezing them for freshness. He was wearing a very dashing bodysuit he said was modeled after the pressurized water-retaining suits the Fremen wore on Arrakis. (FYI—I'm a big fan of these, as you know from previous emails.)

He then gave me a copy of *Dune* with the appropriate pages marked, so I knew he was on the up-and-up. When I remarked on how stylish it was and how I could understand him perfectly, despite the mask and the water tube, he informed me that he just purchased the last suit from DeconByDesign.com, which has a retail shop in SoHo, right next to Louis Vuitton on Greene, off Spring; however, I could go online to order one if I wanted to save on the taxes.

I told him how ironic that was, and began telling him about the lupus situation. He surprised me by saying he knew all about it and, in fact, had already spoken to the Louis Vuitton people about the matter. They assured him, as they did the CDC, that the disease could only be contracted from *fake* Louis Vuitton bags and that they were working diligently with the NSA on a plan that would send all street vendors to secret real-estate investment-club camps. This, they felt, was their only option if they were to totally eliminate the illegal designer bag trade and any threat of a lupus pandemic. Incidentally, funding for this plan would come from the Bill and Melinda Gates Real Goods For Real Women Fund. Bill and Melinda—they had to be sent to Earth by My Supreme Banker, didn't they?

The gentlemen I met at the market is named Usul@Usul.com and he teaches deep-tissue massaging at Morgan Stanley. He's going on a three-year Caribbean finger-strengthening cruise, so I'm not sure where this relationship is going to go.

I would also like to recommend a new book by two Indian psychiatrists called *The Delhi Drop-Off: How To Outsource Your Neurosis*. I want to thank My Supreme Banker for bringing this insightful and beautifully illustrated book to my attention. Through the use of techniques found only in this book, I was finally able to overcome my fear of doorman and the bacteria living in their white gloves. In addition to the book, they have 24/7 phone and web access so you can contact the authors in person if you can't reach your local 9-1-1. They even supply you with ten dollars worth of New Delhi phone cards, so the first minute is on them. And listen to this—if the authors are busy on another call, you can speak with a representative from any one of twenty computer companies, airlines, or McDonald's franchise representatives.

Speaking of My Supreme Banker, he just had LASICK surgery. LASIK stands for Laser-Assisted In Situ Keratomileusis, and is a procedure that permanently changes the shape of the cornea, the clear covering of the front of the eye, using an excimer laser. A knife called a microkeratome is used to cut a flap in the cornea. A hinge is left at one end of this flap. The flap is folded back, revealing the stroma, the middle section of the cornea. Pulses from a computer-controlled laser vaporize a portion of the stroma and the flap is replaced.

My Supreme Banker wanted me to pass this information along to you so that you know that even though he is My Supreme Banker he's just like you and me when it comes to being nearsighted.

Of course, his surgery is but a parable, and its meaning shown to us in the standard eye chart and in the saying *"It is easier to enter the Kingdom of Heaven through the eye of a needle when riding a camel, than to get your insurance provider to pay for elective surgery."* That is why it is so, *so* important to stare into a mirror for at least twenty minutes every single hour of every single day to make sure you're using enough moisturizer and you're skin's not drying out.

One last bit of advice—springtime means migratory birds coming back from far away power lines with all sorts of death things in their beaks. Need I tell you to keep you heads down?

Love from My Supreme Banker Through Cousin Tenderly

From: Laverne.G@Ourmail.us
Date: Monday, March 21, 2005, 10:30 a.m.
To: US@Ourmail.us
Subject: On the run!

Hello, Y'all!

Can you tell we're deep in Jeff Davis country?

"Outlaw Mama" is what little Clara, the demon child, calls me. She is getting to be quite the little thief herself. You should have seen her in Walmart the other day—smiling cutesy at everybody while she's stuffing the latest edition of Chutes and Ladders under her coat.

Of course, little Willie does not have to steal, because he is the *true* Hero Outlaw. First off, the two things he loves most, Dr. Pepper and Krispy Kremes, he gets straight from the manufacturer. Plus, he's got over two million dollars in additional endorsements from the Dallas Cowboys Cheerleaders against Darwin. (Natural selection is against breast augmentation.)

As you may recall, Willie's got this enterprising agent, Pastor "Green Light" Hollywood, and he got the deal. He handles "The Three Foxes" (Glen, Russ, and Bill), but says no one speaks to the anti-government militias like my little Willie.

Most of the endorsement money goes straight to The Daughters of Adam and Eve. That's only fair, because if it weren't for their network of safe houses and salad bars located throughout the US of A at your local Staples, the Feds would have caught us right after Marie blew up the trailer.

In your wildest dreams you just can't imagine all the wonderful things these mothers do besides hiding us and stoning anyone on our trail. For instance, one of The Daughters of Adam and Eve has a very important son in TV. Get this—he's the former coffee wagon guy, now producer, of "America's Most Wanted." No lie! Well, she put in a good word with him, and he made sure we're off their radar and our mug shots off the TV screen.

Daughter Eve (that's the mother's name) even got Daughter Adam (that's her son's name) to kill the story they were going to do on Conrad and the school disappearances. (FYI—all the women are named Daughter Eve and the men, Daughter Adam— pretty cool because you never have to remember anyone's name or face.)

Daughter Eve's smart as a whip, and in the movement since a chimpanzee winked at her during a class trip to the zoo. Right off the bat, she suspected the forensics that put Conrad DNA in the bear's saliva might link him to the missing classmates, and therefore, could be used by Darwin's descendants to smear his brother, Willie. She also informed me that no one would remember Conrad's passion, but only the memory of his political opponents who wanted the job so they could get free candy at the Piggly Wiggly.

Furthermore, she believed that the Ape-Loving Media would beat it into everyone's poor head that Willie has a sociopath for a brother. And it wouldn't end there. There would be full-page ads in The New York Times sponsored by *The Planet of The Apes* Fan Club, or some other neo-Darwinist group, making ugly allegations that, like his brother Conrad, Willie was a serial bad boy.

Sure, the media would look at me, his dad, anyone in the family accused of multiple murders, but that wouldn't satisfy their blood lust. No—it's Willie they would crucify, and they wouldn't quit until he publicly accepted Peter Jackson by embracing him on the red carpet at the worldwide premiere of *King Kong*. Would you believe, they even want him to hug the big ape! Willie's not going to give in, not even if the show's on Nick at Nite, not my little twelve-year-old tough guy. He's my Harry Potter—that's who he is.

You know what my little revolutionary is doing? He's using his web site, that's what he's doing. He's taking some of the endorsement money and making sure that his web site, DarwinAintYourDaddy.com, comes up first on all the search engines whenever you google common phrases like, *I'm not kidding, This time I'm going to kill myself,* or most frequently used words like, *f*ck, sh*t,* and *misanthrope.* He even has his site coming up first when you're doing a search for *The Essential Dolly Parton.*

I'm lending my creative energies by designing the Free Willie T-Shirts. On the front it had a picture of the infant baby Willie being carried to Earth by a stork. He's wrapped in a Confederate flag and the stork's carrying him in his beak. There are little red lights in Willie's eyes that blink on and off, on and off, making him look like Damien in *The Omen*, which inspired the idea in me. It's very festive. On the back is a picture of Darwin, lying face down in a ditch, with a pitchfork in his back. The pitchfork glows red in the dark. Everything's powered with lithium batteries for extra life. Plus, they're waterproof, but I wouldn't recommend putting them in the dryer. At least that's what Marie tells me, and Marie should know since that's how she blew up her sister.

(FYI—Marie's made a duplicate of the varsity school sweater she made for her sister.) Of course, there aren't any lithium batteries in the lettering, so it won't explode, but it's still a nice way to remember her, don't you think? She's selling it on her site, DeadSister.com.

Funny, she wasn't sentimental until she blew up my brother, Jack. I think getting all that insurance money made Marie a different person. You know, much more independent and much more willing to put her emotions out there.

Speaking of selling things on the web, we've added another line of products thanks to The Daughters of Adam and Eve. After Marie blew up the trailer, the good daughters, bless their souls, carted away all the bits and pieces, and now we have the good fortune to sell them on Willie's web site complete with a certificate of authenticity. Some of the sold pieces have ended up on eBay, and let me tell you, the resale prices are insane.

Remember, I told you the hair stylist was blown clear off the trailer? Well—her blow dryer is almost intact, and I hear it's going on eBay for twenty-five large. I'm trying to convince William to set up his own auction, but his anti-*King Kong* crusade is all consuming.

You know, the movie's coming out in December, and all Willie can talk about is decapitating the director. Sure, everyone on his daddy's side is good with a power saw, but I always hoped William would turn his back on Home Depot.

On top of that, the Unintelligent Design court case up in Pennsylvania is also on his mind. The lawyers are just about ready to pick a jury, and I know Willie wants to get up there so he can blow up the school science labs.

I figured marrying Clara would be a calming influence. You know, like she'd let him win at Chutes and Ladders, being she was his wife and wanted to let peace reign in providence. Oh sure, he would miss the occasional kidnapping and all the media hoopla, but I also thought that was just his Attention-Getting Phase, and he would grow out of it, like most kids do. I never figured on Marie, but I guess her always buying them cheese doodles and talking about explosives did it, huh?

I blame myself for not paying more attention to the signs, but I was caught up in those Scratch and Lose lottery cards. Forget about the coffee cups, they're in Reese's Peanut Butter Cups now. Even got 'em in the ATMs, like at Staples and in the Porta-Potties at the revival meetings. Of course, I can't use ATMs, or the Feds will catch my ass in a minute. The first thing they tell you at The Daughters of Adam and Eve Welcome Wagon—rip up your credit cards, calling cards, and throw away those cell phones.

I told Willie, put me on an allowance, or I'll just spend all your endorsement money. One thing I *won't* buy is those King Kong Scratch-Offs everyone's talking about. I didn't tell William. If I did, *ka-boom!* No more coffee, candy or Porta-Potties—you know what I mean?

I did get word to Jerry because William should see his father, but that was a mistake with a capital M—for *Motherfucker*—because that's what Jerry is. You would think being wheelchair bound would soften a fella up, make him realize salvation isn't attained through the magic of crystal meth—but it hasn't. He's as mean and nasty as ever and remembers every single attempt on his life. He also blames me for coming between him and my brother, the one person who he truly loved in the way only a man trapped in a woman's body can love another man who's similarly gender-fucked.

I'm sure that flat-chested bitch (you know the one who doesn't mind sitting on Jerry's face and playing Guess My Weight), is back in his life, poisoning him against me and mine.

I sent Conrad and Judith Ann to see him, but he wouldn't let them in. He was in one of his purple hazes, and swore Conrad was Orville Redenbacher and Judith Ann, Nancy Reagan, and they were out to poison him with caramel popcorn.

I could see the Nancy thing because she's thin as a rail and in her red-dress phase. Judith Ann told me she has to look that way to avoid alien capture. I didn't get her full explanation because it was extremely scientific, but she promised to send me *The Weight Watchers Guide to The Galaxy* and the code to decipher the calorie counts, which would explain it all.

What I did manage to learn was that these extraterrestrials come from a world rapidly shrinking because they ran out of cheese doodles; that they have traveled the universe looking for a world bulging with fatties to feast upon so they could once again turn themselves into aliens with weight issues; then it's their plan to appear on "America's Biggest Loser"—scary, but true.

We move from town to town in a really nice Winnebago The Daughters of Adam and Eve hotwired in Phoenix. You know how I can't resist making art, so, using empty propane gas tanks, losing lottery tickets, and a few odds and ends I stole from a slaughter house in Nashville, I sculpted life-sized metal figures of Willie, Clara, Marie, and me. I painted them different colors using a bag of M&M's for my palate. I made Willie red, Clara green, Marie yellow, and me brown. I was in a shitty mood, that's why I picked brown, but after I thought about it, brown's the color of earth and I'm sort of an earthy person—you know, keeping the family out of jail and all.

All the figures sit on a long metal bench I bolted to the roof of the Winnebago. They're in different poses to express their own individuality. It's the definitive 2005 American outlaw family—at least that's what Uncle Jules said when he I emailed him pictures.

You know, there's nobody in today's art world who can come up with names that will sell product better than Uncle Jules. So, after talking it over with the kids and Marie, we decided to call it "American Outlaw Family." Just so there's no confusion, I painted our names in gold glitter paint under each figure so you'd know who's who. I attached a photo, so you all can see it.

Oh yeah, we're high-tech and in the digital world big-time. A real smart techie put it together for us. Daughter Adam's his name, but I guess you already figured that out. His mother's the treasurer of the Tupelo Mississippi Chapter of The Daughters of Adam and Eve, so he gets the bootleg copies of Photoshop and gray-market cell phones. The Feds can trace regular cells, but Daughter Adam gave us fifty "one-time-only" throwaways. Marie and Daughter Adam hit it right off. You should have seen his eyes bug out when Marie rigged the cell phone to explode.

We're in a truck stop just outside of Mobile, and I've left the kids with those bikers long enough. One thing you learn when you're on the run—you don't ever want to overstay your welcome.

Love to all,

Laverne

P.S. Remember, if you want to contact me, do it via Ourmail.us. I can just hack in from a stolen device without being traced. Neat, huh?

From: Jules@JewelerToTheStars.us
Date: Monday, March 21, 2005, 10:40 a.m.
To: US@Ourmail.us.
Subject: Laverne—I'm so proud of you!

Dear Laverne,

I'm glad I could be of assistance in bringing your plight to the attention of those who really care about great art. I know my friend, the Monsignor Def Rev, feels the same way and extends not only his grace upon thee, but also the grace of the Holy Father, who has been a close and personal friend since they met in Graceland nearly thirty years ago.

Laverne, honey, I can't tell you how proud I am of you. Not since Lady Godiva has there been anyone with your grace and aplomb.

I am excited to tell you your *American Outlaw Family* rivals anything Michelangelo created during his "Rebel Without an Italian Patron" period made famous by the *Bocce Balls of Padua*, which I know is one of your all-time faves.

There is no doubt, art historians the world over would agree that if Charleston Heston were alive today, he would be lying on his back and shouting, *Bravo, bravo!*

Your use of glitter was a real risk, but you pulled it off . . . and made me think when compared to your work, what I was doing for the Brooklyn is embarrassingly *too, too conventional*.

Your art inspired me to leap up from my desk, run to my studio, and throw caution to the wind! I quickly covered the platinum Barbie's tiny arms and legs in sparkle paint, using Frank Sinatra Old Blue Eyes Blue for the left side of the body and Moira Shearer Red Shoes Red for the right; then using Gene Simmons Pink Tongue Pink glitter paint, I drew a circle around Barbie's diamond-impaled navel.

I immediately observed how my eyes now followed the natural curves of the human form and traveled downward from the Pope's emerald encrusted tiara, to his ruby eyes, to his silver nose, to his onyx lips, ending its decent at the Barbie, nestled so sweetly inside the Holy Father's see-through stomach, instead of what my eyes were once forced to do—remain on the jewels and miss the wonder of the Barbie altogether.

Now when Grow Baby Juice with Calcium is injected into the Pope's stomach cavity, The Barbie Magic Grow Baby expands from a darling fetus to Barbie America, woman extraordinaire!

Each of my ten Holy Father's is ten feet high and made of gold, except for their stomachs, which are fitted with Fiat shatterproof windshield glass. Everything is original Italian, including the Pope's clothing.

I have to thank my Monsignor Def Rev for providing complete access to his personal collection of Vatican holy treasures, relics, and clothing he has so passionately and carefully collected during his service to Mother Church in his role as father confessor to the mistresses of the top-ten U.S. pro bowlers, as ranked by the PBA.

Def Rev and I have formed a fifty-fifty partnership, and listen to this—not only do I have access to his collection, I also have entrée to whatever remains in the Vatican Collection.

Laverne, talk about timing! Before the Holy Father wanted to simplify his life, this kind of deal would have been impossible to secure. Fortunately, when the Pope made the commitment to downsize, Def Rev was able to convince him I was a better choice than either Elton or Steve.

It was touch-and-go with Steve, because he and the Pope are Keno buddies, and the Holy Father loved the idea of his stuff being displayed over at the Golden Nugget. Unfortunately, Steve went too far when he told the Pope he was going to rename the Nugget "Wynn's Vatican."

As far as Elton was concerned, he bowed out when I agreed to let him continue borrowing outfits for his appearances on Sesame Street. Of course, any outfits I was using for my work were off the table.

News on the media front is just as good. Def Rev sent photos of the *Ten Popes A- Popping* series to key members of The Christian Coalition for their pre-damnation approval and announced whoever came to Brooklyn would a receive three-carat clear-diamond necklaces that spell out *I Rumble For Goddess,* as well as two free tickets to Letterman. As I guess you have already surmised, that's the name of the series—*Ten Popes A-Popping.* Catchy, isn't it?

Speaking of timing, Laverne, I wish you could be in my studio in about ten minutes from now so you can see me put the final touches on the injection mechanisms that will get all ten Barbies pumping up and down as they expand and then contract—expand and then contract—inside their Holy Fathers, in such a superbly syncopated rhythm, you just want to break out your tap shoes and dance along to the happy beat.

Camera Ferrari, my dear friend who was responsible for getting me the show, is extremely enthusiastic about what I've accomplished and wants to purchase the entire *Ten Popes A-Popping* series for the museum's permanent collection. While I'm charging twice what he would pay if he bought them individually on eBay (where he is a professional seller and marriage counselor), it guarantees he won't have to use the museum's PayPal account, and instead, rack up double points on his own AmEx.

Camera's been sending out his own press releases, and from the initial responses I've been receiving (dead bodies on my doorstep; notes saying, *After the post modernists are gone, you'll be next*), I am extremely confident attendance records will surpass even those of *Live Coffee Bean Art,* and believe me, that show still gives me nightmares.

I have to thank Bubbeh Esther (*pronounced* Granny Smith Apples) for taking my business where no business has gone before by encouraging me to form a LLC with the Finest Doctor, whereby I incorporate his surgical techniques, and he grows jewel-encrusted stem cells.

I'm forming this association with the Finest Doctor because, Laverne, I have a Promethean responsibility to bring to the world *the next great big thing* in jewelry transplants. Sure, I could just rest on my laurels and forget this responsibility, but I couldn't live with myself, or ever face my dwindling bank account again.

It would be unethical to divulge my client list, but I can assure you they are household names: leaders of scandal-ridden companies; scions of the richest robber barons; royal dynasties and despots who have squandered fortunes the likes of which a million men couldn't earn; and, of course, our leading politicians—both up on charges and likely to be charged.

Unlike my bling customers, these patrons are not showy, and have chosen to tastefully have their appendices, spleens, and single lungs removed and replaced with faux organs of gold, silver, platinum and onyx.

For my more *out-there* clientele, i.e., *show-biz folk*, I have accommodated their needs of self-expression by transplanting both complete and incomplete sets of arms and legs, toes, fingers, as well as noses, mouths, lips and eyes; the former procedure has become as commonplace as LASIK surgery.

Laverne, I know I can trust you, as I can trust all my relatives when I let you all in on what *the next great big thing* in jewelry transplants is going to be: *gold blood*. You heard me—*gold blood!* Isn't that fantastic?

Now, remember, this is all hush-hush. The Finest Doctor and I have been working on a process whereby we can liquefy refined gold to the point that we are able to add to it sufficient red and white cells and have this precious new substance run through the human body, as easily as I go through money in the men's department at Barneys.

So far, we have been successful with the model Gisele, but we're hoping by the end of day tomorrow to be able to transfuse our first full-size show-biz client, who I can't name, but I can tell you *is* someone who *is* just a pretty face.

You know, my dear Laverne, in the final analyses, all my jewelry successes are bittersweet, because the true artist inside me aches to break with the conventional. Oh, I know, *Ten Popes A-Popping* shatters post-modernist rules of ecumenical symmetry, style and synchronicity—but that's not good enough when I look at your work and see art that *everyone* finds repulsive.

Oh, Laverne, to be free like you—to explore new frontiers using raw sewage. How I wish I could throw away these diamonds and pearls, emeralds and sapphires—throw them right into my safety deposit box—and pick up medical waste and create—JUST CRE-ATE—like I did when I was two years old; when I was unencumbered by the art of Charles Bronson and the unshakable influence his hair has had on my life.

Other days, when the sculptor in me pushes the painter aside, I want to take a crowbar to my BMW 720 and just smash it to smithereens.

Dear, *dear,* Laverne—I hate to think what my art would be like if I didn't have another artist to whom I could rip open my soul. I thank you, and the world thanks you.

Love and respect,
Uncle Jules

From: SisterChanelSize6@SistersOfTheRuinedFeet.com
Date: Monday, March 21, 2005, 11:00 a.m.
To: US@US.us
Subject: You've been warned!

(FYI: THIS EMAIL WAS WRITTEN IN ONE MINUTE AND THIRTY SECONDS AND WITHOUT TAKING A BREATH, A CIGGIE, OR A PEE EXCEPT FOR A FEW AMENS! FOR BEST READING RESULTS I SUGGEST YOU READ IT AT YOUR OWN PACE, AND TO THOSE WHO KNOW WHO THEY ARE, A RAPID RESPONSE IS REQUIRED.)

I am sorry I have been unable to respond in a more prompt fashion to the full-of-lies-and-slurring-innuendo emails that continue to drag the good name of the former Aunt, known as Bea, through the mud of vilification. Please do not think for one moment that my silence is in any way a vindication of this ugly and completely unfounded slandering of my character. It is only within the last five minutes that these defaming electronic blasphemes have been translated into Hieroglyphic Hittite, the only language I am allowed to read while I am in a religiously induced coma that allows me to leave my body so I can discover who was the first woman to get a man to pay for her by rubbing her stilettos against the inside of his thigh and thus fulfill 1a of The Three Prophecies Of The Golden Shoe Trees.

CAN I HAVE AN AMEN!

Now that I am awake and in full control of my mental faculties, I can, in the most vigorous fashion, deny the heinous accusations made by the Jealous Bitch Branch of The Family Ginsburg (*pronounced* Du Pont) against my good former name, and thus, to the present *me*. While the story about me being in sanctuary lockdown for allegedly pilfering a pair of Manolos provided the authorities with further proof that their forensic evidence (i.e. the said pair of size-4 chestnut-brown crocodile 4-inch Manolo pumps with my DNA embedded in its sole) put me at the scene of the botched assassination attempt on my niece, Cheryl, that narrative was completely fabricated by the same people who falsely planted my DNA. Unfortunately, you bitch bastards who believe you can destroy my metatarsal *chakra* with this fairy tale never bothered to check my *current shoe size*—for if you had, you would have discovered I'm a *size 6*—and as any woman who paid over $500.00 for a pair of Manolos would tell you, it is damn near impossible to sneak up and attempt to strangle someone in 4-inch pumps two sizes too small. Total and unequivocal absolution is the only thing I expect from these defamatory attackers. Without their admission of guilt, these horrible harridans will suffer unspeakable retribution. This act of contrition must come within the hour. After that time, I will no longer have any contact with the outside world until I complete the task of installing a Starbucks Rain Forest in the main chapel of the Sisters of the Ruined Feet Sanctuary. This monumental undertaking, entrusted to me by Sister Prada Size 6, our Mother Superior, fulfills 3a of The Three Prophecies of The Golden Shoe Trees.

CAN I HAVE AN AMEN!

Upon my completion of the three prophecies, Mother Superior will personally hand me the sacred Golden Shoe Horn, with which only I can unlock the hallowed shoe sepulcher of Imelda Marcos. Once inside this holy tomb, I must immediately remove my favorite Manolos and leave them out of respect and as part of the price of admission. Then, I will have ten seconds to choose any pair of Imelda's shoes that go with my outfit. Upon the putting on of her shoes, I will be given the Gift of Enchanted Feet and will immediately attain Glass Slipper Enlightenment. I will then leave The Sisters of The Ruined Feet Sanctuary, accompanied by four wise personal shoppers, and begin a journey by foot that will take me heel and toe, far and wide. I will travel to places like Madison Avenue, Rodeo Drive, and other high-traffic areas where high-income women who cannot control their desire to buy expensive shoes that ruin their feet can come into my presence and be healed. When I arrive, I will set up the first state-of-the-art Foot Worshipping Center and matching Handbag Chanting Garden. I will make myself available by appointment only. I will play footsies with those who will pay my price and bestow upon them the Gift of the Everlasting Strut, which will allow them the ability to comfortably wear any pair of designer shoes, no matter how high the heel, narrow the toe, or slippery the floor surface.

No mark, bruise, bunion, corn, lump, or bump shall they ever encounter, if they take *ME* unto their feet and *walk with me*. And in accordance to The Three Prophecies of The Golden Shoe Trees, we will no longer be called the Sisters of the Ruined Feet Sanctuary. Our new name will be *The Wearers of The Strappy Shoes* and our mantra will be . . . *I'll take them in all colors*.

CAN I HAVE AN AMEN!

I will also be endowed with supernatural foot power so I can kick your jealous-bitch branch of The Family Ginsburg (*pronounced* Du Pont) ass into the next state if you don't stop accusing me of trying to garrote the old elephant woman, who should have died 404 years ago (give or take), or trying to off Cheryl outside of Shirley's Sister's Ex-Mother-in-Law's Market. Again, if you had done the research, you would have learned that one of the reasons I was chosen to join the Sisters of the Ruined Feet Sanctuary was my exceptional score in the Choking-from-Behind and the Sharp-Shooting-with-Eyes-Closed parts of the entrance examination. Trust me, If I wanted to garrote Bubbeh Esther (*pronounced* Granny Smith Apples) or shoot my niece, Cheryl, they wouldn't be here to bitch and moan about it, or be doing spinoramas in a weapons-enhanced mobile wheelchair. While I'm at it, enough with this Angelina business! Who among us hasn't once walked down the street and hoped they'd be mistaken for this angel in human form? Or, even one time, stared long and hard into a hand mirror hoping to see plump, ass-cheek-lips the color of cherry wine, and not some set of candy-red Botox-inflated lips? Before you accuse me, you yellow rat bastards, take another look into that floor-to-ceiling mirror and ask yourself this rhetorical question: *If I were Angelina for twenty-four hours, endowed with special gifts given to me by the Goddess, wouldn't I want to go where I could do the most good?* To do otherwise would be only lip service. Who knows what peccadilloes you'd have chosen, but don't condemn me for being turned on by

Amish men ever since I saw Harrison Ford in *Witness*. Here, in my tiny cell, completely surrounded by floor-to-ceiling racks of my shoes, I kneel barefoot in front of all I hold most holy and I vow the woman formerly known as Formerly Known as The Aunt Named Bea (who may, or may not be the person on the black-and-white grainy Gap surveillance video) no longer exists.

CAN I HAVE AN AMEN!

To prove that all is forgiven, I want everyone to come to my Foot Worshipping and Spa Spritz Sanctification Party for some champagne, a complimentary healing, and 20% off on selected pairs of designer shoes.

CAN I HAVE ANOTHER AMEN!

In all humility,

Sister Chanel Size 6, Formerly Known as the Aunt Named Bea

From: YoungerTheElder23@Ourmail.us
Date: Monday, March 21, 2005 11:07 AM
To: US@Ourmail.us
Subject: Update from Your Humble Servant

Dear Members of the Family Ginsburg (*pronounced* Du Pont),

It's almost 12:00 a.m., and I'm still at the office working ever so diligently on the family portfolio. You know I am not saying this just to blow my own horn. I am only the faithful and most humble servant of the Family Ginsburg (*pronounced* Du Pont), as was my father, his father before him, and his father before him, all the way back to Younger the Elder by One Ginsburg (*pronounced* Du Pont), may they be inscribed in *The History of the World: Book Of Ratings*, Chapter 11, The Great CPAs of History.

I want to thank those of you who called my office as soon as you received my fifty-page memorandum regarding the recent changes in the U.S. Tax Code and how they favorably impact our family fortune. I formally apologize for not being able to personally answer the calls immediately. I can assure you they were taken in the order received. I am in the process of reviewing the LUDS, but I don't believe the waiting time ever exceeded twenty minutes.

The day in question had been a particularly grueling one for everyone here at the firm, so please forgive me if my manner was unusually formal and business-like. I am just thankful Nicky wasn't more seriously wounded, and Agent Marsh survived the twenty-five-floor plunge, and that life-support measures won't be an issue.

I don't want any of you to misunderstand the reason for my retelling of these events. It is not my intention for you to think I am using the Securities and Exchange raid, or our alleged link to the Senate Extortion Scandal as an excuse for not addressing your needs in a more expeditious manner.

I know you were pleased to learn that despite these inconveniences, we never outsourced your calls to any accounting firm *not* being investigated or already under indictment.

These events behind me, and with my own bail set at five million dollars, I now appreciate why none of you thanked me for my lobbying efforts resulting in the fact that no one from The Family Ginsburg (*pronounced* Du Pont)—no matter how much income they receive—will ever have to pay taxes again. I also understand why many of you decided not to phone yourself, but had attorneys—or in one case, a personal trainer—place the calls that threatened my life.

In reviewing my memorandum, I can see how one could falsely assume one did not have to file a return. I can also appreciate your desire to know how quickly you would receive your refund, and if it would be automatically deposited in your offshore banking account.

Again, I must assume full responsibility for not making myself more transparent in regard to the salient points of the memorandum. I also want to clear up any misconceptions my communiqué may have caused.

Firstly, I want to address the issue of the memorandum itself—and its self-destruction mechanism that was activated two minutes after you took it out of its envelope. This was done on advice of counsel, both theirs and ours, and was not meant to be a magical trick, an admission of guilt, or a way to light up.

Secondly, unfair on its face, the fact we wrote the tax code does not mean we are exempt from filing a return.

Thirdly, and for all of us who have homes in the foreign lands, overseas shell accounts can only be accessed via our Bentley or Rolls Royce keyless entry fobs until January of 2006, at which time The Family Ginsburg (*pronounced* Du Pont) will be able to use their Ferrari, Lamborghini and Maserati sports-car fobs. (FYI: shell accounts are never to be referred to as "F*ck You Accounts," as this is not professional.)

I am just sorry that none of you had the opportunity of seeing Nicky before he fled the country. Nevertheless, I can assure you that he didn't take the slight personally, and truly appreciates your support. I know firsthand how much he agonized over the decision to take the job offer in Monaco, but when a king calls, you have to answer the bell. Nicky also wanted me to inform you that once he is settled in, you will all be invited for cocktails. (Aren't you sorry you didn't see him off at the border crossing?)

In case you did not receive my phone message, or Blackberry email, once it is officially proclaimed that royals can't be guilty of anything, Nicky will take his rightful place beside his king.

All I can say is, we are all better off for knowing Nicholas Graham, and having him plan and successfully execute the Vending Machine Coin Drop that would have forced senators and congressmen to drink *sugar-free soft drinks* had they not agreed to vote for our recommended tax code changes.

I realize that in the beginning, many of you were skeptical of Nicky because of how well he spoke English without ever once watching "Masterpiece Theater." Then, there was the little matter of his bad-boy reputation that was unfairly used against him when, a week after he joined the firm, Nicky was embroiled in one so-called "escapade" after another: Bubbeh Esther's (*pronounced* Granny Smith Apples's) stolen jewelry scandal; the counterfeit paintings indictments; and more recently, the St. Patrick's Cathedral incident where Nicky used his likeness to Cardinal Egan to access the confessional whenever he wanted to avoid NSA surveillance.

Bermuda will be the one person who will miss him more than most. It is not every day that two people who loved whipping so much so foolishly mistook love for a successful extortion operation.

I don't want to beat a dead horse, but I would like to go on record for the very last time and say that I never exactly threatened Bubbeh Esther's (*pronounced* Granny Smith Apples's) latest "companions" with deportation if she took Google public.

I won't deny I had my trepidations when she financed the initial startup, but it wasn't because I thought the business model unsound. At the time, I was more concerned with our matriarch's personal relationship with two underage programmers (see photos of the trio at Disney World licking their way, and each other, down the Mr. Fudge Sugar Slide).

Obviously, the Google IPO was, excuse my mixing of metaphors, one of the high-water marks of last year's financial windfall, and a gift that keeps on giving.

I do want to thank you all for your concern, but none of the bail money came from any of our twenty-five thousand (give or take) shell corporations, FEMA insurance policies, or Fort Knox gold reserves. Instead, I was the beneficiary of the President's Emergency War on Poverty Act, where huge amounts of untraceable taxpayer dollars are set aside for exactly these types of misunderstandings.

I can also assure you, my being on bail in no way interferes with this firm's ability to handle your Canadian prescription-drug shipments. More on that later, but first I would like to get back to Mr. Nicholas Graham. As Nicky was making his escape, he wanted you to know that even though his relationship with the King of Monaco will obviously mean assuming many royal duties afforded to one of his station, he is first and foremost my *go-to guy*. In that capacity, Nicky will continue to fully execute his duties and conjure up innovative and completely illegal ways of creating new revenue streams that will become accepted methods of doing business when our lobbyists get them into law.

Nicholas Graham's contributions to our firm, while engaging in so many criminal activities, proved him to be one of the premier multi-taskers in the business world today. This ability illustrates to me that not only will he be able to continue to be my *go-to guy* while being the king's *go-to guy,* Queen-like Nicholas (as we are to call Nicky after the coronation) will also have no trouble assuming his new rank of Finance Minister and CEO of The Bank Of Monte Carlo. These are important new power grabs that will allow The Family Ginsburg (*pronounced* Du Pont) to get back into the European gaming industry. It is for this reason that I have elevated the soon-to-be Queen-like Nicholas to the position of The Family Ginsburg (*pronounced* in Europe as Schleswig-Holstein-Sonderburg-Augustenburg and Windsor)—*Go-To Guy Europe, Too.*

As an aside, the soon-to-be Queen-like Nicholas wants you all to know neither he nor the king, are, as Sister Chanel Six puts it "light in the loafers." This is yet another example of "shoe humor" we have come to expect from The Aunt Formerly Known as Aunt Bea, who, despite her objectionable jokes, always sends her Schedule 9 in on time.

I don't want to be the one to re-write The Family Ginsburg (*pronounced* Du Pont) History, but I think our esteemed matriarch is forgetting the important role Younger the Elder by Four—may he be inscribed in *The History of the World: The Book Of Ratings*, Chapter 11, The Great CPAs of History—played when he was Finance Minister under Louis XIV. To tax anyone who got a suntan while in the presence of the Sun King may have been the matriarch's idea, but the banning of sunscreen was pure Younger the Elder by Four, may he be inscribed in *The History of the World The Book Of Ratings*, Chapter 11, The Great CPAs of History!

I want to thank all of you who supported me in my denying Cousin Tenderly's dubious investment suggestions. Until one is able to breathe without the use of an oxygen mask, I don't see any reason to "go buy it on the mountain."

As you know, I am normally against any kind of speculation. My business philosophy has always been, and will continue to be, one where I let the other fellow assume all the risks, and when the land has appreciated significantly, come in and seize it through the right of eminent domain. However, this does not preclude me from doing a little "investment-opportunity scouting" on my own, so to speak, so when new opportunities present themselves, The Family Ginsburg (*pronounced* Du Pont) will be properly positioned to take full advantage of the situation. With this in mind, I have been quietly gathering information regarding land values contiguous to flood plane areas. I know what you're thinking. If you're not paying attention to Cousin Tenderly's mountain madness, why believe her warnings that hurricanes, nor'easters and other weather phenomenon threaten to destroy our coastlines? All I can say in response is that when Nostradamus comes to you in a dream and tells you, "They weren't talking shit at The Kyoto Conference on Global Warming," you have to say, maybe—just maybe—Cousin Tenderly is onto something.

One final note: I want to thank those of you who emailed me during my arraignment, expressing your surprise, your support, and your suggestions as to who turned me in. Your concerns regarding the confiscation of my passport were also touching, as were your insistence that you had no choice but to go along with the in-house audit, surveillance cameras, electronic ankle bracelet, and hourly water-boarding. I would have ordered the same, plus the rack, had any of you been arrested.

Dear Family Ginsburg (*pronounced* Du Pont), I thank you for this opportunity to communicate my thoughts to you.

As always, your faithful and humble servant,

Younger the Elder by Twenty-Three

From: LawyerUp@AbeSues4You.edu
Date: Monday, March 21, 2005 11:15 a.m.
To: US@Ourmail.us
Subject: Big news from Uncle Abe!

Hello, everybody!

Can you guess where Uncle Abe is right now? If you guessed General Motors Headquarters, GM Renaissance Center in Detroit, you would be right—but as of 12:00 p.m., you'd be wrong! That's right, in two hours, there's going to be a new name on the door, and that name is going to be The Family Ginsburg (*pronounced* Du Pont) Center.

I bet you didn't think Old Uncle Abe could do it, did you? Well, you know what Uncle Abe always says, "Throw enough shit on the wall, and something's gonna stick."

Uncle Abe got them to change their name as part of the settlement Uncle Abe reached just about five minutes ago. Uncle Abe doesn't want to bore The Family Ginsburg (*pronounced* Du Pont) with all the legalese, but in a nutshell, Uncle Abe agrees to drop the class action sexual harassment suit against GM and its dealers, and in return, Uncle Abe gets the family name on the door, plus every person in the class action suit gets a free GM car of their choice.

Laverne, Uncle Abe doesn't want Uncle Abe's nephew, William, getting into any more trouble than he's already in, so please, whatever car he chooses, make sure he only drives it in empty parking lots until he gets his license.

Let's see, what else? Uncle Abe also got GM to rename its 2006 Cadillac Escalade *Esca-Abe*.

Oh yes, Uncle Abe got GM to give Uncle Abe a pension and health insurance, and naturally, they're paying all legal and travel expenses. Oh, GM refinanced Uncle Abe's condo to the tune of seven hundred and fifty thousand—at no interest, and to be repaid when Uncle Abe feels like it.

Finally, and this bruised some egos, Uncle Abe's going to replace Jeff Gordon in car #24, the Dupont Chevrolet (no relation, and *pronounced* the same as our name), at the NASCAR NEXTEL Subway 500 at the Martinsville Speedway.

If you've been reading Uncle Abe's racing-car webpage at AbesASpeeder.com, you know Uncle Abe has won NASCAR events before: NASCAR Ralph Nader Drivers with Seat Belts PlayStation Invitational Cup, for one. The NASCAR Jack Daniels Mothers Against Drunken Video Gamers 2004-05 XBOX for another.

You can bet your last dollar Uncle Abe knows the Martinsville Speedway inside and out, and while Uncle Abe doesn't want to blow his own horn, Uncle Abe is confident Uncle Abe will be the first person since Buddha to demonstrate that the world of virtual reality and the real world "meet the road and become one" on a NASCAR track.

By the way, Uncle Abe's going to rename Uncle Abe's car in honor of Uncle Abe's screen name, LAWYER UP.

Uncle Abe also agrees to become VP In Charge of All Lawsuits Against GM, with an annual salary of three hundred and fifty thousand, not including a signing bonus of one hundred thousand, as well as incentives that could go into the millions depending on how many lawsuits Uncle Abe helps them get tossed.

GM's already ahead of the game because Uncle Abe had, all by himself, thirty-five additional lawsuits against GM, their dealers, suppliers, and ad agencies; the total of which ran into the billions.

Uncle Abe wants everyone to know that Uncle Abe couldn't have done it without the support Uncle Abe received from the Family Ginsberg (*pronounced* Du Pont). Filing a couple of hundred lawsuits a day can be a pretty lonely job unless you have your family behind you.

Of course, the person who really made Uncle Abe's win possible was Brad Pitt. As far as Uncle Abe is concerned, every man in America should toot his car horn to Brad, who put his career on the line so that no car buyer would ever again suffer sexual harassment at the hands of an exotic-car salesmen.

To Uncle Abe, Brad Pitt is Betty Friedan with a touch of Ralph Nader thrown in. When Uncle Abe has some down time, Uncle Abe is going to write a screenplay about this epic event, and you can bet your bottom dollar Uncle Abe is going to personally hand it to Brad so Uncle Abe can star in it.

Another thing that makes Brad so terrific—he didn't let this "thing" about Aunt Bea get in the way of his friendship with Uncle Abe. And, let Uncle Abe tell you this—Brad even put Angelina on the phone with Uncle Abe, and she told Uncle Abe that if she could forgive *Hooked on Crochet* for printing photos of her thumbs without even giving her a few extra issues for her friends, she could forgive Aunt Bea. Oh, yes—there's another reason she doesn't have any hard feelings toward Aunt Bea. Angelina's just happens to be a huge fan of The Sanctuary of the Sisters of the Ruined Feet, and—get this—at one time considered joining the order, but instead decided to try crocheting, a choice Uncle Abe for one, is glad she did.

On top of that, when Brad told Angelina about Uncle Abe's screenplay idea, she said she wanted to play the late, great Betty Friedan—who, as those in the know, know–is the only person Angelina let comb her hair when Angelina was a child.

Uncle Abe wishes Uncle Abe had the same kind of good news regarding Uncle Abe's daughter, Clarice. Who in a million years would have thought Uncle Abe would lose—certainly not the judge, who jailed the jury for not reading between the lines when giving them his final instructions, i.e., "Hannibal the Cannibal Must Pay."

What Uncle Abe believes did Uncle Abe in was the fact the jury had never seen an English knight in shining armor before. As if Sir Anthony's entrance wasn't enough, once Court TV came back from its commercial break and resumed proceedings, Tony really showed off his National Theater training that just blows the socks off of anything Americans can do, although, Uncle Abe thinks Al's performance in *Scarface*, particularly in the Chainsaw Scene, comes close. When Hopkins started doing his kindly "Dr. Frederick Treves Routine," Uncle Abe could see this CBE (Commander of the British Empire) had the jury eating right out of his hand—just the way he had movie audiences lapping it up when he made friends with John Hurt in *The Elephant Man*.

The actor-provocateur ended his performance with his fussy old C. S. Lewis imitation, weeping before the jury just like he did when he was in front of the closet in *Shadowlands*, when he finally realized there was no magic that could bring Debra Winger back.

Unfortunately for Uncle Abe, this time "Knight Bachelor" had the magic, and he certainly used it to put a spell on Uncle Abe's jury. Can you imagine how many lawsuits Uncle Abe could win with that Welsh bastard by *his* side?

Well, you know what Uncle Abe always says: "What one jury won't, another will."

Uncle Abe's class action suit on behalf of every Trekkie against William Shatner, "Boston Legal," ABC, and the affiliates who pick up the show for alienation of affection and the resulting psychosis from such feckless casting, is now on the calendar for early next year.

This week in the highly respected medical journal, *Science, Smience*, Uncle Abe's case will be documented, and for the first time, there will be incontrovertible proof that Uncle Abe's bipolar condition was brought on by the massive and destructive disorientation Uncle Abe suffered while watching a dashing but portly middle-aged man in a custom-made suit, shirt, and very snazzy tie inhabit the young body of Captain James Tiberius Kirk. The article quotes many people like Uncle Abe, who for no explainable reason, stopped saying, "Beam me up, Scotty," and instead, blurt out when encountering strangers on the street, "Hi, I'm Denny Crain."

One noted doctor thinks it's a new kind of Alzheimer's; another, mass hypnosis; still others believe it's subliminal messages imbedded in Travelocity.com commercials.

Uncle Abe is sticking with bipolar, and this has nothing to do with the consulting fees Uncle Abe's getting from the pharmaceutical companies.

Talking about commercials leads, Uncle Abe would like to share with you Uncle Abe's thoughts regarding the settlement of Reagan's case against the BBC and their American affiliates, who recklessly chose to portray her as one of the London Subway Bombers. Only some of the more radical members of the Anne Rice Stake and Ale Investment Club (a.k.a., Daughters of Darkness, a.k.a., D.O.D.) seem upset with the settlement. (See below.)

Regarding punitive damages, Uncle Abe wants to remind The Family Ginsburg (*pronounced* Du Pont) that the dollar amount, as represented in Euros, not dollars, was more than we asked for.

As far as the award for pain and suffering, Uncle Abe would like to point out that Reagan was given her choice of jewels in the Royal Collection. Uncle Abe thinks the one she picked out, while not the one Uncle Abe would have chosen, is highly prized and will attain astronomical figures if ever put on the open market.

As to the final demand, which Uncle Abe eluded to above, Uncle Abe had to agree with Reagan's British barrister when he said, "There is no way in hell the Queen would allow members of the Anne Rice Stake and Ale Investment Club (a.k.a., Daughters of Darkness, a.k.a., D.O.D.) to go down into the Royal Crypts and drive a stake into Churchill's heart, even though there was cigar ash linking him to The Vampire of London's last victim."

Cheryl, you know Uncle Abe loves you and Reagan, but this Vampire of London business is a separate matter and should not be included in Reagan's settlement demands, plain and simple—end of story.

And please, Cheryl, would you change your message on your answering machine? Because if Uncle Abe has to listen to the entire version of "Bad Moon Rising" one more time, Uncle Abe will have to drive a stake into *your heart!*

Love,
Uncle Abe

From: LuLu-LuCrawford@PleasureIsWhereYouFindIt.org
Date: Monday, March 21, 2005 11:40 a.m.
To: Bubbeh.E@US.us
Subject: That's a big ten-four from Miss Lulu-Lu Crawford *(pronounced the way it looks)*

Dear B. E.,

Gosh darn, I, like, promised myself I wouldn't like get all riled up with what's been goin' on with your family, but you are like the first real New York City family I know and you sure are a plumb crazy bunch—*you* excluded, a course.

B. E., thanks for talkin' to Bermuda 'bout my email and all. Bermuda's been right understandin' since then and, like you know, she got that freak Uncle Clayboy—who sure ain't like no uncle I ever seen—offa my back and outta my life.

She also, like, squared things with her mother, who sure does reminds me of a slow-witted boy cousin name a Hugo—he's, like, got my eyes so I know we're kin—I had back in Hogs Breath who was, like, real good with settin' thangs on fire. Why, that good ole boy could set a keg a ice a cookin' with, like, two little puffs a breath.

B. E., it's the Goddess's honest truth when I tell you I once seen him set a hog's tail a fire from two hundred feet, just by him shootin' his breath through a peashooter. I swear, you could see that trail a fire whooshin' across the marsh, hangin' there like the clothesline in your mama's backyard.

Like I said, Hugo was the poor child's name; and, like, he always had a hard time getting' a girl no matter how much he, like, paid 'em, 'cause the last thing a girl wants is to see her pussy hair set a fire. Hugo finally got, like, his sister's second mama, Betty-Jean Boulevard—she's, like, got my eyes so I know we're kin—to, like, shave down there, so the most she ever got was some charcoal-like marks that, like, ended up on old Hugo's face. Everybody, like, used to call him Barbeque Breath and Black Lips, but my favorite was Hot Shit 'cause he could, like, blow smoke signals outta his eyehole just as good.

B. E., I just wish, like, I could take you Ginsburgs (*pronounced* Du Ponts) down to Hogs Breath Alabama for some foot-rattlin' and some of my Uncle Nester's—he, like, got my eyes so I know we're kin—fine-tastin' sour-strawberry whisky mash, and, like, the most garl darn'd delicious barbeque, grits, and okra south a the Mason–Dixon Line. And, like, the pukin' afterwards. Lord have mercy, B. E.—I'm, like, homesick just thinkin' about it!

My goodness, girl, what am I thinkin', rattlin' off about foot-rattlin' and supposin' you know what it means when, like, you probably don't.

Well B. E., you heard of foot-Beaglin', I know you have, 'cause when I got up here one a my clients said they do it up in Greenwich and lots a fancy places instead of, like, fox huntin'.

Well, you know in foot-Beaglin', like, the Beagles go after rabbits. Well, instead of Beagles, we use rat'lers. Man, is it some fun!

Now B. E., *you* could use your trunk to snatch up them little rabbits. Wouldn't that be special?

I'm thinkin', like, maybe you could mention my invite, 'cause from you it would, like, have impact. Naturally, it'll have to be after I get my mechanical head, but, like, that's OK 'cause, like, the fall's the nicest time in Hogs Breath, what with the new sour-mash crop, and, like, the rat'lers rarin' to go and all.

I was watchin', like, Lou Dobbs—I, like, love that man—and he was sayin', like, how the economy's so bad 'cause a the government—and, like, people are tradin' stuff to each other jest to stay alive, only he's callin' it barterin'.

Well, B. E., it, like, hit me right between the eyes, and I said to myself—*Miss Lulu-Lu, that man is, like, talkin' right to you* —*so you email the Finest Doctor and you tell 'im what Lou said and you tell 'im how, like, you'd be willin' to give 'em two freebies a month for, like, five years, so long as he, like, paid the travel and, like, gave you a week's notice.*

I don't have to tell you how nice the Finest Doctor is, but boy, I thought he was, like, gonna cry when he got back to me and said he was sorry, but he couldn't take me up on my more-than-generous offer.

Man alive, for somebody with a foreign accent, that boy can sure sweet-talk the sugar right out of your coffee, can't he? Never you mind, B. E., he tells me in, like, the nicest way he's really got a hard-on for Clarice and doesn't want to, like, mess it up.

I, like, respect him for that, don't you, B. E.?

So, like, we came to another agreement where Bermuda, bless her kind heart, puts up $150,000, and I'd put up the other $150,000. Sure, I'm gonna have to, like, work my little butt off, but I figure what with my new head and all, I'll be givin' better head—if you get my meanin'—and, like, pay her back in a year. Sure, I could, like, take the easy way out and take a job in, like, a hedge fund, but I like to make my money the old-fashioned way, and besides, it's not every day a girl from Hogs Breath, Alabama, gets to live out her dream.

Never you mind neither about him postponin' the surgery 'til September when the Finest Doctor says it's, like, really nice in Mount Cedar.

Hey, B. E., listen to this. The Finest Doctor doesn't think I'll need, like, a head-shrinker afterwards, which is OK by me, let me tell you—'cause between you and me, like, they really mess you up.

B. E., I can put my own new mechanical head on, thank you very much, and I don't need no over-schooled, under-fucked stuffed shit tellin' me how, neither. I mean, have you ever, like, done a shrink?

Now B. E., I don't mean, like, for you to get all offended, but I know you're, like, a woman of the world, what with all the years you lived and all the men you known and all—so maybe you can get what I mean?

B. E., say, like, a man comes to me for—you-know-what. OK, they tell me what they like. Sometimes, it's, like, really weird, but it can be a turn-on after you've had five guys about excitin' as a cold pitchfork handle in an unheated barn.

But B. E., *head-shrinkers*—jumping Jehoshaphat—like, they come from a different planet, don't they? Gosh darn, these guys not only tell you what they want, but then they're, like, askin' what you think of *what* they want. Man, B. E., if there's such a thing as, like, diarrhea of the mind, these shrinks got a double dose.

Now B. E., you got to understand, the first time this, like, ever happened I was still bein' raised up by Uncle Horace and his wife—they, like, got my eyes so I know we're kin—and, like, some head-shrinker comes by school wantin' to, like, talk to me 'cause he understands Uncle Horace was into hog fightin' and, like, all that violence might be the reason I'm, like, writin' what I'm writin' in English class.

Now B. E., you tell me, what the hell does me writin' about a little southern girl who likes to have sex with older men have to do with hog fightin'?

Well, shit B. E., halfway through the interview this big-city A-hole finally takes his beady little eyes off my titties and, like, gets to the meat of the subject, which is wantin' to see me after school for a little you-know-what.

Now, I'm not gonna pretend I didn't, like, lead this fella on, or didn't, like, keep scrawling "$25.00" all over the piece a paper I had in front of me. Heck, just 'cause I'm, like, in the eighth grade don't mean I'm, like, ignorant.

Naturally we meet, and do it, like, in the backseat of his Ford, which is also the first time I ever did it in, like, a car, as all I'd ever been in was, like, pickups and motorcycles, but they don't count 'cause—well, like, they don't.

Never you mind, I'm doin' just fine, and tell you that Bermuda's doin' just fine, too, and yeah—*we're* doin' fine, too.

I won't pretend I wasn't a might perturbed when she went on "Montel"—I, like, love that man—behind my back and without tellin' me, which is mean and low-down and somethin' I cannot tolerate.

B. E., you know how I found out? One of my city commissioners (I got me three of 'em—Water, Sanitation, and Transportation; this one was Water), like, he tells me he wants me to flog 'im, and then, like, make 'im eat the licorice whip he saw Bermuda use on "Montel."

Oh yeah, B. E., he also wants me to be yellin', *I'm Zoro, you piece of shit!*—in fuckin' Spanish—like I speak a foreign language! I nearly bit his you-know-what off I got so garl darn'd flustered.

After I, like, calmed down and stitched the poor fella up, he shows me the program, like, on his cell phone, and there it was—as big as life—Bermuda showin' Montel *our* line of hand-made chocolate and licorice squirters, strap-ons, dongs with and without balls, whips, chains, and bondage bakery products we're selling downstairs—not once mentionin' these wonderful products were, like, made from my kin's secret recipes.

Not only that, B. E.—Montel, like, gets her to fess up to the fact she, like, signed a deal with QVC; and, like, the Food Channel's gonna give her her own show, which she tells'em she's callin' Dr. Wanker's Chocolate Factory. For fuck's sake—like, she's as much a doctor as, like, my left nipple.

B. E., what really gets me, like, madder than a raccoon caught with its pecker in a trap is, like, we just spent all night in bed makin' whoopee and all and even talkin' about, like, gettin' hitched—and maybe, like, adoptin' a Chinese baby.

Now B. E., you gotta believe me on this, but, like, this Chinese baby stuff is somethin' she brought up, and I swear I had nothin' to do with it 'cause to tell you the truth, I been, like, a little taken up with gettin' my mechanical head. Go on, like, call me Little Miss Selfish—and all the time she's, like, got this stack a secrets she's keepin' from me.

Damn B. E., I'm just a little ole country girl that's good at lickin' men's balls, but that don't mean I should, like, be taken advantage of—and the secret recipes handed down from kin to kin with eyes like me shouldn't be, like, stolen by someone you thought was, like, your soulmate.

My Goddess, B. E., my folks must be turnin' over in their graves knowin' someone, like, outside the family's makin' soft chocolate mouth gags, or red licorice floggers with pecans so, like, you get them nice-shaped welts, you know.

B. E., I was so damn mad I, like, nearly made up one of my great-grandma Cleola's death mixes—they say I, like, got her eyes, so I know we're kin—and if it wasn't, like, for Oprah—I, like, love that gal—talkin' on the TV about forgiveness through listening to Elvis, I would have put that death mix on the tip of Bermuda's favorite Jack Rabbit vibrator and watched as she, like, came and went—if you get my meanin'.

I remember my kin used to, like, make our own Jack Rabbit model, like, with white chocolate and marshmallows. Boy B. E., that's a real Easter-time treat, I tell you. B. E., I swear, everybody from, like, nine to ninety wanted one of them babies when they went egg rollin'.

Like I said, thank the Lord Goddess for Oprah—I, like, love that gal—who said to forgive and to listen to Elvis, so I went back to that sassy bar in Chelsea and remembered that first moment I met Bermuda and, like, how *she touched my hand what a chill I got. Her lips were like a volcano that's hot. I'm proud to say she's my buttercup. I'm in love, I'm all shook up. Mm mm oh, oh, yeah, yeah! You're in love, you're all shook up, a hah, a, hah, you're all shook up.*

Anywho, B. E., Bermuda and me got everythin' settled and we'll be, like, fifty-fifty partners, so you look for me on the QVC and the Food Netty, course this'll all be in, like, the fall, and way after I, like, get my head, which I may have already mentioned.

B. E. don't you go frettin', I'll still have the weekends so I can still meet you down in Hogs Breath for some serious funnin'.

By the way, the Finest Doctor is gonna make sure my new head don't reflect too much light so I'll be able to, like, look my best in front the TV cameras. Ain't he, like, the sweetest? Love you like the family I ain't never had . . .

Respectfully, yours,

Miss Lulu-Lu Crawford (*pronounced* the way it looks)

JUNE 21st, THE FIRST DAY OF SUMMER

From: Cheryl.G@Ourmail.us
Date: Monday, June 21, 2005, 9:00 a.m.
To: US@Ourmail.us
Subject: *Été est ici!* (Summer's Here!)

Ma chére famille, (My darling family,)

Quel matin glorieux! (What a glorious morning!) As I sit out on my terrace in my scooter and wave across the street to the Prince and Princess of the Duchy of Lichtenstein as they tend their rooftop terrace, I thank my lucky stars I changed medication.

Oh, what a great feeling to know I was born a Ginsburg (*pronounced* Du Pont) Girl, endowed with bountiful beauties that make it so easy for me to make friends and influence men, as summed up in the words of She Who Brings Forth Life, the Great Baleboosteh Ginsburg (*pronounced* Eleanor of Aquitaine): *Abiistis, dulces caricae.* (You're finished, sweet figs.)

Even though I feel I could float right off this roof, don't for a second think I don't appreciate how these twin peaks have made it possible for me to live richly in the wealthiest of all New York City zip codes and on the most desirable of streets in a townhouse I received as part of my divorce settlement back in the early seventies from Prickface #3 (now worth one-hundred times more than he paid for it), BECAUSE I DO! (If you think my D-cups look great now, you should have seen them then!)

Across the street and one next townhouse down, the King and Queen of Spain have a little *pied-à-terre* for when they come into town and simply want to kick off their royal slippers and be like everyone else who owns their country and a nice piece of ours.

Talk about people who make this a kinder and gentler world. *Tellement vers le bas à la terre.* (So down-to-earth.)

How many times have they sent me something marvelous from back home? Why, when they heard I was shot, their first thought was to fill my house with Goyas. (They just backed a truck up against that museum of theirs and pulled those paintings right off the wall.) *C'est vrai!* (It's true!)

You know what demonstrated how clearly they understood the very core of my being—they chose the exact same cheer-me-up paintings I would have picked. For instance, the one they put in my bedroom, *Guernica*—wow! Let me tell you, nothing makes a room come alive more than a painting that picks up the colors in your rug.

And listen, how many kings and queens do you know who would cancel a royal musical performance and fly up in their royal jet just for *your* birthday party? Case closed! I know, *I know* the Stones came back with them on the plane, so the concert wasn't a total washout, but you can't compare Mick's rooster walk at their palace to a stroll up an airplane aisle, even if it was in a Boeing 747-200B modified to meet the needs of a king who's a direct descendent of the pharaohs.

And, the gifts I got! *Incroyable!* (Incredible!) I can't tell you how many times I tried to give the King back his grandfather's crown. But, *noooo*! He just kept putting it right back on my head, insisting his father, King Ferdinand II (he called him "The Ole Cocker") had so many crowns that when he himself became King He Himself & I, after his older brother, King Isabelle the Confused, abdicated (everyone knows the story of The King Who Would Be a Queen), well, "Toots," short for Tutankhamen (that's the secret name I call King He Himself & I) said he just didn't have any more room at the palace for these heavy headdresses and, well, he knew from the way I was salivating at last year's Halloween party how much I admired the crown he was wearing, and well, so, the king gave me one! *Quel gentil type.* (What a nice guy.)

I'm so excited, I hope I'm making sense! Hold on, I have to adjust my morphine drip. Don't want to fly off the old roof, you know . . . That reminds me, I'll get to your birthday cards and the balcony mishap in just a *minuto* (minute).

I can't say enough about the king's—I mean Toots's—lovely young bride, Carmen Santiago Chile, who has taken the name "Just Carmen from the Palace." "Taco Bell" (that's the secret name I call Just Carmen from the Palace, because she just adores their hot sauce) won me over when she insisted on doing my hair, saying it was her special birthday gift to me. *Quelle femme, huh?* (What a woman, huh?)

Well, I happen to know Toots doesn't do anything without "You Lucky Bitch" (that's the other secret name I call Just Carmen from the Palace, a.k.a., Taco Bell), so that's *two* wonderful gifts I received (the crown being the other).

I remember when she first did my hair. I'm telling you, I can see why Toots grabbed her out of that Barcelona salon and married her the very next day in Vegas. This girl gives some cut. And the way she colors! I'm telling you, she could put Frederic Fekkai out of business in a New York City heartbeat. (Don't you say a thing, or Frederic will put all the gray back in, and I'll look like George Whipple in drag.)

Of course, you know that Toots and That Lucky Bitch (a.k.a., Just Carmen from the Palace, a.k.a., Taco Bell) are going to dance together on "America's Most Wanted" and then offer a reward of ten free dance lessons, or the cash equivalent, to the person who brings me THE BITCH-BASTARD WHO PUT ME IN THIS FUCKING WHEELCHAIR SO I CAN CUT OUT HER TONGUE AND USE IT TO BITCH SLAP HER TO DEATH!

LA MORT AUX CHIENNE-BÂTARD! (DEATH TO THE BASTARD!)

I'm feeling much better now, thank you very much.

This morning the mayor (who you know lives right up the street) came by on his way to City Hall and dropped off a magnificent bouquet of *Viola cryanas* (Cry Violets) he had his Bronx Botanical Garden people make up special for my day-after-my-birthday-gift. I was a tad disappointed (I know I shouldn't have been), but you see, I couldn't help but compare them with the magnificent bouquet of *R. gallica violacea (La Belle Sultane)* roses they sent for my birthday. Don't think I didn't tell "Arnold" (that's the secret name I call the mayor, because he thinks he looks like Arnold Schwarzenegger), but he swore today's flowers were as rare, and after they were tossed down the incinerator, would become just as extinct.

Arnold isn't tight like other billionaires I know, and no one had been more generous, both with his time and his police details. (My own Delta Force guys had to go back to Baghdad for some secret thingamajig.)

You know there is so much trash talk about how the mayor and the governor don't see eye to eye on how to take care of people here in the city, and that's all it is—*trash talk*—because they have certainly been in sync when it comes to looking after my welfare.

As you all know, Arnold has so thoughtfully provided me with around-the-clock police protection. Well, the governor has been just as generous. "My Cheesy Mac" (that's the secret name I call the governor, because he loves mac and cheese) stationed state troopers at my summer house in West Hampton and at my winter place up in Tuxedo Park. Not only that, whenever I leave the city I always have six troopers, plus a state police helicopter watch over me until I leave the state. *Combien délicieux est ce?* (How delicious is that?)

I told Madison not to use her influence, but does she listen to her mother? I said, "Since when does a Supreme Court Justice have nothing better to do than to put the arm on the Commander of the Joint Chiefs of Staff?" Well, the next thing I know, Madison has *him* on the phone, and *he's* pulling Delta guys out of Baghdad and sending them to protect *me*. (I'm not supposed to know, but a mother always does, doesn't she?)

BOY—AM I FEELING GREAT! THIS MORPHINE IS REALLY TOP GRADE!

Kudos go to Monroe for getting one of his F15s at such short notice so he could fly up here from Palm Beach. I'm just sorry he couldn't stay longer, because no one knows how to rub my back like my "Magic Fingers" (that's the secret name I called Monroe when he was a little boy), but he had to go up to Washington to pick up the president and his family. (Goddess knows how he's going to squeeze everyone into that back seat unless "Big Boy's Babe" (that's the secret name I call Mrs. President) is going to sit on "Big Boy's" lap (that's the secret name I call the president), like I did with Condoleezza when we flew to the Dinah Shore Nabisco Cookie Classic.

As you probably know (if you listen to Fox News), Arms and

Ammo is putting on their annual Religious Retreat and Grenade-Fishing Weekend this Saturday. What makes this weekend extra special is it will be the first time since becoming CEO that Monroe has the honor of hosting the event.

Of course you know he and the president are old pals. Wasn't it fun when Big Boy surprised Magic Fingers with the Liberty Bell at the Nobel Peace Prize ceremony? I keep asking Monroe when he's going to find a home for it (he's renamed it "Ma Bell" in my honor—isn't that sweet?), but his new job's got him traveling non-stop. So, he's just living out of presidential palaces all the time. It's a tough job, but somebody's got to keep countries at war. *Droit sur!* (Right on!)

Well, I suppose until Monroe settles down, Ma Bell will just have to stay in storage. I was thinking of having her sent over to my place in West Hampton (it weighs a ton, but that darling fellow from FEMA promised he'd get the National Guard to move it for me), but until the Finest Doctor fixes me up, I'm staying put right here. (More on this later.)

WHAT'S THAT RINGING? OH SHIT, THE MORPHINE DRIP SHUT OFF! OH WELL!

Sylvia, I don't know why Book 'em Dano didn't tell you he was going to be there for Presidents' Weekend, but I imagine it had to do with his pardon. I know you have mixed feelings about the government returning Book 'em Dano's passport and allowing him back into the states to surf, let alone back in your life, but I think you have to consider Bermuda. A daughter needs to have a father. *C'est la verité.* (It's the truth.)

I know, *I know,* I'm not the one to talk. Looking back on it, perhaps it wasn't right for me to have Giuseppe castrated, but he didn't have to sneak back to Montevideo like a whipped dog. He could have stayed in Reagan's life. (FYI, I know you didn't push Book 'em Dano's "friend" off the balcony.)

Dr. Phil told me he believes Reagan's preoccupation with machetes and warlords can be traced back to that castration incident. I think that's too, *too* conventional an explanation. After all, we know life is not that simple. (Wouldn't it be wonderful if it were?) *Telle est la vie* . . . (Such is life . . .)

Speaking of wonderful, I feel I have grown in self-awareness since I began playing Truth or Dare with "Dr. Phil," so I imagine if I resumed my sessions (fucking impossible until I'm off the morphine drip), I'd see things more clearly and probably come to agree with his analysis.

I can't tell you how much I miss "gaming" with that man (he is a *goddess*), but not as much as I miss having FUCKING MOVEMENT in the right side of my body. And let me tell you another thing, I'll never again underestimate how important FUCKING WALKING is, no matter how many car services I own!

Oh m'excusent (Oh excuse me), I promised I wouldn't be feeling sorry for myself anymore, didn't I? Well, you know how birthdays can do that, don't you? (Page Six called it *The Pity Party to End All Pity Parties*.) It's times like this I'm sorry Bubbeh Esther (*pronounced* Granny Smith Apples) sold *The Post* because I could make up cleverer headlines. (See "Headless Body Found in Topless Bar".)

By the way, when "Dr. Phil" came to my birthday party, I almost didn't let him in. What threw me off was his curly blond hair. (I always thought he was a goddess, but now he looks like one.) It wasn't until he opened his shirt and I saw the tattoo of the serpent swallowing the little girl that I recognized the big lunkhead.

I just wish Dr. Phil could have met the Finest Doctor in person, not because of the operation (obviously Dr. Phil is capable of a little self-surgery, and with video conferencing even a child can do it), but because they both love the Cleveland Indians, and Dr. Phil is just yearning to have coffee and cake with someone who loves Bobby Ávila the way only a man can love a second baseman.

I thought Madison looked beautiful, and I'm happy to see she's loving it up with our new attorney general. (Is he an accomplished equestrian, or what?) I know others would disagree, but I thought the most exciting part of the evening was when "Speedy" (that's the secret name I call the attorney general) showed us how he won the Indianapolis 500 Steeplechase by hurdling over the sofa, the dining-room table, the center table (with the candelabra), and twelve out of the thirteen chairs (he's so, *so* superstitious) without once breaking stride or a sweat. *Je jure! Je jure!* (I swear! I swear!)

I have to applaud the way my Maddy hung on. Bubbeh Esther (*pronounced* Granny Smith Apples), you would have been so proud. My little girl just hiked up her black robes and jumped right on Speedy's back, jabbed those six-inch Manolos into his legs, gave him one quick whack across his ass with her gold-studded Gucci belt, and off they went—just the way you showed her when she was a little girl and she wanted to know why you liked men so much. Oh, I wish for those days . . . WHEN I COULD FUCKING WALK!

Madison was wearing the most darling La Perla garter belt, but instead of Veletta Pink, I want something a little more shocking for summer. I might be in a FUCKING WHEELCHAIR, but that doesn't mean I still can't show off a little leg with my D-cups.

What a nice coincidence, wasn't it, that Speedy was there to handle the cops? Sure, the police commissioner could have bribed them, but "Jawbreaker" (that's the secret name I call the police commissioner because he loves them, especially the green ones) was getting his hair cut by the Lucky Bitch (a.k.a., Just Carmen from the Palace, a.k.a., Taco Bell).

Of course, by then, the body had been auctioned off on eBay and already picked up by UPS. It's unfortunate it had to land on the trunk of French Ambassador's brand new Rolls and set off its darling alarm ("La Marseillaise"). Otherwise, the boys in blue wouldn't have been any the wiser. It worked out in the end. Speedy autographed several hundred-dollar bills, and then the cops had sponge cake and champagne with Arnold and My Cheesy Mac.

I'm just thankful we had enough champagne, because later on I learned "Big Boy" (that's the secret name I call the French Ambassador, *pronounced* with a distinct French accent so as not to be confused with the secret name I call the president, which I pronounce with a distinct Texas twang) couldn't get the last case out of his car; something to do with the way the body bounced off the trunk and jammed the lock. *Quelle tragédie!* (What a tragedy!)

Lucky Alan Greenspan, the old darling, was there, because he's quite the little burglar and had all the tools to open the trunk without so much as a scratch.

Yes, everybody, I had my little talk with Alan about the books, and while he didn't come right out and say it, I did get the distinct impression that if he were *famille* (family), he would immediately vote to remove *That Putz* from sitting on the board of the Federal Reserve. I could also tell by the way he wouldn't look me in the eye when he scarfed down those canapés (made in the shape of gold bars), he wouldn't be lowering the interest rate for the Bank of Monte Carlo anytime soon (and he certainly wouldn't be sharing a hot tub with Mr. Nicholas Graham in the near future, either).

By the way, "Big Boy" (that's the secret name I call Alan Greenspan, but I say it in a whisper so as not to be confused with the secret name I call the president, or the secret name I call the French Ambassador) has a thing for robbing homes protected by the Slomin's Shield, which is a very East-Coast thing. I asked him what he did when he traveled to the West-Coast and he whispered in my ear, *LoJack*.

Big Boy (said in a whisper, naturally*)* is the father I never had, so I know he wasn't the one to push Book 'em Dano's "friend" off the balcony. Besides, the security cameras placed him in my bedroom trying to open my safe with a Ouija board. I know the odds were two to one he did the dirty deed, because back in the day, he was known to throw bankers off balconies whenever he raised interest rates. He told the media, *"It was a yin-yang thing."*

Actually, my security cameras caught the whole thing in hi-def, so this is how it went down:

Book 'em Dano's "friend" walks out onto the balcony and gently places the Anna Nicole Smith doll on the railing. He is dressed in the same outfit as his American Girl and looks every bit as good. (By the way, Book 'em Dano said his "friend" has the largest collection of American Girls outside of Finland.) When I asked where he keeps all his matching outfits, Book 'em Dano said he has two entire rooms devoted exclusively for that purpose. Not only that, but Book 'em Dano says every month his "friend" has every garment cleaned (his and the dolls), regardless of whether they're worn or not. And get this: his "friend" has his own cleaning establishment right there on the grounds in the same mall as a Marine training facility, the second-largest Sam's Club, and the largest doll carousel outside of Finland (naturally). *C'est la verité!* (It's the truth!)

The next thing you see is Book 'em Dano's "friend" lighting up a Cohiba Lanceros. Anna Nicole becomes agitated, rolls up her sleeve (she's battery operated), removes her Nicorette patch, and grabs the cigar right out of Book 'em Dano's "friend's" mouth. She proceeds to jam the cigar into her mouth, coughs, then suddenly, Anna Nicole loses her balance and tips backward.

Book 'em Dano, oh, I mean Book 'em Dano's "friend" reaches out and grabs onto the Cohiba Lanceros, but the cigar's red-hot tip burns his hand and he lets go.

Anna Nicole lurches out of frame, and the last thing you see of her, or the cigar, is the cigar's glowing red tip disappearing into the night. Of course, there's sound, but it's too frightening to describe. (For anyone interested, you can go to my web site, click on "Web Gems"—scroll down to "Cigars"—click on that—then scroll down to "Balcony"—click on that until you come to "Anna Nicole Takes a Header"—and click on that. FYI, for best viewing I suggest Quick-Time Holographic Version 10^6.)

OK, to continue . . . Book 'em Dano's "friend" becomes agitated. He reminds me of the bald-headed detective in *The Shield* (as you know from previous emails, this is a show with special meaning because of my connection to Glenn Close, but I'll leave that for another time). Book 'em Dano's "friend" looks around, and all he can see are people taking pictures of him with their cell phones. There must be hundreds of flashes in windows and on balconies, twinkling like stars in the heaven above. (They're on SuicideMatch.com if you're interested.)

Book 'em Dano's "friend" calmly takes out his last Cohiba Lanceros and lights it with his gold Blackberry (he's got a special app for it), which suddenly begins flashing a text message. Out of the darkness, a smooth, gray, snake-like arm wraps around Book 'em Dano's "friend's" leg and with the strength and agility of an elephant's trunk, lifts him up and dangles him upside-down high over the darkened street. *C'est coeur s'arrêtant, je vous dissent.* (It's heart stopping, I tell you.)

I have never seen the kind of courage I then witnessed: hanging, upside-down, five stories above the pavement, calmly smoking a Cohiba Lanceros, Book 'em Dano's "friend" responds to his latest text message, and then checks his email before the trunk slowly unfurls and he plunges down to earth. (He was so good-looking in the way only Book 'em Dano—I mean Book 'em Dano's "friend"—can be.) *Quelle perte!* (What a loss!)

What I still can't get over is the sound quality. I'm telling you, when that car alarm goes off, and you hear "La Marseillaise," it sounds just like the soundtrack of *Casablanca,* but get this—you still can hear "Die you bitch-bastard" in the distinctive Ginsburg (*pronounced* Du Pont) Latin vulgate. *Incroyable!* (Amazing!)

Oh, there's the bell! I think it's those darling people from the Brooklyn Aquarium with something very, *very* exotic, thanks again to Arnold, the most wonderful mayor I know.

Entretien à vous bientôt. (Talk to you soon.)

Cousin Cheryl, A Very Proud Mom!

P.S. I've just completed my first twenty-foot onyx vase. I had a specially constructed crane and harness set up on the roof so I could be lowered down to work on the piece, which has as its motif the trajectory of a bullet as it flies through the air. Of course, this is not a literal translation of the bullet that struck me down in front of Shirley's Sister's Ex-Mother-In-Law's Market, or else it wouldn't be art, but just a Jude Law movie. The story is just as much about the trajectory of the bullet as it is of those it hit along the way. I named the piece "Travels with My Bullet." *American Art and Hand Creams* calls it "Tender as the night, and just as explosive."

I hope you get a chance to see it before it goes on display at the

Met. I can't wait for you to spot your own figures. *Très magnifique!* (Very magnificent!)

P.P.S. Remember… *El amor nos guardará juntos.* (Love will keep us together.)

SING IT LOUD! SING IT PROUD! SING IT NOW!

From: Bubbeh.E@Ourmail.us
Date: Tuesday, June 21, 2005, 9:07 a.m.
To: Cheryl.G@Ourmail.us
Cc: Us@Ourmail.us
Subject: I'm good to go!

Mein darling Cheryl,

Good news, my darling! I'm standing here with the Finest Doctor, and he says I'm good to go for another twenty years (give or take), fifty thousand miles. I haven't felt the earth move under my feet like this since that wonderful day back in September of 1961—the thirtieth, I think—when I purchased the rights to the earth's continental plates and, just for fun, shifted them just a smidgen; so if you happened to be standing on the borders of France and Belgium, you had to do a tiny split for just a sec, until I pushed them back into place. I was a hell raiser, wasn't I?

I remember at the time I was involved with Juan de Fuca, and to show you how head over heels I was in love with the rapscallion, I named one of the plates after his lovely gluteus maximus—or was it in loving memory of his great-grandfather, the first man who made love to me on a moving dog sled?

It was July 4, 1791—Saskatchewan. Check it out. See if your Bubbeh Esther (*pronounced* Granny Smith Apples) is making it up like some doubting Younger the Elder by Twenty-Three in this family complain I do—*That Putz*. Why? Because, *mein* darling Cheryl—*er drayt sich arum vie a fortz in russell*—excuse my French—he wanders around like a fart in a barrel and has nothing better to do then pooh-pooh me and mine.

Mein darling Cheryl, I should have done to *That Putz* what you did to Giuseppe, but you know my hands were always too small to comfortably grip a machete, so cutting off a man's *cojones* was always a distant second to injecting a man's *shvantz* with peyote until his balls began hallucinating—an endearing poetic kind of justice my Indian friends taught me to unleash whenever I was in the mood for revenge.

You don't agree? Well, perhaps it's a generational thing. Let's face it, a woman of a certain age can't help but be a bit nostalgic for the way things were back in the day.

No, *mein* darling Cheryl, I never did that to Younger the Elder by Twenty-Three. After all, *That Putz is* family. I'm not saying what you did to Giuseppe was wrong, and what I *didn't* do to *That Putz*—which was nothing—was right.

Darling, you know what it says about bad boys in the *Second Book of the 999 Books of She Who Brings Forth Life, the Great Baleboosteh Ginsburg* (*pronounced* Eleanor of Aquitaine), twenty-third psalm, first chapter, third verse (written in her own hand and genetically imprinted on our magical gifts—visible only to us after vigorous rubbings of Oil of Olay while repeating the mantra: *Jack and Jill went up the hill, each with a buck and a quarter; Jill came down with two-fifty, think they went up for water)*: *"Caesar si viveret, ad remum dareris."*

If Caesar were alive, you'd be chained to an oar. Are these words to live by, or what?

Talk about fireworks going off on the Fourth of July. All of Western Canada still talks about how on that day, the earth shook, the sky turned red, and oil started shooting up from the ground like a scene from *Giant*. Of course, since 1791, the land belonged to me, but it was still nice to see The Heap of Big Oil in the Ground prophecy come true, and know I hadn't had a three-way with the chief's one-eyed father and his ninety-seven-year-old grandfather merely because they turned me on. *Yingeh tsats-keh!*—excuse my French—I was some living doll!

Incidentally, *mein* darling Cheryl, I never believed a moose puking in the full moon was as effective as the morning-after pill, but I'm living proof *it is*; and maybe something *you* should consider, since a bathtub full of Cristal and Häagen-Dazs is a non-starter.

And another wonderful memory from those exciting times: I still have "Big Bazooms of Sturgeon Lake" tattooed on my scalp, which, I tell you, gave me terrific street cred when I built the Fulton Fish Market in 1835.

You know, don't you, that when Alaska achieved statehood I sold them the oil leases for the exclusive rights to their air space, which I tell you became the gift that kept on giving once, as the chief's one-eyed father said, "The great white man who smelled like shit, sprouted wings and came across the North Pole, because it was shorter and saved on fuel." Naturally, I have to kick back a percentage to OPEC, but that's OK, as long as they keep jet fuel prices up. Otherwise, airlines will return to the old routes, and the only ones using my air space will be hang gliders—and go try collecting from someone who has a death wish.

Mein darling Cheryl, let me tell you that what they say about explorers is so, *so* true, as long as *they like going south.* Oh, now a woman my age shouldn't be talking so naughty, should she? But after seeing the Finest Doctor, I simply feel wicked, and not because of the altitude—*or* the drugs.

I haven't thought about Juan de Fuca in ages, but I tell you one thing, he was a Big 6 on my love barometer. Of course, top honors still go to Charles, who first rocked my world back in 1935. It was an earth-shattering event, and to show my appreciation, I named my love barometer the *Richter Scale* after that human jackhammer.

Charles was my first seismologist, and if he taught me anything, it was: *size really does matter.* To show you how good a judge of talent I am, to this day his name *still* measures up.

However, *mein* darling Cheryl, long before Mr. Charles Richter made my G-spot ripple (imagine a boulder being dropped in the middle of Lake Meade), I got a taste of how well explorers could *discover things.* There I go being naughty again.

It was when I had Magellan, or shall I say, Magellan *had me.* That crazy Go-Mambo-Italiano showed me what it's like to go around the world like no other five-men-at-a-time ever did, and loved me for *me* and not my magical mounds. Although, I warmly recall he did love to put his head between them for hours on end and say he'd discovered the passageway to my heart.

Exhausted from sucking my rock-hard nipple mountain peaks until his lips finally cracked and his jaw locked up tighter than a bank vault on a holiday weekend, my adorable explorer boy fell off to dreamland. Oh, I don't know what's making me say these sinful things—shame, *shame*, on me.

Fortunately, like all Ginsburg (*pronounced* Du Pont) Girls, I'm a great multitasker, so when that happened, I simply levitated out of my body and took my second shape, which, *mein* darling Cheryl, is another way I use the gift of being in two places at the same time.

By this time next year I want to take more advantage of this particular talent, so while I continue writing my memoirs here in Mount Cedar, I will be taking frequent trips to places in my past, and want you, *mein* darling Cheryl, to accompany me. By then, you will be back on your feet, so get ready for some fun, because your Bubbeh Esther (*pronounced* Granny Smith Apples) has lots of gas left in her old tank.

Mein darling Cheryl, I know you've become a bit superstitious about mentioning your surgery, but I'm afraid the cat's out of the bag, no thanks to what happened this morning with the Finest Doctor.

Before you go blaming him, you have to hear both sides of the story. The Finest Doctor was just finishing my tune-up and adjusting the eyes in back of my head (when I happened to mention the time and place of your operation.)

Well, what I didn't know was that the music playing "Where Did Our Love Go," wasn't coming from his stereo, but from the speaker in the Finest Doctor's cell phone implanted in his head. (Remind me, will you? I want to get one as soon as he works out all the bugs.) Anyway, before I could say anything, Clarice (she was the one on the cell phone, if you haven't guessed already), stops singing and begins making luncheon plans for everyone.

Say what you want, but trust me when I tell you I know Clarice has always looked up to you in the way only an adoring little sister looks up to her big sister.

I know, *I know*, you don't agree, but you only see the jealousy and the resentment. But honestly, can you blame her? Before you get angry and walk away from the computer, listen to me, because I'm telling you this out of love. It's only natural Clarice feels the way she does when she sees how you've made your life work by channeling your anger *into* the men you've married and making them suffer horrible illness, or outright death. *Mein* darling Cheryl, don't say anything, it's *emes*—excuse my French—but *it is the truth.*

Just listen to what your Bubbeh Esther (*pronounced* Granny Smith Apples) has to say and take a good hard look at your poor little sister Clarice with all her clogged channels. When she desperately needed you to help her unclog, you didn't lift a finger to help her kill your father and Uncle Maxie, did you? No you didn't, and you know full well when you have clogged channels you're really in for it. No wonder the poor child needs to stare at a Yule Log to feel good.

They say you are only as happy as your saddest child, so you can imagine how this clogged-channel thing is making me nuts.

Mein darling Cheryl, what I'm suggesting is that Clarice accompany you to Mount Cedar, and before you get really get out of control, relax a moment, take a few deep breaths—in and out, in and out—then increase the morphine drip, open your mind, and just hear me out for a minute. Try to see the plusses and minuses of what I'm suggesting.

For one thing, you know as well as I do, your sister's terrific when it comes to drug smuggling. OK, maybe not as good as Sylvia, but if you should have any trouble concerning the amount you're carrying, Clarice, who has a mouth on her, will straighten the Chinese border people out so you won't have to be imprisoned like the last time.

I know you had your heart set on Sylvia going, but she can come later and still be there for the operation. In the meantime, you and Clarice can get to know each other again and maybe put an end to some of the other *unclogging* issues that have come between you two—and I'm not just talking about why you didn't follow through and kill her first husband after she killed yours, because that's water under the bridge, like they say.

Right now your sister needs a shoulder to cry so she can work through her disappointments, pull herself together, and go forward on the appeal instead of carrying out her threats, because the last thing we want is for her to kill the entire cast of "Law & Order: Special Victims Unit." *Um-be-shrien!*—excuse my French—Goddess forbid! And not because I own the Federal District Courthouse and blowing it up will just balloon my insurance on my other nearby properties, but because you can't stop Dick Wolf from creating spin-offs.

I don't know if Clarice's passport problems are still an issue, but if they are, I'm certain Grant can take care of them. Which reminds me—you destroyed the tapes like I told you to, right?

If I weren't in such a hurry to get my second self back to Mount Cedar, I would have taken care of it myself. So check into it, please. It would make me rest a lot easier knowing there's nothing to indicate an elephant was involved in *you know what,* especially when the circus is coming to town and that kind of publicity would just hurt the kids.

For the record, when I agreed with Sylvia when she said "some men just need killing," I was *with my friend,* and when I'm *with my friend* I'm just not myself.

I have to lie down now, because the Finest Doctor wants me to take it easy for the next four hours, even though he knows I'm a fast healer, especially in the summer when the moon is in my second house.

I love you all as only a Bubbeh (*pronounced* Granny) can!

Bubbeh Esther (*pronounced* Granny Smith Apples)

From: TenderlyThroughMySupremeBanker@MySupremeBanker.him
Date: Tuesday, June 21, 2005, 9:30 a.m.
To: US@Ourmail.us
Subject: Summer greetings and ominous signs!

Hello and happy summer to my loving family!

May My Supreme Banker, known by many names and different faces, bring you all love, peace and harmony, and remind you we are all connected by credit-card debt.

I am now made of pure joy after learning my prayers to My Supreme Banker have been answered, and Cousin Cheryl will finally have the operation that will enable her to walk again.

I have also been appealing to My Supreme Banker for a miracle that would reunite Cousin Cheryl and her sister Cousin Clarice, and, thanks to the wise counseling of our esteemed Bubbeh Esther (*pronounced* Granny Smith Apples), that will now take place.

Unfortunately, my other pleas have gone unanswered and during this time, when the living is supposed to be easy, summer's been no picnic.

Where do I start?

I could begin with the undeniable fact that no one in the Family Ginsburg (*pronounced* Du Pont) has gotten their cholera or typhoid fever shots. Or, I could start with the troubling news that none of you are taking your Lariam (Mefloquine). This is particularly shameful, considering I sent you each PharmaKarma.com *Hanukah gelt* that would have saved you 40% on these wonderful anti-malaria pills, as well as a host of other psychotropic pharmaceuticals phenoms.

And please—I don't want to hear the excuse that the drugs you're on now prohibit you from taking these meds. I know what you're using, and provided you haven't copped from other dealers, there is no one in the Family Ginsburg (*pronounced* Du Pont) who cannot continue self-medicating. Naturally, this does not apply to Cousin Cheryl, who is preparing for surgery.

So, where do I start? I think with the disturbing news that has reached these ears that many of you have not yet heeded my American tsunami warnings (hurricane to end all hurricanes).

I am most worried about those family members who continue to reside in your waterfront properties and marinas. By not seeking higher ground immediately, you risk being swept under, or smashed to bits against the wreckage of your block-long yachts, or impaled upon the masts of your equally huge sailboats. Remember, too, a tidal surge also brings with it a myriad of waterborne illnesses, so anyone living within a fifty-mile radius of the raging, roaring waters should also escape to higher elevations.

How ironic that I have been able to save the millions who have paid attention to my End of Life As We Now Know It column in *Body Building and Hot Rod Today*, while my own family is determined to ignore my entreaties. (See Cousin Younger The Elder by Twenty-Three's fall email.)

When My Supreme Banker elevated me to the position of Media Rep on this earthly plane, I rejoiced as only a child would, but in light of these disturbing developments, I have little to cheer about. I worry about all of you, so, *so* much. In fact, it takes me nearly a full night of chanting in a hyperbaric chamber just to get my juices flowing and myself psyched enough to get out of bed and face the next day, knowing *my people* have chosen the wrong path and are still in harm's way.

I will not give up. I will continue to be *His* voice. That is why I want to take this opportunity to pass along My Supreme Banker's latest forecast. Cousin by Younger the Elder by Twenty-Three, pay particular attention, because this is directed at *you*. *You Will Die! End of story*.

There—you heard it from My Supreme Banker.

Staying with the tidal-wave theme for another moment, please—I beg of you—when you go out, keep your cell phone on vibrate, because I will be texting the up-to-the-minute polar ice cap melting measurements.

Of course, when you go mobile, all this info and more is available on your End of Days Last Alert Wristband and Heart Defibrillator that I sent out to each of you in June. I never go out without mine, and am constantly discovering wonderful features like the iPod adapter that allows you to listen to podcasts relating to your rising toxicity levels. This is especially relevant when one is within fifty miles of a nuclear power plant.

(FYI—at home you continue to have the option of retrieving messages via the various personal messaging services and spyware I installed on your hard drives, or by clicking on the folder *How I Get My Drugs.*)

As you know, every season family members want to know, where can I vacation and what can I eat when I get there? Well, as you are aware, summer has always been my favorite time of year, and because I'm a water sign, I have a natural affinity for the ocean. I love to body surf, and recommend it to one and all as long as one takes the proper precautions. (I refer you to my email regarding spinal injuries and sexual prowess entitled: "I Rang the Doorbell, Didn't I?: Things I Can Do From a Wheelchair.")

What can one say about the joys of taking long walks on the beach with the sea breezes blowing in your face and the salt air filling your lungs? Only this—you must always be on guard against those who wish to sneak up on you and carry you away to do with you what they may. (I refer you to Louisa May Alcott thought provoking e-book, *The Shark Who Kidnapped Me: How I Talked My Way to Freedom.*)

Since that inspiring story appeared, I am happy to say that Southern girls with two first names now have bodyguards when they go walking on Myrtle Beach.

Summer-getaway destinations like Cape Cod and other shoreline communities are tranquil oases that fortify our very soul, but that doesn't mean you shouldn't be wearing your Fremen Summer Breathing Suit and accompanying footgear that now come in beautiful, summer colors.

That said, with the impending American tsunami (the hurricane to end all hurricanes) and ensuing tidal waves caused by the rising water temperatures, in addition to previous requests, I recommend anyone living along the East Coast to think *mountain climbing—very high mountain climbing.*

I know, *I know,* for years I have been warning against killer African bees, and how they can sting an entire family to death before anyone can yodel for help. What about high altitude hit-and-run fatalities? You mean to tell me skiers, snowboarders, and all those crazy hang gliders aren't mowing down unsuspecting mountaineers faster than you can order something from this year's Eddie Bauer catalog? What about mountain caves that harbor, within their dark, dormant recesses, the deadliest of diseases like the Marburg and Ebola viruses you alert us to on the hour, every hour?

Hey, everybody—all good. Look, I'm not saying stick your nose where it doesn't belong—unless you want to risk the most horrible death so unimaginable, no one will even burn your body, much less bury it. What I am saying, through My Supreme Banker, is unless you want your lungs to explode like those trapped souls in *The Poseidon Adventure*, you must head for the hills, and I as said—*the higher the better.*

You will be glad to know that in preparation for the move to the mountains, I am using the America's Next Top Model Satellite to triangulate avalanche activity. This orbiting info will be available via all your electronic devices, including your End of Days Last Alert Wristband and Heart Defibrillator.

Happy summer, and please, *please* get your vaccinations and take your pills.

Love from My Supreme Banker Through Cousin Tenderly

P.S. Drink plenty of bottled water, but only at room temperature, and only after you have removed the water and heated it in a basic oxygen furnace to a temperature of 2,000 degrees Fahrenheit and then rebottled it in your Fremen canteens.

P.P.S. Fremen canteens are available only at DeconByDesign.com.

P.P.P.S. All day, all night, you give me ten minutes, and I'll give you pandemics, epidemics, avalanches, hurricanes, tornados, even sound bites from Mel Gibson's *The Passion of The Christ*.

P.P.P.P.S. I, for one, believe in giving people a second chance, and that goes for even someone like Aunt Bea, who, to my mind, has turned her life around.

From: Sylvia.G@Ourmail.us
Date: Tuesday, June 21, 2005, 9:40 a.m.
To: Cheryl.G@Ourmail.us
Subject: Getting things off my chest

Cheryl, I don't want you to worry about me, because the last thing I need is for you to get upset right before your surgery, but I'm sure I'm being followed and I was thinking—could I come over and borrow one of your guns? It's been a long time since I tried to shoot myself, but I think I remember how to use one. If you want to give me a few pointers, great. If you're not up to it, I understand. I know what it's like to be on a morphine drip. Goddess knows, some days I couldn't even brush my teeth, which was still a lot better than thinking they were falling out every time your husband sticks his tongue down your throat. I didn't say anything to you about the *gun thing* at the party because, well, it was a party and I didn't want to rain on your parade. Then—there's Bermuda. Didn't she look radiant? She was watching me like a hawk—coming up and hugging me—telling me what a wonderful mother I was, when what she was really doing was patting me down for a weapon. Tell me—where has the trust gone? Thank Goddess she had a job, otherwise I wouldn't have be able to sneak into your bedroom and look for the plastic gun you're always getting through airport security. I know, *I know,* I was taking a terrible risk with Bermuda cutting the police commissioner's hair in your dressing room, but I just couldn't get what you said out of my mind —you know—*that with the right ammo, the gun could stop an elephant in its tracks*—not that I still wanted to seek revenge and put the old proboscidean down. Well, it did sound like the perfect gun, but you never told me it wouldn't fit it in my ivory clutch purse—you know, the Judith Leiber with the diamond elephant-shaped clasp you're always admiring. It was my intention to tell you everything when I got home, because I promised my shrink I wouldn't hold back anymore, especially to you, my dearest friend. Unfortunately, things went blurry after Bubbeh Esther (*pronounced* Granny Smith Apples) threw Book 'em Dano's "friend" off the balcony. All right, the four tequilas with a Percocet chaser had something to do with it. The three Long Island Ice Teas in the car coming over didn't help, either. I know, *I know*, I promised to get more exercise, and walking the block to your place would have been the smart move, but you know how I dislike the streets when they're filled with those *museum people*. Can you please tell me why the Met doesn't just send them out the back door and into the park instead of permitting them to cross Fifth and gawk up at our homes, as if *we* are part of their exhibit? I need a ciggie and a pee.

OK, I'm back!

I also felt a tad uncomfortable asking you for a weapon with my two boys flitting around and moving furniture here and there. How many times have I complained how embarrassing it's been for me, watching those two go into a neighbor's apartment and begin redecorating, willy-nilly. When they started doing their *thing*, I thought it was cute. And let's face it, for five and six-year-old boys, Hill and Dale had such a well-developed sense of color and fabric. Now—I just think they can't help themselves. Cheryl, darling, can you tell *me why they do it*? They're both rich and famous; they shouldn't be giving it away for free—it's not sex. All right, Cheryl—you don't have to say it. That was a mean, ugly thing to say, but you know when I'm under stress I say nasty things about my family instead of addressing the real source of my anger. This is something Dr. Peck wants me to do, and believe me, I'm working on it. This is another reason I want a gun. I need to pee again.

OK, I'm back!

Where was I? Wait! Give me a sec. I got it! My pointy-headed shrink! That's it! Well, I just saw Dr. Peck today, and it's his professional opinion that setting my apartment on fire is an expression of self-directed anger and not an attempt to simplify my life. I don't think he has any idea in hell how difficult it is for me to throw anything out. Dr. Peck says a person is defined by *what he can't get rid of*. I asked him if he meant Book 'em Dano, and that pointy-headed little fucker just smiled in the smug way pointy-headed little fuckers do. This is another reason I want a gun. Oh—you think I've really become paranoid, do you? Well, let me let you in on a little secret: Right after I left his office, one of those voices in my head that I'm always telling you about told me to go onto HighSchoolReunion.com and look for any unholy-for-me alliance between Caroline Peck and my Dr. Peck, and guess what—*as usual, my voices were right on.* The bastards are *brother and sister!* There it is again, *six degrees of desperation!* Well, you know me, Cheryl, when I get hold of a bone, I don't let go. So—you know what I did next? No—I didn't call Clayboy. Just because I'm having a *relationship* with him doesn't mean I have to rely on him for *everything*. And no, for the last time, we're not having any problems now that Book 'em Dano's coming back to the States. Clayboy has promised me it's over between him and Book 'em Dano, and I believe him. What I did do, Cheryl, was I went onto HighSchoolGossip.com, and do you have any idea what I further uncovered? THE FUCKING AWFUL TRUTH, THAT'S WHAT! My dear, sweet, caring, high-school friend Caroline, that kindhearted, sympathetic soul who introduced me to Book 'em Dano—well—that—*that slut* not only knew him, but *dated* him for two years— and, *and* according to several unnamed sources, went *all the way* with him *under the football stands*! I need another ciggie and a pee.

OK, I'm back!

And—*I'm mad as hell and I'm not gonna take it anymore!* The story doesn't end here, not by a long shot! Listen to this. According to HighSchoolGossip.com, my *dear, dear* friend was giving herself to my husband-to-be since the very first day they went to sleepaway camp! I didn't need any voices in my head to know my next move had to be to log onto CampGossip.com—so that's what I did. Never in a million fucking years are you going to believe this shit. Are you sitting down? My shrink, Dr. Peck, with degrees up the yin-yang, was also at the camp. *Six degrees of desperation*, my ass. It's *six degrees of degeneration* and a goddamn conspiracy to destroy me! Can you see now why I need a gun? I need another ciggie and a pee!

OK, I'm back!

"The Big Pecker"—his camp nickname; wait until I call him that at our next session— can you believe, was in the same bunk as Book 'em Dano? First, they were Onondaga Scouts, then Onondaga Warriors, and for the last two years, Onondaga Chiefs. Cozy, isn't it? When I tried to discover if they went on to be camp counselors, the web site warned I wasn't cleared for that information. If you think this was going to stop me, think again.

Remind me, will you Cheryl, I have to get Happy Endings With Lucy a little something for bribing her brother to hack into the camp site. She's the lovely little girl who washes hair with Bermuda at the salon. (I wonder if I should also get the brother something? I just don't know what you get an FBI agent who has access to everything, do you?) Are you ready for this? When I told Bermuda what I wanted, she broke down and confessed she already knew about The Big Pecker and her father. How, you ask? I asked the same question. The answer—when Bermuda was doing her film-school thesis. You remember—about her father's gun-running? She was looking for a backstory and figured if she did a background check into her father's childhood, something might come up. Now, Cheryl, you know that since Bermuda was a child, she has told me absolutely *everything,* and I have been equally honest with her. Why, you know, we're more like best friends than mother and daughter; not the way *we're* best friends, but *second* best friends—you know what I mean.

For Goddess's sakes, she could light my cigarettes before she could walk! I need another ciggie and a pee.

OK, I'm back!

And—*I remember exactly where I left off.* It was at the point in the story where I was wondering what could I do to repair the damage done to my mother-daughter relationship when I glanced over the sealed court papers documenting the Bondage and Sodomy Color Wars and the trial that eventually led to the camp owners' imprisonment. Even—*even* when I finally read through the testimony of over *one hundred* Broadway choreographers—all five hundred lurid pages—recounting, in graphic detail, how the memory of those color wars were the ones they still, to that day, *cherished the most*—and how that those events definitely turned them onto wearing their hair like *Gwen Verdon*—EVEN THEN, I DIDN'T GET THE PICTURE! Cheryl, you know when the little switch finally turned on in my head, and all the voices stopped screaming? When my about-to-be-disinherited daughter came over and threw me into the cold shower, shoved a wet No-Calorie Tree Bar with Berries Attached—you know the ones you shoplifted at Oh, Natural (a.k.a., Bark and Barf) down my throat—that's when my world was shattered into a million pieces (not to mention she forget my shower cap and ruined my $250 birthday cut That Lucky Bitch gave me). THAT'S WHEN! I need a ciggie and a pee.

OK, I'm back!

Cheryl, I guess what I'm trying to say to you is that I won't be angry, or hurt, or even mildly disappointed if you decide to take Clarice to Mount Cedar instead of me—me—SYLVIA—the ONE and ONLY PERSON to stick by you through all the shit—thick and thin. Me—SYLVIA—the ONE and ONLY PERSON to offer you her own throat and aortic artery after our crazy Aunt Bea nearly severed yours at the Gap.

Me—SYLVIA—the ONE and ONLY PERSON to offer you her own spinal cord and lower half of her body after you were shot in Shirley's Sister's Ex Mother-In-Law's Market and lay half-frozen in that pathetic lump you now call *your body*. So, you go take Clarice, because that's what Bubbeh Esther (*pronounced* Granny Smith Apples) wants you to do, and you do everything Bubbeh Esther (*pronounced* Granny Smith Apples) wants you to do—DON'T YOU? *"Bubbeh Esther (pronounced Granny Smith Apples) wants me to go with her to Mount Cedar so she can have eyes put in the back of her head."* Yadda, yadda, yadda. So, you run off, without so much as a goodbye, leaving me to be nabbed as the brains behind my husband's gun-running operation; the one that misogynist from "America's Most Wanted Bitches" called "The West Hampton Gun Cunt"! What about the time Bermuda was facing jail time for the hit-and-run *thing?* I needed you, but NO—you did some running of your own. REMEMBER THAT? What—it was more important to go with Bubbeh Esther (*pronounced* Granny Smith Apples) and have her feet fixed so she could walk on water? When Bubbeh Esther (*pronounced* Granny Smith Apples) calls, Cheryl, her little puppy dog runs after her, doesn't she? What about Sylvia, caregiver to all, but cared by no one. Go on—go. I'll probably be dead anyway—murdered by persons unknown. At least that's what the voices in my head keep echoing on . . . *over and over and over and over* . . . I need a ciggie and a pee.

Love,
Cousin Sylvia

From: Sylvia.G@Ourmail.us
Date: Tuesday, June 21, 2005, 9:47 a.m.
To: Cheryl.G@Ourmail.us
Subject: One more thing . . .

Oh, I almost forgot to tell you. The photos I took of Bubbeh Esther (*pronounced* Granny Smith Apples) on the balcony are *hidden* in a galaxy far, far away, and if I should die, or be injured for any reason, they will be sent to PETA and to The Vatican, where we all know, Book 'em Dano's "friend" was voted the Prettiest Prelate of 2005 in its very own *Body Builder Summa Theologica.*

Love, Cousin Sylvia

P.S. I don't want to start any rumors, but has anyone ever seen Book 'em Dano and his friend together in the same room?

From: Bermuda.G@Ourmail.Us
Date: Tuesday, June 21, 2005, 10:10 a.m.
To: Sylvia.G@Ourmail.us
Subject: Aunty Cheryl's party

Oh, Mama, you think the silliest things when you have had too much to drink. Of course, *I wasn't patting you down* last night at Aunty Cheryl's birthday bash. Why would I—you were practically naked in that yellow silk-and-satin see-through, banana-shaped, Carmen Miranda bodysuit from Dolce & Gabbana. And, I might add, Mama, the envy of all the women and quite a few men, including the poor guy who took a header off the balcony, who everyone thinks *is really Daddy*, but how can that be when everyone knows Book 'em Dano hates heights.

I think the choice of the Judith Leiber ivory clutch purse with the diamond elephant-shaped clasp you know I would kill for, was oh, so perfect. The way it just blinded you! And where in the world did you find that pair of ivory Jimmy Choo lovelies?

I was just in there two days ago, and Jimmy was near tears telling me how the airline mixed up his bags with those of Deepak Chopra; putting his Vuitton steamer on Deepak's flight to Palm Springs and giving him Chopra's cylinder of natural healing laughing gas. (FYI—until the airline people bring him his trunk, Jimmy's using the forty-foot silo to show off his kitchen magnet collection.) I asked him why he couldn't just get his factory to FedEx a new shipment, and he said the entire Ivory Coast was closed so everyone could go to Disney World.

Tell me the truth—are you leaving the shoes to me or to Brothers Hill and Dale? Just kidding, Mama. You're going to live forever— Bubbeh Esther (*pronounced* Granny Smith Apples) will see to that.

I can't believe I missed all the excitement, but Aunty Cheryl sent over tapes from the surveillance cameras, and tonight I plan to have a look-see. Don't fret, Mama, I won't be alone. I plan to open a pint of Healthy Choice Chocolate Cherry Mambo and a delightful Krug Clos du Mesnil '88 one of my clients so generously gave me last Christmas. (FYI—he just loves the way I rinse.)

Aunty Cheryl thinks the footage might be perfect for the opening of her Reality TV Assassination Series, but I don't think we want anyone to see Bubbeh Esther (*pronounced* Granny Smith Apples) during *that time of the month*—if you know what I mean?

By the way, didn't you think Aunty Cheryl looked absolutely ravishing in her Harry Winston diamond body armor with gold-and-silver-threaded chain-mail trim? And tell me the truth—wasn't that absolutely gorgeous platinum and titanium breastplate to die for? Am I going crazy, but didn't I see something just like that in *Gladiator,* or was it the one what's-her-name wore at the Grammys when she sang "Walk Like An Egyptian"?

And, Cousin Madison, that sly she-devil, she. I can see why the senate confirmed her appointment to the Supreme Court without even taking a single vote. You know, I talked to Maddy two days ago, and she swore up and down she was not going to do anything to dress up that black robe of hers, but that gold studded Gucci whip she wrapped around her waist was right out of Abu Ghraib, and did you see the size of those heels! Liar, liar, house on fire!

Oh, Mama, I didn't mean you!

Oh, heck, I hope I don't get a nosebleed.

Quick—where's my quarter!

OK, I'm OK!

As I was saying, those heels—my Goddess, you could commit suicide by just jumping off of them. And, you tell me, Mama—those spikes—they *were* made of real diamonds and not that cubic zirconium, right?

And, how about the Scales of Justice gold headdress! Well, of course, she has the height to pull it off, but can you tell me how in the heck Maddy kept it on when she was whizzing around the room on Speedy's back? The scales were flying up and down and sideways, and the whole thing must have weighed a ton, plus it looked like Cousin Maddy put on a few pounds since her appointment to the High

Court, so you wonder how the AG never missed a jump, or worse, break his back every time he landed. You'd have to go back to Aaron Burr to name an attorney general who ran like Mr. Speedy Gonzalez.

Mama, you stayed longer than I, but if Daddy's so-called "friend" just went swish into the night instead of squash on the pavement, Maddy's mad ride would have made it to above the banner on Page 6. Instead, all the talk was of Amber Alerts and wounded elephants that speak in Hittite. (FYI—I will address the issue of my missing father later in this email.)

Thank Goddess for our friend, Mr. Bill O'Reilly, who put the kibosh on that story by revealing the entire incident to be the work of outsourced Elephant Agitators in the employ of the publishers of the Babar series. Bill and Bubbeh Esther (*pronounced* Granny Smith Apples) go back a long way. (FYI—it was on her recommendation that he got into Harvard over the objections of the football coach, who foolishly believed Bill was just another Geraldo and better suited for Columbia's outside running game.)

Honestly—did you like my outfit? It wasn't too, you know—HEY-LOOK-AT-ME? I was trying to get that teenage-tramp-whorish-lesbian look that is so, *so* appropriate for someone of my age, yet still retain the Paris Hilton/Lindsay Lohan innocence bulimic spirituality one automatically gets by wearing a vomit-stained Martha Stewart jailhouse apron, ripped black mesh stocking with rhinestone smiley faces and fleece-lined Hillary Clinton fuck-you combat boots, mirror-shined so you could see your reflection.

Keep in mind, Mama, I had to go to wash hair later, so I had to wear something sensible.

Mama, before I forget, I have to thank you for my good taste in clothes. I remember the time I was five—when Brothers Hill and Dale and I would anxiously anticipate your arrival so you could model the clothes you brought home that day.

We would make ourselves comfy on the couch, the three of us, side by side, our bare feet dangling off the $75,000, 18th-century, Louis XVI canopy; not quite touching the thick, plush, 16th-century,

$250,000, Aubusson carpeting; mesmerized as we listened to you rhapsodize about the latest *haute couture* fashions, their exotic fabrics, the expert European tailoring, and which designer loved to do it out of their genetic pool.

While Brothers Hill and Dale cherished the moment they could put on the clothes and prance around, I couldn't wait to hear how you stole them, and which of your gang got nabbed that day.

Mama, do you remember how we moved the furniture to make the living room look like a dressing area at Bendel's or clothing racks at Bergdorf? I would play the sales ladies, Brother Hill a gang member, Brother Dale the store detective, and you—why the brazen thief, of course.

In the beginning, names like Chanel, Balenciaga, and Elsa Schiaparelli were unpronounceable, and oh, how you would laugh, when we said them, in accents just as strange as the names; with colored French cigarettes in long ivory holders dangling from our lips, feather boas wrapped round our necks and hanging to the floor; heads covered in huge, saucer-shaped hats, bedazzled with silk flowers, semi-precious stones and multi-colored beads.

Mama, I still say you should write a book about your exploits before Marty steals your story and does *Gangs of New York II*. Actually, I think Leonardo does have your features, and I can see him twirling around in a strapless Schiaparelli evening gown saying, "As far back as I can remember, I've always wanted to be a gangster."

OK, OK, so that's what Daddy said at his trial, but it's really a Ray Liotta line, and Daddy used it as a way of saying how sorry he was for having my knees broken, because he knows my beach-tracking shots were a *homage* to Marty's Copa entrance in *Goodfellas*.

Now, Mama, don't say you don't remember any of those shoplifting days. I started taking stills around then, and didn't you tell me going through the photo albums and seeing all the clothes you stole made the drugs go down better? Besides, your memory is sharp as a tack since you've been siphoning off Clarice's elephant stem cells and replacing them with Just-Like-Elephant Stem Cells—the new, non-fat version.

Oh, don't deny it, Mama! You were caught on tape! *That's right, you were caught on tape!* You thought you were safe when you turned off the lights before spiking Clarice's high colonic, but you didn't know I installed CCTV cameras that can see in the dark! How else do you think we got what went down on the balcony? Oh Mama, don't you worry, all is safe; and I'm happy you took Clarice's stem cells because, as the one who first taught me the secrets of self-medicating, you know all too well the terrible consequences when one can't get the drugs they need, when they need them—witness the multiple times you tried to castrate your husbands. (A completely different scenario when you resolved your difference with Daddy by doing a few peyote buttons and then wading into the middle of the Hudson River, singing "Blue Bayou.")

It was only after you divorced Daddy, the first time, that you started listening to the life-size wooden steer outside The Cattlemen Restaurant. I can understand how the first incident caught everyone off guard when you told them it was for your husband's bris. The waiters naturally thought you said *brisket,* but how you got them to keep bringing out five-inch steak knives is a tribute to your way with people, and not, as you swore, because *The wooden steer made them do it.*

Mama, *I know* there are things mothers shouldn't tell their kids, and I guess even though you're my best friend, and *I tell you everything,* it's a parent's duty to hold back when dealing with a borderline psychotic; however, I hope one day you'll tell me where they took the "talking steer" after The Cattlemen went out of business.

Oh, Mama, I know you can't wait to bring up Lulu-Lu, but how many times do I have to tell you that I don't know anyone by that name? Look, Mama, didn't Clayboy back up my story and convince you those emails are the work of either a foreign intelligence agency, or some ugly, simply envious of the way I wash hair?

Speaking of washing hair, it looks like you were right and there is something in the soap causing my hands to crack and bleed, so to remedy this, I'll be moving to South Florida where the water is *kashrut,* and the Rabbis allow the wearing of latex when you give a Jheri curl to Jews.

I know you think I'm going because the ATF's using The Miami Beach Botanical Gardens for their next sting operation, but I swear, I'll only see Book 'em Dano at Passover and only in the presence of Uncle Maxie and Uncle Abe.

They want to return to the Boston Market on Hallandale. I told them to check first, because the Philippine cashier they want to wed may have relocated to Aventura.

In closing, I have to say these last months have made me a better person. I'm not sure if turning inward did the trick, or if it was due to joining the TiVo Community.

Love ya,

Bermuda, your newly saved daughter.

P.S. (FYI—Mama, the reason you think Daddy looks like the person who "fell" off the roof is because the NSA electronically altered the image as an attempt to discredit his upcoming testimony as part of their diabolical plan to prove the man testifying is *not* Daddy, because Daddy's *dead*, which of course *he isn't*, because he's testifying—*right?*

From: Laverne.G@Ourmail.us
Date: Tuesday, June 21, 2005, 10:10 a.m.
To: US@Ourmail.us
Subject: It's hot as hell here!

How y'all doin!

I'll tell you one thing about summer in the South, it's f-ing hot! And humid! Bitch yes, it is!

Lord, the air's so thick, when you see a mosquito zeroing in, you got time to get to the Winnie, find the swatter, go back out, sit yourself down again, and kill that SOB dead in plenty of time before he reaches your nose. No lie! Thank Goddess, we'll be leaving the sweat zone for Pittsburgh, but more on that, and what Willie's aiming to do, after awhile.

Goddess bless Southern folks, they don't give a damn how hot and humid it is. They're out in their backyards drinking beer, or at the state fairs, drinking beer, or at the flea markets, drinking beer.

Willie and Clara just love flea markets and drinking beer. You should see'em sashaying around the booths. They're like kids when they're rummaging through piles of Confederate uniforms, trying on this ole bullet-ridden shirt, or that ole blood-encrusted coat, even if they are five sizes too big. And, when they're going through the goodies at the local chapter of Witness Protection, trying on fake mustaches, putting on wigs, or sunglasses—why, they are so darling, you almost want to take them home with you.

They just act so normal, why, it's times like these I believe they are. And maybe I'm their normal mother and I'm the president of the normal PTA. And, I have a normal husband, with a normal job, and a normal SUV—a Beemer, and it's light blue. And we live in a normal home and belong to a normal church, and nobody in my normal family ever killed a relative. And if pigs could fly, they'd be eagles!

Jerry's been giving me a hard time about how I don't discipline the kids enough. I told him to shut the f-ing up, or I'll get Marie to blow up his wheelchair while he's in it.

First off, under the law, when your kid kidnaps another kid, this other kid *is not* your responsibility—even if the kid—*your kid*—marries the kid he's kidnapped, and makes the kidnapped kid *your daughter-in-law*.

Second off, as far as I'm concerned, a mother-in-law should not interfere between a husband and wife. You've heard it on "Oprah," you've heard it on "Montel," and now—you've heard it from *me*.

Third off, don't tell me how to do things unless you walk a mile in my shoes, and since you're still paralyzed, that ain't gonna happen anytime soon.

You think it's easy disciplining two 10-year-old outlaw heroes? F-ing A, it ain't! You've got their agents, lawyers—criminal and civil—PR people, and don't forget the multi-nationals doling out endorsement money; all telling you to step away from the kids with that steak knife, or we'll haul your ass into court.

If it's near impossible to keep a ten-year-old in line when they're at home, that's a Krispy Kreme compared to what it's like when they're on the run. Why, to them, every day is a goddamn vacation. *"I don't have to do my schoolwork—we're on the run. I don't have to go to sleep at nine o'clock—we're on the run. I don't have to brush my teeth, take a shower, comb my hair—we're on the run."*

Willie won't even listen to Conrad or Judith Ann when they get on the phone, or we meet them at a rest stop. It used to be that Willie looked up to his older siblings and would fall over himself to please them. Not anymore. *"I'm on the run, I'm on the run."* If I hear that whiny little anarchist say *that* one more time, *I'm going call the Feds and turn him in myself.*

Then you got The Daughters of Adam and Eve. Don't get me wrong, without the DAE we'd be under the jailhouse, but if a bear don't poop in the woods, they're a bunch of apple-eating thugs. Can you imagine anyone who would slit your throat just because you throw salt over your left shoulder before you eat?

I don't think it's only a Family Ginsburg (*pronounced* Du Pont) *thing*, but if I don't throw salt over my left shoulder before a meal, I get the acid reflux so bad I can't breathe.

I told those punk-ass Daughters of A&E exactly that, and even brought them a doctor's note, but they said acid reflux was a sign from THE GARDEN. And what f-ing sign was that, I asked? Course, I don't curse around them, 'cause they'll slit your throat for doing that, too. But, I do talk *Southern,* and they eat that drippy shit up.

Listen to this crap in a cup, willya. They said THE GARDEN wants me to breastfeed again. When I started to make a face, they made me open *The Farmers Almanac* to page whatever, and had me read, and I quote, "When in THE GARDEN, do not touch condiments, but use willingly thou milkers to breastfeed."

You could have put a pitchfork through my you-know-what and told me I was done. When I told Marie, she got so pissed she wanted to go right out and dynamite every damn Staples from here to the coast. I said, what good would that do? These wackadoos would just set up safe houses in Walmart or Williams-Sonoma.

Speaking of blowing up, if the kids keep gorging themselves, they're going to end up as floats in Macy's Thanksgiving Day Parade. Before we went on the run, Willie was a skinny thing. He could eat three or four Krispy Kremes and two Dr. Peppers and wouldn't gain a pound. He hardly ate anything for breakfast except some Fruit Loops. For lunch it was always Skippy Peanut Butter and Welsh's Grape Jelly on Saltines, and for dinner, whatever I'd put on the plate, he'd eat like maybe half. Except pork chops. I never seen anyone put away pork chops the way Willie does. I always said he took after the men in my family, because the Family Ginsburg (*pronounced* Du Pont) Women can take 'em or leave 'em.

My brother, Jack, dearly loved his pork chops. I think he was eating pork chops when Marie blew up the trailer, otherwise, why would that half-eaten pork chop bone be stuck into his chest like a goddamn Indian arrow? It's a damn shame Marie didn't set the timer so at least Jack could have finished.

Daddy loved his pork chops, too. Come to think of it, the police found a pork chop stuck in his chest after the explosion. Daddy was the fastest eater alive, so I bet his pork chop was bare to the bone. I'll have to check the autopsy report.

Conrad and Judith Ann were always watching their weight and didn't go in much for pork chops. They were very sensitive when Jerry called them fatties and made hog-calling sounds.

The kids never said anything, but I know it made Conrad madder than hell, and I wouldn't be surprised if he didn't take it out on the missing kids. I'm not saying he killed them, but imagine how you would feel when your father yelled, "Sooooey," when he wanted you to come to the dinner table? That anger's gotta go someplace, and judging by all the Wood Pet Urns we dug up, I thought the answer to the missing litter of puppies was clear . . . but when the forensic people said the ash came from hashish, it was a mixed blessing, don't you know.

Judith Ann never let anger get the better of her, either, but don't fool yourself, she has a temper, and many a time I saw her take a towel and twist it and twist it until the damn thing shred up into a million pieces. And a will of iron . . . If my baby said she was going on a diet, believe you me, she went on a diet and she stuck to it. Then, of course, like I told you before, she unlocked the secret messages in *Weight Watcher's Guide to the Galaxy,* and knew if she went over the calorie limit, those saucer people would beam her right up and feast on her white bread/Cheese Doodle cells until they turned up on "America's Biggest Loser."

You never saw my Judith Ann eat two loaves during a game of Chutes and Ladders, or tell me the empty bags of Cheese Doodles I found stuck behind the toilet helped soften her stool, but hey—I'm not her mother.

Judith Ann warned them, but you know how kids are, they think they're immortal.

Willie never ate that junk until he started going shopping with Clara. She's Miss Piggy in a 10-year-old girl's body. She won't eat any veggies, hates fruit, and thinks eating land-based animals will make her lips small.

You know, I got so desperate I emailed Cousin Tenderly. She got right on the case and emailed me back a list of childhood maladies "kids on the run" were most likely to get.

Did you know "kids on the run" have a 50% higher risk of becoming part of the "South Park" cast than kids on Ecstasy? That's a fact. And listen to this: because "kids on the run" cross so many state lines, they have no regional accent, so if they're handsome, or pretty enough, they can do the evening news on TV. Scary thought, isn't it?

Since the little demon child's been with us, she's gone from a size 3 to a size 14. And, she's a little bitty thing. I don't think she's five-one, if she's an inch.

Willie's gained, too. He's almost at 100 pounds, but thank Goddess, he's almost 5'8. That's over twenty-five pounds in, what—five months? He won't use the exercise bike I bought for the Winnebago. Course, if he were in school, he'd be still on the track team *and* the wrestling team. He's nowhere near as good as Cheryl's kids, but then again, who is?

The thing is, I don't want being on the run to mean he can't lead a normal kid's life, like getting Willie into an Ivy League school. I know I can count on Bubbeh Esther (*pronounced* Granny Smith Apples) and her connections up at Princeton, but I'm not sure little Willie wants to apply for the Albert Einstein Energy-Saving Scholarship. On the other hand, he was just asking Marie how many sticks of dynamite does a woodchuck chuck, *so* maybe Princeton isn't such a reach. Goddess knows, the boy already knows his way around explosives.

Speaking of explosives, I want to thank Book 'em Dano for sending us the C4 and I also want to thank him for the trip in the F16 Falcon. You know it's been a week, and the kids are still talking about it, especially when they see a plate of fried Twinkies. I don't think they'll ever forget watching their vomit go sideways as they pull 5Gs. Well, Book 'em Dano, you did warn them.

Kids, you just can't tell them anything, can you?

I don't want to beat this thing into the ground, but it ain't easy raising two outlaw kids without a male figure. I know Marie points to lots of lesbian couples who are doing a good job, but the last time I checked, neither of us signed up for the Dinah Shore Invitational Pebble Beach Pussy Rub, so I don't know what the hell she was talking about. Hell, half the time I don't know what the hell that woman is saying, but if you think I want to argue with her and end up with a pork chop in my chest and the rest of me spread across the Great Mall of Georgia, you need to think again.

Since the gas attack, Jerry's brain isn't working half as well as his feet, and we all know Jerry's feet don't work at all, what with him being completely paralyzed from the waist down. At least that's what they said on the police report he filed the last time he accused Conrad of trying to kill him. I had to hear this from Judith Ann, because Conrad was too ashamed to tell me. I knew that Jerry's brain would finally turn to dog shit, just like his father and his father's brain cells before him, that's why I'm f-ing amazed that Jerry's been able to memorize over five hundred TV and radio commercials. Can you believe this shit? You know how I know? Every time we stop for gas, the kids call him. You should see how red their faces get when they can't stump him.

Did I tell you, the kids are finally getting to meet Pat Robinson? Yep, it'll be a dream come true. Twice, meetings have been called off, but we're on again for next week, when Pat loses his FBI bodyguards.

In case you don't know, Pat's been under federal protection ever since he threatened to kill Zorro, but that's going to end because of pressure from Pat's long-time love child, Donna Karan. According to Page 6, Donna really lost it when the Feds refused to leave the Hacienda Streisand until George Hamilton showed everybody how he gets a perfect tan, which pissed off Pat, Babs, and Donna, who hate the sun, and just wanted to sing old Mexican love songs without the Feds joining in. Donna immediately called Shirley MacLaine, who channeled J. Edgar, and in twenty-four hours were having a cold one, and Shirley had his promise the guards would be gone by next week.

Anyway, getting back to Pat, Willie and Clara can't wait to meet him. They've collected all his Pat Robinson Bible Death Cards and want to talk to him about his marketing plan. The kids want to make sure they haven't missed a trick when they roll out their own Willie's Kidnapped Kids Trading Cards, "Willie's Kidnapped Kids Game Show" and the accompanying Willie's Victims Stickers and Willie's Victims' Redemption Books.

I don't know where these kids come up their ideas? I mean, at their age, I was just learning to kill a relative with my bare hands, but these kids—talk about salesmanship!

I really can't go into it any further, or the kids won't let me be part of the IPO, but I can tell you plans are in the works to kidnap Darwinists and hold them for ransom. And get this—all the money goes to building The Garden of Eden Theme Park and Serpent's roller coaster ride. Sweet, huh?

Oh, and you must keep this under your hats: I'll be working on designing the signage for Beggar's Beach, where former *SI* Swimsuit Winners can panhandle naked, and visitors can touch the models and have drinks with them at a wet bar in the shape of Kate Moss's lips.

Oh, shit, gotta go now—Alabama State Highway Patrol's waving us over.

Love,
Cousin Laverne

From: YoungerTheElder23@Ourmail.us
Date: Tuesday, June 21, 2005, 12:58 a.m.
To: US@Ourmail.us
Subject: Update from Your Humble Servant

Dear Members of the Family Ginsburg (*pronounced* Du Pont),

It's almost 1:00 a.m. and I'm still at the office working on the family portfolio. You know I am not saying this just to blow my own horn. I am only the faithful and most humble servant of the Family Ginsburg (*pronounced* Du Pont), as was my father, and his father before him, and his father before him, all the way back to Younger the Elder by One Ginsburg (*pronounced* Du Pont), may they all be inscribed in *The History of the World: The Book Of Ratings*, Chapter 11, The Great CPAs of History.

I have just concluded my conversations with our Swiss banking friends, and they are signing off on the Alaska pipeline contract. In the end, the purchase of the entire state of Alaska (a throw-in), will ultimately be to our benefit. Recognizing the booming real-estate market, particularly in the U.S. and its Territories, I see no reason why we can't flip it before we take ownership. In a worst-case scenario, I am looking at eBay and The Bank of New York as possible rental candidates.

As I expected, any negative feedback resulting from our hostile takeover was limited to Juno and Dawson City. This is due to the wonderful work of We Put Horses Heads Into Your Bed, made available to us through the generosity of The Godfather Properties, and their former, CEO, Michael Jackson, who, before going over his credit limit, signed off on the deal.

One of the Juno papers ran that old story about how we bought and sold Jerusalem with the headline "Raiders of The Lost Ark Strike Again!" Before the boys could squash it, it was picked up by the AP and put over the wire. Fortunately, it didn't receive any play because of all the attention paid to Tom Cruise, and his call to put psychologists out of business by surgically removing their patients' tear ducts so they couldn't be sad.

I have to credit Bubbeh Esther (*pronounced* Granny Smith Apples) for putting the Tom Cruise story out, which she had privy to because she was the one to turn Tom onto the idea in the first place.

I'm not sure of the dates, but I'm certain that if Bubbeh Esther (*pronounced* Granny Smith Apples) wasn't the first one to have the procedure done, she was certainly in the top five. There are so many stories floating around as to why she had the Finest Doctor perform the surgery. One story says she did it so during her spying days she could withstand the torture like a man. I prefer to believe it was because she became so emotionally distraught whenever one of her younger companions "left," it was either have the operation or one day drown in her own tears.

I know there are some of you who want to keep the Alaskan pipeline intact, while others, such as myself, believe it would be more profitable to break it up and sell it off to different buyers. I'm in that camp, and not only because that business model worked so well in Saudi Arabia, but because it makes for an international scandal which ultimately leads to a bestseller and finally a blockbuster movie.

Speaking of blockbuster movies, I have gone ahead and had my acquisitions people acquire the rights to the name "Raiders of The Lost Ark," as well as registered "Raider of The Last Arc" *before* Hollywood gets wind of our plans to purchase and then to connect all the Archipelagos in the world. I'm looking on my calendar right now, and closing dates on the Greater and the Lesser Antilles should take place in about two weeks' time. Construction on our seasonal rental units should begin soon after.

I want to take this opportunity to mention that the reason Bubbeh Esther (*pronounced* Granny Smith Apples) was not informed of the Alaska deal until it was completed should be obvious to all those who are aware that *she* once owned Alaska, and the emotional baggage she still carries from the sale of said property should be left unpacked, so to speak.

I want to thank the Family Ginsburg (*pronounced* Du Pont) for your unwavering support during the trial. That support enabled me to access *your* various shell corporations, and through them funnel the necessary cash payments, assuring the judicial process proceed in a fair and equitable manner that would have made the Founding Fathers proud to be members of the Family Ginsburg (*pronounced* Du Pont).

Notwithstanding Cousin Tenderly's objections to my objections to her real-estate suggestions, I am indebted to her for My Supreme Banker's taped message. She deserves all the credit for putting it together and then getting the airtime on The Disaster Channel so it could be shown every hour during my one-day trial. Although I thought the choice of "Where Have All The Flowers Gone?" for background music to be a bit heavy-handed, I have to admit, by the third showing it grew on me.

The King of Monaco's opening statements also buttressed my spirits. I was especially touched by his willingness to forgive the judge's gambling debts. I nearly broke down in tears when he so graciously said, "We've extended your credit by $500,000."

Of course, I recognized Nicky's hand in The King's eloquent statement. The part about "life on a respirator" was pure Nicholas Graham, as was the phrase "And don't call the cops if you want to see your children again."

Coincidentally, the very same judge is also handling Nicky's case. I was pleased, as you must have been, when after pronouncing my innocence, the judge told the court Nicky's extradition charges would be dropped, befitting his royal station, and he wished to invite Nicky and the King to be his guests at Le Cirque. This is good news for Monaco and its chance to repeat as alpine snowboarding champions. (FYI—the judge's middle daughter by his first marriage, Madrid, is going to compete with Nicky in "The Dead Man's Pipe Snowboarding Pairs," putting an end to the rumors she is eight months pregnant with his love child.)

As this family's faithful and humble servant, I find it is my duty, as it was the duty of my father, his father, and his father before him, all the way back to Elder By Younger One Ginsburg (*pronounced* Du Pont)—may they all be inscribed in *The History of the World: The*

Book Of Ratings, Chapter 11, The Great CPAs of History—not to become involved in internecine disputes within the Family Ginsburg (*pronounced* Du Pont). However, I do believe it is my obligation to address any cynosure that endangers the financial well-being of the family. That said—let me begin by declaring that nobody is more a fan of Cousin Laverne than me. Let me also remind you all, it was with the best of intentions that I cleaned out her accounts and settled her ten-million-dollar debt with Mozambique's Scratch and Sniff Lotto for Lovers. Sure, if I had it to do again, I would have asked her, but unless you were a mind reader, who would have thought she planned to stiff Mozambique. And I resent the accusations that just because I'm the CEO and majority stockholder in the Mozambique Scratch and Sniff Lotto for Lovers, I somehow managed to put money into my pocket

I am completely innocent of all charges, so then, why, I ask myself, should anyone affix a stick of dynamite to my X5I Cross-Trainer w/ Interactive Console by Life Fitness? Or, more to the point, why should Marie affix a stick of dynamite to my X5I Cross-Trainer w/ Interactive Console by Life Fitness?

I would also like to take this opportunity to say nobody in the Family Ginsburg (*pronounced* Du Pont) is a greater Free Willie fan that me. I have all his T-shirts and have purchased his entire line of products from his web site.

I believe, and the audits Laverne's attorneys ordered will substantiate, how prudent the investments were I made on behalf of William and the entity known as Darwin Ain't Your Daddy, LLC.

Further proof of my sincerity and the deep regard I have for Willie is reflected in how closely I worked with his agents and corporate sponsors to effectively guarantee that this entity receive all the tax considerations normally entitled to any member of the Family Ginsburg (*pronounced* Du Pont). This was no easy feat considering the total number of liens that have been filed against Darwin Ain't Your Daddy, LLC, by The American Academy of Science and other faithless-based organizations.

So, I ask myself, why should anyone affix a stick of dynamite to *my* La Pavoni PRH Professional Copper-Brass with wooden handgrips? Or, more to the point, why should Marie affix a stick of dynamite to *my* La Pavoni PRH Professional Copper-Brass with wooden handgrips?

I must reiterate, I do not want to toot my own horn, but—and I address this to Cousin Laverne—if you look at both your son's and daughter's stock portfolios, you will see an almost 500% return on their investment, due primarily to our ability to borrow funds from Darwin Ain't Your Daddy, LLC, and invest them in Mayor Bloomberg's Re-election Campaign IPO.

Laverne, on a personal note, I am also a major contributor to The Daughters of Adam and Eve on a national level; in addition, as you and William "visit" local chapters, this firm automatically sends each local a donation.

I want to also remind you that I have always enthusiastically supported your artistic efforts, starting with your *American Outhouse Series,* and have many of your works displayed in our street lobby entrance, as well as in our boardroom. Finally, have you forgotten I purchased *Two Apes Pulling Darwin's Arms From His Sockets* for which I agreed to refund to you all your stocks, plus interest? Furthermore, it will be at my own expense that I pay for the crane that will lift the two-hundred-and-fifty-pound sculpture eighteen floors and swing it through my forty-foot balcony windows.

So, I ask myself, why should anyone affix a stick of dynamite to *my* Sony KDF-60WF655 60-in.LCD television? Or, more to the point, why should Marie affix a stick of dynamite to *my* Sony KDF-60WF655 60-in. LCD television?

Could it have anything to do with helping your husband, Jerry? I only bring this question up after receiving two separate batches of photos. The first, in an envelope marked *BEFORE* contained photos of my three vintage Rolls-Royce automobiles, my Fifth Avenue condo, the summerhouse in Westport, and my yacht, The USS *Younger the Elder by Twenty-Three.* The second, in an envelope marked *AFTER,* contained the same photos, only now retouched to show what my possessions would look like after being blown up and totally destroyed. Strewn amongst the wreckage are unidentifiable pink *things,* circled in red, with an arrow leading off to the margins and pointing to the words *JERRY'S BODY PARTS.*

Laverne, as I have so painstakingly outlined in three different memorandums, I do believe that in the long run, you will come to appreciate what I do for Jerry in terms of how it will ultimately reflect positively on the children and their perception of me. Obviously, if he does keep threatening your life, if he attempts an assassination, successful or otherwise, we will reevaluate the situation.

Dear Family Ginsburg (*pronounced* Du Pont), as always, I thank you for this opportunity to communicate my thoughts to you.

Your faithful and humble servant,

Younger the Elder by Twenty-Three

From: Maxie.Ruthie.4Ever@Ourmail.us
Date: Tuesday, June 21, 2005, 10:30 a.m.
To: US@Ourmail.us
Subject: Strong as an ox!

Hi, everybody!

Good news! I just had my checkup, and my PSA's 2.8, LDL 100, HDL 91, and my triglycerides 93. Can you imagine? *Emes!* No bullshit!

I go to the finest doctor in South Florida, Mark Green—same name as the guy on "ER." Can you imagine? *Emes!* No bullshit!

I was driving down and saw his billboard, right before the Pompano Beach exit—*9501 BISCAYNE BLVD, AVENTURA. IF YOU WERE HERE, YOU WOULDN'T BE SCRATCHING.*

Like they say in the Torah, "When a Jew gets sick, the finest doctor will appear." Believe you me, when Dr. Green showed me those *things* crawling in the microscope, you'd have to kill me before I ever go near a gas-station toilet.

I guess you can tell he's a skin man, but he's got all sorts of doctors working for him, so whatever the problem, I go Green. You should see his operation. He took over the entire Aventura Mall and got different doctors in all the stores, restaurants, even the Cineplex. I got my annual in Urban Outfitters, and get this—they give you a nice discount on selected items with each checkup. When you're finished, you go by tram to the main office in Saks—you know—where all those *Watusis* sell cosmetics? As soon you get there, they come over and give you a *spritz*. Watch out: stare up at them too long, you'll throw your neck out. I did a few times. Can you imagine? *Emes!* No bullshit!

Listen to this—they're from Africa, and you know what else, they're *lantsman!* Can you imagine? *Emes!* No bullshit! You know how I know? They wear the Star of David; they sell 'em, too. Ruthie—may she rest in peace, *aleichem sholom*—bought so many, I swear, they should have named a village after her. Can you imagine? *Emes!* No bullshit!

Bermuda, it just came into my head, I bet they'd be good for business—you got basketball players coming by, don't you?

You know what else is so great about Dr. Green—you know how doctors like to rush you in and out? Not him. Took me right down to where he parked his Maserati and—get this—let me sit in it. Now, you tell me—does your guy care about you like that?

And listen to this: if you pay cash, the gift hostess gives you an extra goody bag. Can you imagine? *Emes!* No bullshit!

Now, I don't have to tell you I got good hair and how I made sure I combed it a lot, because it's a known fact that combing keeps you from getting bald. You remember Ruthie—may she rest in peace, *aleichem sholom*—was always jealous of my hair, saying stuff like, *"It's not fair Ginsburgs (pronounced Du Ponts) have better follicles than anyone else."* Can you imagine? *Emes!* No bullshit!

I used to say to her, *"You take care to comb your hair, and your hair will take care of you."* You think she listened? She just told me, and I quote, to take my "fucking comb and shove it where the sun don't shine," and if she wanted advice from a *faygeleh*, she "would ask Gianni." End of quote. You can bet I gave her a double *schmear* a schmaltz for that, the bitch-bastard. Can you imagine? *Emes!* No bullshit!

You know, don't you, every Friday she went to Gianni and got herself a dye job? That's why her hair kept falling out. OK, maybe the chicken fat helped.

A couple of days ago I noticed a little thinning around the top so, naturally, when I went for my annual, I casually mentioned it to Dr. Green. You know what he does? He tells his personal hostess to make sure when she gives me my goody bag to include TWO sample bottles of his Dr. Green Surfer Boy 16 with Follicle Testosterone and Sexy Wavy Hair Steroids. Can you imagine? *Emes!* No bullshit!

Did I tell you, I tried it last night and what a difference! You know, my hair's a little salt and pepper, right? Not anymore! You should see—bleached blonde, and so natural looking. And thick! I swear a bird could make a nest up there. Can you imagine? *Emes!* No bullshit!

The doc's got me using his hair dye and face creams, too. Imagine if Ruthie—may she rest in peace, *aleichem sholom*—was still alive—she'd be running to tell her girlfriends, and they'd be pointing and giggling every time they saw me, the bitch-bastards!

You know, I'm not dumb—I wouldn't use this stuff if I didn't see how it worked on Dr. Green. He's—what? forty?—but his hair looks like he's fifteen. And listen to this, there's not a goddamn wrinkle on his face. Can you imagine? *Emes!* No bullshit!

When I asked him, you know, about getting rid of some of my wrinkles—you know, around the eyes maybe . . . not saying I'll do it—he told me he would prescribe his Dr. Green Surfer Baby *Toches* Moisturizer and Skin Cleaner with Buns of Steel Steroids in preparation for his non-evasive Dr. Green Liposuction Tar Wrap and Wrinkle Remover that *he also uses on his Maseratis.* No wonder they shine like they do! Can you imagine? *Emes!* No bullshit!

Oh, another thing. Green knows how much I love cigars, so he says I'll love the girls who do the facials because they used to wrap Cohibas in Cuba. Can you imagine? *Emes!* No bullshit!

I'm going next Tuesday. He does the procedure in the Ralph Lauren Polo shop, where you also get a nice discount, but not as big as Urban Outfitters. You recover in the AMC Theater, and listen to this: he says it's so painless you're eating popcorn and drinking soda right after. I think you get a nice book of coupons, too, but I'll let you know. Can you imagine? *Emes!* No bullshit!

Oh, you know what else? Listen to this—we're going into business together and building medical centers in the Dominican Republic with all the big-name stores—Prada, Gucci, Hooters, plus their own golf course, tennis courts, spas, and lap-dancing facilities.

Jewish doctors from Florida are going to do the billing, and get this—their Russian trophy wives will run the spas and give messages when they're not out buying jewelry or sleeping with their personal trainers. The brochures are nearly ready, and don't worry, everyone in the Family Ginsburg (*pronounced* Du Pont) will get one, plus a booklet of discount tickets so you can fly down and see it for yourself.

I'm telling you, it's going to be paradise. Can you imagine? *Emes!* No bullshit!

Talking about Russian trophy wives, that's who takes your blood, does the cardiogram, checks your blood pressure, and gives you a rectal. I can see why Turpin, that bitch-bastard, goes Green once a week. Can you imagine? *Emes!* No bullshit!

They all wear tight, red, low-cut silk uniforms. I'm surprised my blood pressure doesn't go through the roof, but the doc says it's 100/80. Can you imagine? *Emes!* No bullshit!

Did I tell you about the receptionists? They're Incas. He's got one—Chasca. I swear, Bermuda, you got to hire this woman. She's always learning over when you come to the desk and—get this—grabbing your hand and putting it to her breast and asking how your car is, and when you're going to take her for a ride. Now that I'm blond, don't think I'm not going to ask her, either. I might just want to get some work done, first. Yeah, I know, I always said that stuff was for sissy boys.

Dr. Green says I shouldn't be saying sissy boys, because we all have male and female chromosomes so we're all . . . *sissy boys.* Can you imagine? *Emes!* No bullshit!

That little thing about seeing Lenny—I mean Jerry—Jerry Orbach—may he rest in peace, *aleichem sholom*—in South Beach the other day: Dr. Green says it was just a case of mistaken identity that is going around in men my age. I don't have Alzheimer's, or anything like that, but just to be on the safe side he gave me some seizure stuff and told me not to worry about the date because samples never go bad if you take them in quantity. I take five, five times a day. Can you imagine? *Emes!* No bullshit!

I tell you, the next time I think I see Lenny—I mean Jerry—Jerry Orbach—may he rest in peace, *aleichem sholom*—I'm gonna handle it different. Instead of running up to him and pinching him on the cheek to see if he's alive, I'm just gonna calmly walk over and say, "TNT—it's all about the drama." And then, just like that, go back to my table and eat my stone crabs. Can you imagine? *Emes!* No bullshit!

If you don't believe how good my Doctor Green is, go check him out in *New York* Magazine. He's number one on their list of the richest doctors who make their money in South Florida real estate. Can you imagine? *Emes!* No bullshit!

I tell everyone, it's worth a trip down here just to have him check you out. Even if he's not in your plan, I say, spend the money—land is everything, right? I don't mean you should be like Ruthie—may she rest in peace, *aleichem sholom*. She went to the doctor every goddamn week complaining about her feet. I never saw anyone have so many goddamn corns. I said to her, who wears high heels to the pool? But, you know Ruthie—may she rest in peace, *aleichem sholom*—she knew everything. She just told me, and I quote, "Maxie, it's my fucking feet, so fuck you and the horse you rode in on." End of quote. Can you imagine? *Emes!* No bullshit!

I used to wonder if all the chicken fat was what was making her corns grow so big and ugly, because they were so mushy when she squeezed them, but then when her sister Rosalie, the bitch-bastard, came down with her ugly feet the size of mobile homes and her rows of squishy mushroom-looking corns that she stuck right up on my new glass coffee table, I could see it was genetic. Those corns were so bunched together her feet looked like goddamn hoofs. Can you imagine? *Emes!* No bullshit!

That's when I finally figured out why Ruthie—may she rest in peace, *aleichem sholom*—and her sister, Rosalie, the bitch-bastard were so good at picking the horses at Hollywood Park. Can you imagine? *Emes!* No bullshit!

Listen, Tenderly—I got your message about tropical storms Arlene and Bret, but other people besides our cousins have those names, so I don't see what the big deal is.

Yeah—in fact, did you know I dated a woman from Tower Two named Arlene? Arlene Schneider: she lives on the eighteenth floor in a gorgeous wraparound facing south. But, get a load of this: her second husband was named Bret—short for Bratislava, or something like that—may he rest in peace, *aleichem sholom*. So there you have it, a husband and wife both having the same names as these two storms. Can you imagine? *Emes!* No bullshit!

Bret dropped dead two months ago—a cerebral hemorrhage. The notice they put up in the elevators said it happened while he was screaming at the cable company. Don't get me wrong, I'm not saying the old *cocker* deserved it, but I couldn't understand him half the time, so how do you expect some poor *schmuck* in India to know the Yiddish words for *Disconnect me again, I'm going to kill you, your family, and your cow*. Can you imagine? *Emes!* No bullshit!

The last of the snowbirds, those bitch-bastards, went back, so it's only us regulars who have to put up with all the bullshit rules. The office, the bitch-bastards, sent around a notice they'd be sending someone up to make sure the porch furniture is off the terrace. I told them, nobody's coming up to my apartment without me being there and without a day's notice—you know what a pain in the ass it is to move Ruthie, may she rest in peace, *aleichem sholom*. Can you imagine? *Emes!* No bullshit!

Arty Gottfried's another pain in the ass—that bitch-bastard *mamzer*, shoving that cruise lines crap under the door. He thinks he's such a know-it-all, smoking his fake Montecristo Prominente and grabbing up all the goddamn pool chairs—the *mamzer*. When I see him leave, I take his cruise ship towels and dump 'em in the *coca-dodo* kiddie pool. Can you imagine? *Emes!* No bullshit!

One day, when he didn't have anyone else to bullshit to, he sits his fat ass down next to me, tells me nobody sees Ruthie anymore, and they're wondering if I killed her. Before I can shove his cigar down his throat, he leans over and whispers that he hopes I did a good job getting rid of the body, because without a body the cops have no case. What, I don't watch "Law & Order"? Can you imagine? *Emes!* No bullshit!

Then he says how I should have come to him because the *gentse kener's* figured out the perfect way to kill his wife. In fact, he said, not only did he get rid of Loretta—may she rest in peace, aleichem sholom—but her *whole goddamn family*. Can you imagine? *Emes!*

No bullshit!

He pulls his chair closer, tells me about Going Overboard Cruise Lines, and says they didn't care who gets thrown off the ship so long as you're a hundred miles out to sea, in pre-paid groups of ten or more, and haven't tossed anyone else overboard in the last year. Can you imagine? *Emes*! No bullshit!

You should see Artie's new wife. She could be his daughter, only she's a gypsy, or something—from Bulgaria, I think. What a knock-out! I heard somebody said she used to do his tarot cards in Coconut Grove. Can you imagine? *Emes!* No bullshit!

Bermuda, I'm telling you, these gypsies are smart cookies. You should meet this one. She'd be great for your business, and I bet she's ready to leave Artie because, I hear, she's got a thing for a weightlifter over at Bodies by Juan on U.S. 1. Can you imagine? *Emes!* No bullshit!

What was I talking about? Damn—I think it's those seizure pills. Dr. Green says I shouldn't do anything too taxing after taking them, like meeting up with Pearlstein, the president of the condo, the bitch-bastard *mamzer*.

I said, "Lenny"—and then I stopped myself, because when Pearlstein wears a suit he looks just like Jerry—Jerry Orbach, may he rest in peace, *aleichem sholom*—shook the cobwebs loose and said, "Forget about the goddamn pool, worry about the goddamn garage." He said, "What are you worried about the garage for?" and I said, "I'm worried about the goddamn *underground* garage because, goddamn it—if the goddamn ocean comes over the goddamn beach, it will run right down the goddamn ramp, fill up the goddamn garage, weaken the goddamn concrete that is supporting the goddamn condo. *That's goddamn why—you dumb SOB, bitch-bastard mamzer!*" Can you imagine? *Emes!* No bullshit!

You gotta talk tough to this bitch-bastard *mamzer*—otherwise, he'll walk all over you like he did to fat Jackie Jacobs, who's just so happens to be a real sweetheart.

"Oh," he says, "I never thought about that." . . . *Oh, he never thought about that!* The goddamn bitch-bastard *mamzer!* Then he's got the *chutzpah* to tell me he's going to call up his son-in-law's construction company. Can you believe the balls on that one?

Oh, don't you worry, I could see Pearlstein's eyes lighting up with dollar signs, so that's when I told him I just invited Myron Bernstein (as in the new Broward County District Attorney) to come to the next meeting. Then I informed him, very nonchalantly, that Mr. District Attorney Myron Bernstein is thinking of moving into the building because his sister, Helen, and her husband, Sam (who is old enough to be her father), live here; and an invite would make Mr. District Attorney Myron Bernstein feel like we want him to not only move in, but join the condo board. You should have seen Pearlstein's eyes glaze over on that one—the *mamzer*. Can you imagine? *Emes!* No bullshit!

Now, thank Goddess, most of Ruthie's girlfriends are up North—may she rest in peace, *aleichem sholom*—and I can put her out on the deck and let the sun set her on fire. Can you imagine? *Emes!* No bullshit!

I got the idea after I read in the papers that the Lauderdale cops are banning the annual Jews Gone Wild Holiday Break because of all the chicken-soup self-immolation. Listen to this—I'm reading from the article now, and it says, "Kids, after a night of chicken-soup bingeing, are passing out on the beach, and before they wake up, the sun heats up their gold Rolexes, igniting the chicken fat that's oozed out and greased up their naked bloated bodies." End of quote. Can you imagine? *Emes!* No bullshit!

You know I've always kept Ruthie—may she rest in peace *aleichem sholom*—in a dark place, and when I look at her, I only use a flashlight; and since the hurricane warnings I wrapped up in her raincoat and moved her away from the window—otherwise the sun would have got to her and the whole condo would have gone up! Can you imagine? *Emes!* No bullshit!

After I read the article, I wrapped her up real good in wax paper, covered her in aluminum foil, and wheeled her into the closet until summer. I got a dozen room fresheners in there, but for half an hour a day, I still open the door and let the five ionic-breeze things I got from The Sharper Image, air it out. I also got the windows open and the central air on 24/7. The trouble is, the room's like an icebox, and I'm thinking maybe that's not such a good thing for my suits. Can you imagine? *Emes!* No bullshit!

I also got to be careful, because one day Hazel Blumenfeld from next door, the bitch-bastard, rings my bell and asks if she can see my wife's new face lift because she smells the homemade chicken fat and knows Ruthie must be back—may she rest in peace, *aleichem sholom.* Can you imagine? *Emes!* No bullshit!

Love,
Uncle Maxie

From: Clarice.G@Ourmail.us
Date: Tuesday, June 21, 2005, 10:41 a.m.
To: Cheryl.G@Ourmail.us
Subject: FYI

Well, Big Sister Cheryl, you can tell Sylvia, that arsonist auntie of ours, she can stop wetting her pants. I'm not going to Mount Cedar—now, or ever. And trust me, if you think it was because *he* threw me over for the real Diana Ross—it *wasn't*, and he f-ing *didn't*.

(FYI—he still thinks I'm still *Supreme!*) Go ahead: ask him when you get there. And while you're at it, ask the Finest Doctor to read you his love poems to me, begging me to come—threatening to never again touch a Petri dish if I don't take his pleas seriously.

And don't worry—Bubbeh Esther (*pronounced* Granny Smith Apples) is in the loop, so don't you stop reading this and think about how you are going to put another one of your *"I'm gonna kill you, and you won't know when"* messages in my alphabet soup.

Sure—when I was a baby it scared the f-ing poop outta me, but compared to *Clarice—Clarice . . . wash your mouth out with soap. . . Clarice . . .* —it's f-ing amateur hour.

Besides, the Finest Doctor didn't mean it. He sent me a fresh set of stem cells to prove it.

Oh, what—you don't believe me?

I can email you a photo of the shipping container, plus the pics the FreshDirect guy took. He's got the same camera phone as me, so the pictures came out real good.

Oh, don't f-ing worry—Bubbeh Esther (*pronounced* Granny Smith Apples) will tell you I'm telling the truth. Like I said, she's in the loop.

Jesus, Mary, and Joseph, she did one of her "Be in two places at the same time" routines, and then when she got here used her special eye skills to see if the f-ing impregnation worked.

I don't know why she had to come. I'm not an f-ing amateur. I've been doing the "self-serve" ever since I watched your hand disappear down your pants the minute Fabian started singing "Turn Me Loose" on "American Bandstand."

I miss my girl capris. They were perfect when your fingers did the walking, weren't they?

After Bubbeh Esther (*pronounced* Granny Smith Apples) looked my ovaries over, she ordered up a magnum of Cristal Brut 1990. I have to say, I was *mucho* impressed that after only one sip, the Fresh-Direct guy (he was still taking pictures) knew the year—and I told him so. I can see why the Finest Doctor has them on speed dial.

Don't go ballistic on me—I *was* going to notify Auntie Sylvia, but I have it on the down low the fire marshals still have her on the f-ing wire. Of course, *you* don't have to worry about surveillance—you're in a wheelchair. Everybody loves a cripple, but then you know that, because ever since we were little girls you've worked the f-ing pity angle—haven't you Big Sister?

Our wonderful daddy called. Bubbeh Esther (*pronounced* Granny Smith Apples) must have put him in the picture. I told him if didn't want me to sing like Diana Ross he should have spent more time at home, and then maybe—just f-ing maybe—instead of doing "Someday We'll Be Together," I could have been studying to be TV lawyer and turned out to be Angie Harmon.

He told me not to be so hard on myself, and that maybe the Finest Doctor really loves me for me, and not because he thinks I'm Diana Ross. Imagine: our father being sweet when there isn't a jury around?

What you all don't know is that the love street to the Finest Doctor is already full of bumps, and for me the rubber meets the end of the road when I see the sign *VEGAN SPOKEN HERE*.

STOP! I know what you're thinking. Did Mr. Curie let a little bad breath stop him from marrying his Marie? No—he went out and got his brilliant Madame a Pez dispenser. Maybe for my own set of wings, and the chance to fly faster than Lara Croft parasails across Hong Kong Harbor, I should do the same. . .

Love,

your sister, Clarice

From: LawyerUp@AbeSues4You.edu
Date: Tuesday, June 21, 2005, 10:50 a.m.
To: US@Ourmail.us
Subject: Uncle Abe's alive!

Hello there!

To paraphrase Mark Twain, Uncle Abe would like to say the report of Uncle Abe's death has been grossly exaggerated. Already, Uncle Abe would be suing all the major networks and wire services for printing stories about Uncle Abe's untimely demise *um-be-rufen*, Goddess forbid, pooh, pooh, pooh. Naturally, the news frightened the Family Ginsburg (*pronounced* Du Pont) members half to death, *um-be-shrien*, Goddess forbid, pooh, pooh, pooh—giving so many of you no other choice but to deal with your overwhelming grief by taking all the drugs you poor people could get your hands on.

Uncle Abe can only thanks Goddess *riboynoy-shel-oylom,* and credit the fine work of the first responders for keeping the death toll down to one.

At this time, Uncle Abe would like to extend Uncle Abe's condolences to the family of the deer that was hit by the CNN Hurricane-Chasing News Van on Sunrise, over by Plantation. Prayers continued 24/7 from Uncle Abe's lips, and hope never faded, but when surgeons from Miami Heart were unable to glue the big fella's antlers back just the way he wanted them, we all knew it was over. In lieu of flowers, Uncle Abe asks anyone wanting to make a contribution to send it to: DOEs WITHOUT DEARs, Los Alamos Testing Grounds, Los Alamos, NM 87544.

Next year, on the anniversary of this dear deer's death, Uncle Abe will notify everyone so we may have a memorial service and light *yahrtzeit* candles for a heroic animal.

Uncle Abe's near-death experience has made Uncle Abe see things in a different way and, consequently, Uncle Abe is not going to do sue any media giants for putting out these irresponsibly false and misleading death notices. What Uncle Abe *is* going to do is sue *Uncle Abe*, or should Uncle Abe say, *the Old Uncle Abe.*

Yep, you heard it right. Uncle Abe is going to sue the Old Uncle Abe for gross negligence and depraved indifference, for it was the Old Uncle Abe's reckless behavior that caused the Old Uncle Abe to incessantly talk on the cell phone and use his PDAs so much that when the Old Uncle Abe met someone in person, the Old Uncle Abe had nothing to say, which, as you would expect, caused the Old Uncle Abe so much unnecessary pain and suffering that the Old Uncle Abe actually stopped using these devices for ten minutes, which of course led everyone to believe Uncle Abe (the Old Uncle Abe) was dead, *um-berufen*—Goddess forbid, pooh, pooh, pooh.

Naturally, Old Uncle Abe feels reborn, and naturally, the Reborn Uncle Abe is going to sue Old Uncle Abe's cell phone and PDA manufacturers, plus all providers, for alienation of affection and the loss of minutes Old Uncle Abe (to be referred to in the lawsuit as *Old Uncle Abe*) incurred, or the Reborn Uncle Abe (to be referred to in the lawsuit as *Reborn Uncle Abe*) will lose.

In addition, Reborn Uncle Abe (I've legally changed my name and pronounce it the way it looks) is seeking unspecified damages caused by not being on Old Uncle Abe's cell phone or PDA during those ten irretrievably lost minutes. Reborn Uncle Abe is inviting anyone with a cell phone or PDA, including the Family Ginsburg (*pronounced* Du Pont), to join in a class action suit if they think they would have contacted Old Uncle Abe during those lost minutes.

Reborn Uncle Abe is proud to be an American. Reborn Uncle Abe just wanted to mention that.

Now, Reborn Uncle Abe would like to take a minute to bring everyone up to speed on Old Uncle Abe's hurricane lawsuit, or as the press here in Miami has dubbed it, Fruitcake vs. The Hurricane—that way, everyone will know where Reborn Uncle Abe is now coming from, and going to.

As you remember, Old Uncle Abe made a very nice deal with the Florida Archdiocese and removed Goddess's name from the lawsuit and was only going after the National Weather Service (they never went into Chapter 11—the government bailed them out) and Mercedes-Benz of North America. Mercedes-Benz thing was a late addition because, as Old Uncle Abe told you, Old Uncle Abe has been having nightmares about Benzes flying through the air, causing Old Uncle Abe to fear for his life when Old Uncle Abe is outside, because Old Uncle Abe might get crushed by a falling 3,200-pound SLK 350.

However, since Reborn Uncle Abe's rebirth, the future of any and all of Reborn Uncle Abe's lawsuits has been foretold, and Reborn Uncle Abe now knows what Goddess wants Reborn Uncle Abe to do—and Reborn Uncle Abe quotes: "Bring forth thy Court TV lawsuits tenfold, so that all shall know the Lord, thy Goddess, is alive and well and loves litigation." End of quote.

Ordinarily, Reborn Uncle Abe would be afraid to tell anyone about the dream, what with Reborn Uncle Abe's brother, Maxie, seeing dead actors in crab houses, but since it's in Reborn Uncle Abe's deposition—what the hell.

So Reborn Uncle Abe quotes, "Old Uncle Abe had just finished off his usual bedtime snack of two Fig Newtons and a warm glass of two-percent milk with a touch of Sweet'N Low for some kick; removed Old Uncle Abe's dentures and placed them in a mug Old Uncle Abe got from the University of Miami debating team; closed Old Uncle Abe's eyes for what, ten seconds maybe, when suddenly the deer (the one that got killed by the CNN Hurricane News Van) appeared at the foot of Old Uncle Abe's bed and started talking ordinary English with just a touch of a New York accent. Can you imagine? *Emes!* No bullshit—as Old Uncle Abe's Bubbeh (*pronounced* Jane Austen) used to say.

Naturally, Old Uncle Abe thinks Old Uncle Abe needs to take a tinkle, but the doe shakes her head (yep, CNN got the gender wrong) and says—and Reborn Uncle Abe quotes Old Uncle Abe here—"I am *You-Know-Who,* and if you read between the lines and go forth as I say, but not as I do, I will fix your you-know-what, so you can sleep through you-know-what, until the Angel of Death takes you,

you-know-where, you-know-when." End of quote.

The doe moves Her lips and everything, so Old Uncle Abe knows it's not gas—which it definitely could be, because Old Uncle Abe had, for the Thursday's Early Bird Special at Murray's New York-Style Chinese Deli, the most delicious side of Chinese cabbage with the leanest pastrami sandwich you can imagine.

The doe says—and Reborn Uncle Abe quotes Old Uncle Abe again—"The world was a better place when there were no headlights and *You-Know-Who* could cross the road without getting stage fright and end up as roadkill." End of quote.

Old Uncle Abe suddenly has to pass wind. Come on, don't look at me like that—it happens, especially after eating Chinese cabbage. The doe turns around and runs out of the room and never comes back, even after Old Uncle Abe sprays the place twice with some nice cherry-blossom room freshener with extra cherry that Old Uncle Abe got on sale at Publix.

The next morning, Old Uncle Abe is sitting on his terrace overlooking the ocean and admiring the view from the nineteenth floor, wondering if what happened last night was real, or just indigestion, when a hen flies onto the terrace and sits down in the chair across from Old Uncle Abe. The chicken says—and Reborn Uncle Abe quotes Old Uncle Abe—"She is the doe, who is really *You-Know-Who;*" then, the chicken says with a straight face, "How about some coffee—decaf, with a little half and half? If you got any more bagels, plain, lightly toasted with a *schmear* of Land O' Lakes, slightly salted, that would be fine, too." End of quote.

Well, as *You-Know-Who* is Old Uncle Abe's witness, the hen sounds just like the doe, and believe you me, when a hen that's really a doe that's really *You-Know-Who,* asks for something—you hop to it.

When Old Uncle Abe returns to the terrace, newspapers are all messed up, and She's using Old Uncle Abe's cell phone, calling you-know-where. Not only that—Old Uncle Abe can also see Her beak's covered with the last of the raspberry jelly that Old Uncle Abe got on special from Publix. So, Old Uncle Abe waits maybe five minutes while She complains about how rainy it was, and—this is a direct quote—how in all Her life, she's "never seen the water so warm," and that "maybe Cancun isn't such a bad idea." End of quote and end of deposition.

If you think Reborn Uncle Abe is making any of this up, you can check Old Uncle Abe's deposition, which is online at Depositions.org/Miami/theoldfruitcake.html.

So, as Old Uncle Abe was saying—and this is a direct quote—"*You-Know-Who* gets off the phone, tells Old Uncle Abe that Old Uncle Abe's battery's low, and then proceeds to—excuse the expression, because Old Uncle Abe don't mean to be disrespectful—"bitch and moan" about gasoline prices, and how the Dolphins needed to enlarge their parking facilities because She hates "to wait an hour just to get out of the damn lot." End of quote.

Before Old Uncle Abe can get a word in, *You-Know-Who* changes from a hen into a *Pekingese,* because She says it's just a matter of time before Old Uncle Abe asks Her why She crossed the road, or which came first—the Her, or the egg.

Besides, it was a little chilly out on the terrace, and as Reborn Uncle Abe quotes Old Uncle Abe, She likes the way a Peke's soft hair keeps her "warm and toasty." End of quote.

Reborn Uncle Abe, quoting Old Uncle Abe, continues: She wants to know if Old Uncle Abe wants to pet Her, and Old Uncle Abe tells Her that according to the condo board, no dogs are allowed in The Madrid, and She says, "That's a lawsuit in the making."

Before Old Uncle Abe can say anything, *You-Know-Who* says She is happy with Herself, but didn't think *I* would be until I stopped referring to myself in the third, fourth, or fifth person because, how could I get personal with someone if I wasn't personal with myself?

I have no problem with that, ask if She wants a warm-up. She says no, but She does want an entire bagel because She doesn't eat like a bird. I know this—so naturally, I agree.

We make small talk about the weather, and about how She never had a dog growing up. *You-Know-Who* has a strange look in Her eye, and I say, "What?" She says, "Go on, ask." I say, "What—WHAT?" She says ask me to ask Her if She knows that "*sseddoG* spelled backwards is *Goddess*."

Love,

Uncle Abe

P.S. I had my name legally changed back to Abe Ginsburg (*pronounced* Du Pont)

From: Lulu-LuCrawford@PleasureIsWhereYouFindIt.org
Date: Tuesday, June 21, 2005, 12:00 p.m.
To: Bubbeh.E@US.us
Cc: US@US.us
Subject: Lulu-Lu needs your help B. E.

B. E.,

Oh, gosh darn, B. E! What to do, what to do? I'm at sixes and nines, I tell you. Do I, like, send money down to Hugo and his sister's second mama, Betty-Jean Boulevard—they got my eyes, so I know we're kin—so they can, like, rebuild their place, or do I, like, tell 'em they gotta leave the family homestead and go farther up the Pearl Jam Mountain and get 'em, like, another trailer that won't get blown to shit every time a darn tornado comes a roarin' through Hogs Breath? Then there's Black Lips' little boy, Nester, Jr.—he's got my eyes, so I know we're kin—named after Uncle Nester—he's got my eyes, so I know we're kin—'cause Betty-Jean, like, just discovered that's who her daddy really is—but who everybody calls Black Lips Too, after his daddy, Hugo Black Lips, Sr., which I think is, like, just the respectful thing to do, don't you?

B. E., the name thing, like, has to do with Uncle Nester's disappearance 'round the time of the killin' of the Federal fella twenty years back, but first I have to ask myself, *Are they gonna, like, use the money for a new trailer, or will they, like, drink it up when they go a searchin' for Black Lips Too, who could be, like, anywheres?*

Some say Black Lips Too seen the Federal Fella die, but, B. E., when I was, like, a little more than the height of a rusted ole junker's hood buried in a foot a mud, little Horace—he's got my eyes, so I know we're kin—who everyone called Hiccup 'cause of all his hiccuppin' was, like, only nine months old at the time, and was, like, blown by a tornado clear into Water Moccasin Hollow near five miles down the road and wasn't found 'til he was, like, nineteen, even though when you went into the hollow lookin' for Water Moccasin—like, you know, to kill just for fun—like, you could hear his hiccuppin' and all.

Yep, I still remember the day little Horace came into town dressed head-to-foot like a water moccasin—scared the bejesus outta me, I can tell you.

Of course, B. E., I don't want to be tellin' no tall tales and, like, to be truthful and all, I did hear Black Lips Too weighs a might bit more than old Horace, so I can't see the wind, like, a tossin' him that far, but you know if he was, like, sittin' up in a tree pickin' his nose like I know he likes to do . . . no tellin' where the little bugger could be, 'cause when those tornados pick up a tree you might as well bend over and kiss your ass good-bye. Why—I heard tell a pine tree picked up in a tornado is, like, travelin' faster than a dingleberry in a hibernatin' bear's first fart—and take it from Miss Lulu-Lu Crawford (*pronounced* the way it looks), if you been in, like, an open field when that's a happenin', you know that's, like, pretty darn fast.

B.E, I guess what I'll do is maybe, like, drive down there and lend a hand now that me and Bermuda are, like, quits. I'm not one for blamin' other folks, not when I was the one who, like, picked up the fire extinguisher, but even a uneducated mountain girl from Hogs Breath, who can't even use a calculator without, like, movin' her lips, knows when enough is enough.

Like I said, I'm not, like, a blamin' Bermuda, 'cause maybe—like the radio says—the poor air quality is makin' people act, you know, like, weird-like. For the record, B. E., the pollution's not makin' me pick up other women, no-how. I don't need no more one-night stands with women who had Asian babies without men and just wanna, like, brag about that, thinkin' that's a gonna, like, get my pussy hot.

B. E., when the weather's that bad I, like, just breathe outta a paper bag like I did in Hogs Breath, but heck, the pollution here's gotta get a might worse to be like home, 'cause the smoke from the atomic-bomb plant fire that's a been burnin' there for, like, the last sixty-five years can really suck the air outta a body.

B. E., you take it from Miss Lulu-Lu Crawford (*pronounced* the way it looks): on, like, a good day, the air down home was so darn thick it was like you was buried in a West Virginia coal mine with your eyes taped shut—ask anyone, if you don't believe me.

Anywho, B. E., like Oprah says—I love that gal—*what is is, best no matter how bad your heart aches for love.* B. E., what really sunk the Love Boat was jealousy. I ain't lyin'. I'm a tellin' you things got a little, like, hinky just as soon as I talked about my mechanical head. B. E., I could see it was, like, gnawin' away at her like a mangy dog gnaws at a three-day-old chicken wing, and you know, I never would have figured what was up, 'cause she'd usually boot me outta the room when she has, like, one of those nosebleeds and gets to erase what she wrote on the walls—but you know, one day, like, she was passed out on the bed, and I, like, snuck back in, and on the walls was all this stuff written in nose blood, and I'm not, like, talkin' outta the side a my mouth, neither. Well at first, I thought it was, like, right outta that movie, *Seven,* you know—with Brad Pitt, I, like, love that man—but then I'm thinkin', maybe it's, like, some secret Jewish-holiday thing, 'cause you people are always celebratin' this Bible story, or that, and talkin' in that strange, like, Yiddish stuff, right? Well, if all of you ain't, Bermuda does and, like, so do all those old fogies Maxie sends up—like that rabbi, who's a real nut job, and that's *emes.* See, didn't I tell you I know your words?

Anywho, B. E., I, like, checked my little book of Jewish expressions—which, lemme tell you, is a must-have if you gonna make some serious money in a New York City whorehouse—but if a bear don't shit in the woods, the words *weren't* Jewish—and it was no quickie look neither, 'cause I, like, went through that book *two* times with a piece a paper under each line when I did.

B. E., I don't know what made me want to, like, brush my hair a hundred times, 'cept that's what I do when I'm, like, under stress, but as soon as I looked into the mirror, I could read the words on the wall as clear as I could see the stars in a Utah sky—which is where I, like, lived for six weeks with that school shrink I told you about that didn't go nowheres 'cause I wasn't gonna marry him even after he took me to that place where all the men had more than one wife.

Anywho, B. E., the backwards words on the wall said—,and I

quote, 'cause I wrote'em down——: *Blood, blood on the wall, why can't I have the most beautiful mechanical head of them all?*

Wow, it, like, hit me like a ton of crap in a shit storm! Naturally, I, like, got myself onto the next plane to Mount Cedar where I'm, like, a waitin' on the Finest Doctor, who says he can fit me in tomorrow, which can't be soon enough.

Now, B. E., I want you to tell Bermuda as soon as I, like, get my new head: like, I'm not gonna be givin' any no more, if you get my meanin'. You heard it right. I'm quittin' the life for good, and headin' with my new head back down to Hogs Breath to see if I can make a difference.

B. E., I will continue to, like, communicate with you, 'cause you're my real family and all. And, B. E., you tell Miss Bermuda that Miss Lulu-Lu says, what, like, goes on in Mount Cedar, like, stays in Mount Cedar.

Love you like the grandma I ain't never had . . .

Respectfully yours,

Miss Lulu-Lu Crawford (*pronounced* the way it looks)

From: Jules@JewelerToTheStars.us
Date: Tuesday, June 21, 2005, 12:30 p.m.
To: Laverne.G@Ourmail.us
Cc. US@Ourmail.us
Subject: Laverne—exciting news!

Laverne,

I have just returned from an incredibly exciting event at Le Cirque, where I was wined and dined by the Board of Directors of the Brooklyn Museum, my friend the Monsignor Def Rev, the governor, the mayor, and the Walmart's Executive V.P. in charge of Art and Artifacts Made in Taiwan.

The event celebrated last night's preview, and it could not have been better received. If you haven't already had a chance to see it on cable news, protestors have begun demonstrating outside the museum demanding that my *The Pope's A-Poppin Series* be destroyed, and that I be stoned, pilloried, then hanged, and finally my dead body burned on the steps of the museum in an area they have designated "The Kill Zone."

The Pope's A-Poppin' Series Roadshow doesn't officially open for another week, but already across the street is a two-mile waiting line that is growing by the minute. Naturally, the powers-that-be have instructed the police to allow the media an unobstructed view of the demonstrators, many of whom we have discreetly bussed in from out of state psychiatric institutions. We are supplying these demonstrators with Red Bull and cheesecakes from Junior's so they can maintain their twenty-four-hour vigil. In addition, the museum has provided buses to shuttle demonstrators too old or infirmed back and forth to the Metropolitan Museum of Art, where temporary housing has been set up for them at the Temple of Dendur. This is part of the National Endowment for the Arts' Reciprocal Museum Housing for Rioters Act that hopefully will encourage the masses to appreciate the arts in the same way they appreciate the looting of appliance stores.

According to the bloggers at WaitingOnLineLikeAMoron.com, the numbers threaten to exceed those at the recent Eagles' Last Reunion Reloaded, Reloaded Concert, unless you count the people who died from exposure. Of course, you can never trust the Chinese government, because they have a history of feeding the West misinformation when it comes to liner notes regarding Joe Walsh.

Getting back to Le Cirque. The mayor made several toasts in recognition of the fact that every hotel in New York City is booked for the duration of the six-month show. Not wanting to give himself the evil eye, the governor crossed himself before he made his own toast, boasting that he estimated revenues from collateral damage could run higher than the rioting following the last casting call for "The Sopranos."

Naturally, a state of emergency will be called to access the billions of dollars in federal aid needed to cover the anticipated damages that the governor's family, friends, and anyone who donated more than $10,000 to his campaign will suffer to their beach homes because of the demonstrations.

I'm sure you want to know what's in it for me. Well, thanks to the governor's policy of *No Federal Money Left Behind*, he outsourced the job of supplying three units of the National Guard to one of the Ginsburgs' (*pronounced* Du Ponts') twenty-five thousand (give or take) shell corporations.

I can only thank our wonderful patron of the arts, Bubbeh Esther (*pronounced* Granny Smith Apples), for having the foresight to think this scheme up. You know about jewelers who become artists: we just lose our heads for business, so naturally I was a little hesitant. But Bubbeh (*pronounced* Granny) made a convincing argument when she spun that atlas around and showed me how many Catholics would riot when we brought *The Popes A-Poppin' Series* to a museum near them.

Even a jeweler could see how soldiers would be needed for crowd control, and who better to supply them than Bubbeh Esther (*pronounced* Granny Smith Apples), whose company, Bubbeh's (*pronounced* Granny's) *Boys*, already furnishes the Buckingham Palace Guards, Mexican Border Patrol, and French Foreign Legion.

What really made me believe I was bound for glory was when Bubbeh (*pronounced* Granny) grabbed me up by her trunk and smashed me across a giant globe, screaming, "First Brooklyn, then the world!"

But wait, *wait,* Laverne—this isn't *all* the good news I have to tell you and the Family Ginsburg (*pronounced* Du Pont). After we had our meal and were about to have some very old brandy and equally pricey Cuban cigars, the mayor gets up, makes everyone quiet down, then announces I am to become the new Official Big Apple Jeweler.

Now, Laverne, this is a big honor, because this means anyone who gets married in the city and wants a wedding-ring finger must have the transplant done by me. Furthermore, as the Official Big Apple Jeweler, I'm the designated transplant-jeweler in the City's health-insurance plan, so any city employee or their family member who wants a jewel eye, nipple, foot, etc.—and wants it fully covered by his or her insurance plan—has to come to *me.*

Laverne, because I'm one to give back to the community, I'm offering a 15% discount to all retired City employees, as long as I've already done work on them. Generous, no?

I've got so much art in me, my head's spinning, but before I sign off, I want to share some of the glowing reviews my work has received. *Never on Friday,* the number-one Catholic meat-slapping magazine in the world, and one I've taken a $50,000 full-page spread in, says in its museum reviews, editorials, placards, and death threats—and I quote— "Pregnant with artistic poignancy . . . stomach full of symbolism . . . finally, someone who knows what we want and isn't afraid to give it to us. . . . If your family likes the work of the antichrist, this is for them."

BuddhaHidesCouponsUnderATree.com, the fastest-growing New Delhi web site for mantras and madras, and one I've taken a $25,000 pop-up ad on, says—and I translate from the HTML—"Only someone who has drunk from the waters of the Ganges in huge excesses could create a work of such sublime majesty. . . I can't wait for the bobblehead version. . . "

And from the hit series "Without a Trace"—and I quote— "Barbie's not dead, she's just living inside the Pope's stomach."

Finally, the Holy Father, after seeing the show (how he got in without being interviewed by George Whipple, Goddess only knows), had this to say: "The seats could have been a little better."

I just wish Mom and Pop could be here now; but I know they'd be looking down and they would be smiling on me—that's if I hadn't had a total facelift and they could still recognize their little *boychik*.

Love,
Uncle Jules

From: SisterChanelSize4@SistersofTheRuinedFeet.com
Date: Tuesday, June 21, 2005, 12:30 p.m.
To: US@Ourmail.us
Subject: *Mea culpa*

Dear Family Ginsburg (*pronounced* Du Pont),

I have been six days without bread and water. Sister Susan Bennis Size 4 just applied soothing salves to my back, and Mother Superior (Sister Prada Size 6), forbade me my morning and afternoon self-flagellation in the hope that my leg wounds would be sufficiently healed so that I may resume my penitence, limited as it is, this evening.

I regret deeply the tone and tenor of my last email. My use of profane language brought shame upon my order and me, and served no purpose but to inflame an already incendiary situation.

I also apologize for not respecting or being sensitive to the feelings of my family members. I was so caught up in my own world of diminished hope and damaged dreams that I allowed myself to sink to such depraved levels. You are, nor ever were, *rat bastards.*

It was selfish and self-serving to believe that taking the precious life of *Mein* Bubbeh (*pronounced* Granny), the matriarch of the Family Ginsburg (*pronounced* Du Pont), would bring meaning to my own worthless existence. Through weeks of meditation and counseling, I now realize the injustices, whether real or delusional, should have been greeted with understanding, compassion, and reconciliation. To try and take another human being's life with a Brillo Pad wire was morally reprehensible. I take full responsibility and cannot blame anyone but myself for such a violently disrespectful and horribly bungled act of transgression.

I take no solace in knowing that my sisters here at the Sisters of the Ruined Feet Sanctuary celebrated my resourcefulness by swallowing lighted candles for twenty-four straight hours. Not one of them, they confessed, would have had my presence of mind and looked for a lethal weapon amongst the cleaning supplies. (The fact that I'm always fantasizing about steel wool did nothing to diminish neither their awe, nor their candle swallowing.) Sister Prada Size 6, our venerable Mother Superior, herself a suspect in three *crimes de passion*, thought it took a truly imaginative and counterintuitive person to fight her natural instincts and not grab the fire ax off the wall. After praying for nine consecutive hours while standing on their heads, it came to my sisters—just as it came to me in the Gap—that such a choice would run the risk of breaking a nail.

I must take a moment to recognize Sister Fendi Size 14, who applauded the superior manner in which I treat inferiors that made it easy for me to enter a store that made a mockery of all I venerate and successfully avoid eye contact with woefully under-dressed customers so I could reach Bubbeh Esther (*pronounced* Granny Smith Apples) undetected. Of course, I knew about the mammoth's magical gifts, for they were promised to me if I ate my Wonder Bread which would help build my body 12 ways; however, I also knew the Dry Roasted Planters Peanuts located near the cash register would distract the behemoth and provide me a window of opportunity in which to strike.

To digress a moment—I remember at my sixth birthday party showing my mother my strength by bending a steel bar on the jungle gym, then begging her to fulfill her promise and send me to the Finest Doctor so I could have eyes in the back of my head, just like *Mein* Bubbeh (*pronounced* Granny). I was nine when, despite pulling the Ferry across The Mersey with only a rope attached to my teeth (a swimming feat still unmatched to this day), Mother once more denied my plea. It was only when my blood flowed like a woman that I accidentally discovered it was *Mein* Bubbeh (*pronounced* Granny) who put the kibosh to those—and any of the subsequent hopes I had of emulating the one person in the world who meant more to me than life itself.

During those formative years, a day didn't go by when I didn't write *Mein* Bubbeh (*pronounced* Granny). These letters, on Babar stationery, were the emotional outpourings of a little girl who desired only to be like her Bubbeh (*pronounced* Granny). *Mein* Bubbeh (*pronounced* Granny) would always reply with three blank sheets of her own Babar stationery. Only I knew the cocktail of fruit juices one needed to reveal her message. Her wonderful letters, always full of encouragement, were traditionally accompanied by photos of her and her husband.

It took a day of searching through the Book of Knowledge to learn husbands and wives, at least with each other, didn't attempt such ambitious acrobatic positions, and another of looking through my Gilbert microscope to count the exact number of "companions."

Recalling it now, I have to be honest and say the increased magnification also increased my fascination with *Mein* Bubbeh (*pronounced* Granny's) corpulent body. I clearly remember spending countless hours inspecting every inch of her bare flesh, scrupulously comparing it with mine in only the way a child first examines her own, downy coverings. I wondered if my D-cups would be as large, and if so, how those voluminous mounds would look on my tiny, disproportionate body.

I marveled at their firmness, wondering all the time if my tips would be as red and so pointedly erect. I imagined having the thick and diamond-shaped hair that mysteriously grew between her legs, and wondered if I could keep my skate key in it.

I hid the letters from the world, but shared my imaginings with *Mein* Bubbeh (*pronounced* Granny). Always inspirational, always compassionate, I never once suspected the growing jealousy raging beneath her loving exterior, blazing with the heat from a thousand hellish infernos. How could I know my beloved *Mein* Bubbeh (*pronounced* Granny) saw in me a rival to her youth and beauty, one who had to be destroyed until no vestige of that pure and innocent budding flower existed?

I never would have believed that someone who I loved so dearly and so openly, and who I thought loved me with equal ardor, would betray the trust of someone so vulnerable.

Again, I have to take to heart the words of Sister Prada Size 6: *"Shit happens. Suck it up."* And, draw sustenance from the words of Sister

Novitiate Jimmy Choo Size 4: *"If the Old Shoemaker in the Sky didn't think you could handle it, he wouldn't have given you falling arches."* Can you envision such insight from a novitiate?

Dear Family Ginsburg (*pronounced* Du Pont), please accept my apology for the poorly executed assassination attempt on our illustrious matriarch, for an attack on *one* Ginsburg (*pronounced* Du Pont) is attack upon *all* Ginsburgs (*pronounced* Du Ponts).

In a moment of deep meditation, locked away from all my shoes, I asked myself how come someone who scored so high in "Choking-From Behind," one of the most difficult parts of our entrance exam, failed to garrote a 400-year-old woman.

At first I thought I had chosen the wrong weapon, and the Brillo Pad wire simply wasn't strong enough to penetrate the mammoth's thick, elephantine hide. But if that was so, why, in my dreams, had all my trial runs been so successful? No, I thought—if I could sever those elephant heads clean through at the Museum of Natural History, there was no earthly reason I couldn't do the same to *Mein* Monster.

Could it be possible that an invisible *white light* indeed surrounded her? Naturally, I knew the stories surrounding the infamous *Personal Guide* from *the other side*. The one who looked after our matriarch, and made certain she wouldn't be vulnerable to her enemies during a faith-based blackout.

I now believe, with all my heart and soul, that both of us were being guided that day, and consequently we each learned valuable lessons that needed to be learned if we were to grow as spiritual beings, and if I were ever to successfully garrote someone with steel wool.

As I expose myself to you like the exposed wounds of my oozing, self-mutilated flesh, I also beg you to believe that I had absolutely nothing to do with either of the two badly bungled assassination attempts on the life of Cheryl, my niece.

No one knows better than me how Cheryl feels about Bubbeh Esther (*pronounced* Granny Smith Apples). The closeness of that bond is unmistakable, and for some, unspeakable. I saw this symbiotic relationship up close and personal when we gathered for the yearly Family Ginsburg (*pronounced* Du Pont) Reunion.

Furthermore, I realize the Sisters of the Ruined Feet Sanctuary don't want me to discuss these events unless I'm in a padded cell, heavily medicated and securely restrained. I appreciate their concern, but I'm feeling much better now that the Starbucks installation is going so well, and therefore, believe I can handle the retelling of these childhood memories, no matter how painful.

I was eleven when Cheryl tried to kill me the first time. It happened at the final Ginsburg (*pronounced* Du Pont) Family Reunion to be held at Yankee Stadium. Sister Mary Janes Size 6 said I must have buried the memory deep within my subconscious, because I never thought about that day until I heard what happened to that poor Amish fellow at the Super Bowl. Then it all came back to me in a deadly series of nightmarish levitations in which, naked and wet to the bone, I finally descended back into the safety of our Jacuzzi.

Mein Bubbeh (*pronounced* Granny), *Mein* Aunt Hilda, and Uncle Abe were all standing at the railing of the upper deck behind home plate, looking down at the field. It was a magnificent August afternoon and the Yankees were out of town, playing a doubleheader against the Tribe in Cleveland. *Mein* Bubbeh (*pronounced* Granny) was lamenting the day she sold the Yankees, but all of us knew she had no choice. It was either keeping the Bronx Bombers, or give up her dream of putting the first man on the moon. Thank Goddess that as one of the provisions of the sale she still had the total use of the stadium four times a year, rent-free. Naturally, there were other perks, like her season tickets behind third base, a place you could find me almost any Saturday or Sunday the team was in town.

Mein Aunt Hilda was eight and a half months pregnant with Cheryl, and you can imagine, she was as big as a house. *Mein* Bubbeh (*pronounced* Granny) was beside herself with joy, for she and Hilda were best of friends, and it was she who had made it all happen.

Hilda and Abe had been unable to conceive, and after much convincing, *Mein* Bubbeh (*pronounced* Granny) finally persuaded Hilda to see the Finest Doctor. The fertility experiments he just completed were revolutionary and without question would help Hilda to conceive.

One week after her arrival, Hilda was pregnant with Cheryl. It was only years later when the Sisters of the Ruined Feet Sanctuary returned with the secret files stolen from the Finest Doctor's office that I learned he was the antichrist, and discovered the nature of the side effects *Mein* Bubbeh (*pronounced* Granny) suffered as a result of her seasonal and highly unusual stem cell transplants. I also uncovered another horrible secret—so terrifying I can hardly speak of it today. Of course, on that glorious August afternoon, I knew nothing of the true origins of Hilda's demon child, nor of its diabolically superhuman powers, as I stood on tiptoes at the railing of the upper deck, basking in the warming rays of a sun-drenched sky and eagerly leaning forward to get a better view of my dear, loving relatives frolicking down on the field below.

Blue and gold tents representing The Ginsburg (*pronounced* Du Pont) family colors were set up on the infield grass so everyone could exhibit floor-to-ceiling models, built to scale, of the private residences and commercial real estate they owned. Others in the clan displayed all their jewelry, gold bars, coin and stamp collections, as well as, priceless heirlooms such as their antique silver and china collections.

I especially liked Uncle Younger The Elder Twenty-Two's Indian Head penny collection, the mere mention of which always got *Mein* Bubbeh's (*pronounced* Granny's) blood to boil. I also loved Uncle Jules's modern art collection—a priceless group of work that eventually found a home at MOMA—and really took delight in meeting all his cool friends, who would draw your picture for a rub on the *tushy*, or if you were a teen, a little French kissing.

That year Uncle Jules brought two of his South American buddies, Pablo Picasso and Salvatore Dali. There was also a mariachi band, flamenco dancers, and the artists' girlfriends handed out sangria while you waited to have your portrait done. Everybody was singing and dancing. It was really one of the most festive Ginsburg (*pronounced* Du Pont) Family Reunions I can remember. Pablo didn't care, but Salvatore got really angry if you sat down with your drink, or even worse, took a sip while he was drawing you.

I still have my portrait, although Sister Prada Size 6 said it would be unwise for me to look at it again after what happened the last time. Anyway, it was a magnificent day, made all the more magical when seen through the impressionable eyes of an eleven-year-old girl who was standing in the air space of her revered Bubbeh (*pronounced* Granny).

I don't know what made me turn around and see the arms pushing out from my aunt's swollen tummy. It could have been my internal warning system, or perhaps it was *my Personal Guide* wrapping me in my own protective cloak of *white light*. Whatever it was, I saw the hands a split second before they pushed me backwards, and that saved my life.

The next thing I knew, I was sailing off the upper deck, the warm stadium breezes that blew in from centerfield enveloping me and spinning me around and around in a kind of suspended animation. I didn't panic, but instead began, in the most natural way, to flap my arms as if they were wings, and I was a bird. I felt those warm stadium breezes, that moments ago held me in their centrifugal grip, now gently propelling me up and out into centerfield.

I don't remember, but everyone said I circled the field twenty times before finally gliding down and safely landing in the softest patch of centerfield grass.

I lay in a coma for a month, blinking continuously, until the Finest Doctor, posing as Dr. Scholl's of Mussel Shoals, slipped into the country, looked into my eyes and telepathically transmitted the message—*high heels bring me closer to heaven.*

Waiting for such a sign, The Sisters of The Ruined Feet Sanctuary immediately kidnapped me, for it was foretold in *The Three Prophecies of The Golden Shoe Trees* that "The healer of woman's soles shall come out of a field of dreams and build foot-worshiping centers where tootsies are reborn and high-fashion shoes fit all."

Of course, as a young and naïve novitiate, all I could think about was how I could kill Bubbeh Esther (*pronounced* Granny Smith

Apples) and my niece, Cheryl, before they killed me.

CAN I HAVE AN AMEN!

Had I read *The Three Prophecies of The Golden Shoe Trees*, I would have known my fate was sealed three-thousand karmas ago when I was—Sorry, I must leave this bit of information out, for it is written in *The Three Prophecies of The Golden Shoe Trees* that that will be revealed in the follow-up to *The History Of Our World (Pronounced Life On Earth): The 2005 Emails Of The Family Ginsburg (Pronounced Du Pont)*, entitled *The History Of Our World (Pronounced Life On Earth): The 2006 Emails Of The Family Ginsburg (Pronounced Du Pont)*.

Even now, it is beyond my comprehension how I could have had the prescience to recognize this unborn child—soon to be known to me as my niece, Cheryl—lying within my Aunt Hilda's swollen belly, was, in truth, the unholy product of Bubbeh Esther's (*pronounced* Granny Smith Apples's) egg exchange, secretly placed in vitro by the antichrist to thwart *The Three Prophecies of The Golden Shoe Trees*.

I feel myself growing weary and in need of sleep if I am to fulfill my evening penitence.

I ask only your forgiveness.

Sister Chanel Size 4 Formerly Known As The Aunt Named Bea

SEPT 21ST, THE FIRST DAY OF FALL

From: Cheryl.G@Ourmail.us
Date: Wednesday, September 21, 2005, 6:00 a.m.
To: US@Ourmail.us
Subject: *Joyeux anniversaire à moi!* (Happy birthday to me!)

Ma chère, merveilleuse, affectueuse famille, (My dear, wonderful, loving family,)

Of course, you all know how much I love my birthday month, and how many marvelous and wonderful events always seem to occur under the personal warmth of my Libran sun. Naturally, you recall September 30, 1986, when Miss Maria Callas appeared in my bedroom and told me, I would bear a boy child who would be called *My Little Mister.* His voice would be high, "but of course not as high as mine," said *Le Voix Du Siécle* (the voice of the century), and it would eventually crack—so I shouldn't. He would be hung like a rhino (*an endowment obviously not on his philandering father's side,* thought I), and mothers would learn to lock their daughters up, or their daughters would learn the "hard way" (don't you just love coded messages?), for My Little Mister would use his "gift" well and wield it often. (I can't tell you how the diva's words have inspired me and kept me going.) *Quelle femme!* ("What a Woman!"—And the secret name I call Maria).

It was September 30, 2000, just a year later, when What a Woman! appeared again (this time in my bathroom and a little overly made-up for my taste), showed me exactly where my hairbrush lay hidden, and so gently scolded me for overzealousness when, under the influence of ecstasy, I tried to find things that were lost while downloading a new screensaver. (You can bet that was a multi-task turning point.)

Ben-Gurion showed up on September 30, 1993, while I was ordering Showtime, and told me I should stay away from fried foods. "The Lion of the Hair Salon" (that's the secret name I call Ben—he had the most beautiful head of perfectly coiffed white hair I had ever seen in someone so tan) proceeded to show me how he kept it looking so good, even after he spent a week in the Sinai. (I still think of him every time

I pick up my blow dryer.) *Quel homme*! ("What a Man!"—the second secret name I call The Lion of the Hair Salon.)

On September 30, 1964, Mae West paid me a visit when I was waiting in Dr. Don's office to have my braces removed and reading a fascinating article in *Money* about how to avoid probate. (Mae was the one who told me to hide my diary, because a young girl's secrets, especially when they concern rich older men, are only meant for publication.) "Even Bigger Than Me" (the secret name I call Mae) was annoyed because she thought I was paying too much attention to my D-cups, and wasn't educated to the fact that Allied Soldiers honored her by calling their inflatable life jackets "Mae West." *Honte sur moi!* (Shame on me!)

From that moment on, I vowed no child of mine would suffer a similar historical humiliation, and as soon as an offspring reached their fifth birthday (or craved an afternoon cocktail—whichever came first), I had a life preserver adorned with their monogrammed initials in eighteen-carat gold leaf, tattooed sixteen inches above their left breasts. *Si beau!* (So beautiful!)

On September 30, 1987, when employed as a teller at the New York Bank for Savings up on 73rd and Broadway, a hundred-year-old Cherokee Indian hobbled up to my window. (It was during the months leading up to Bubbeh [*pronounced* Granny] buying all the branches.) He had a full roll of nickels he wanted changed into folding money. After handing him two dollars, he communicated to me (using his blanket to make three enormous smoke signals) that in his next incarnation he was going to be Tommy Hilfiger, and if I became a travel agent, I should keep in touch. (This would never happen in today's smoke-free environments.)

As you all know "Carrie" (that's my secret name for Tommy, because he can throw a model across the runway just by blinking his eyes five times) is still my friend, even though he introduced me to Husband #5 (may his head never be found).

Of course, plenty of special things happened to me on other September days. For instance, on September 12, 1953, Miss Betty Furness appeared next to the refrigerator, whirled around once, then opened it up and said, "You can be *sure* if it's Westinghouse." Ever since that magical moment, I've been whirling every time I open a fridge, and as you also know, have worn my hair exactly like "Miss Furness" (that's the secret name I call Betty), except for the time Clarice drugged me and then shaved it clean. Clarice would have drugged and shaved the entire family if Bubbeh Esther (*pronounced* Granny Smith Apples) hadn't magically appeared and shown her the *three sixes on her scalp* were really *triple nines*. From that moment on, we all looked at numbers in a new way, and after a while became so good, none of needed a mirror.

Some people think I'm unlucky I'm able to remember every last detail of every last minute of every last September day since birth, when other members of *la famille* (the family) have birthdays in more exciting months, and remember every single thing that happened on Halloween, Christmas, St. Paddy's Day, or if truly blessed, April Fool's Day.

Unlike others in *la famille* (the family) who think self-medicating means depriving oneself of oxygen for a day, I never dwelled upon the metaphysical aspects of a September birth until yesterday, September 20, 2005, when, out of the blue, Neil Diamond strolled into my bedroom singing "Sweet Caroline." *Aucun mensonge!* (No lie!)

I don't know what made my half-paralyzed lump of a body suddenly feel feathery light. (I always liked that song, but it never made me want to get up and dance.)

As luck would have it, I was a high as a kite, otherwise, I would have totally freaked when, just as I stood up, my fucking wheelchair—*oh m'excusent* (oh excuse me), my fucking *scooter*—flew straight across the room and *fucking disappeared* into Neil's guitar (as if a giant magnet had sucked it right up)! *C'est vrai, c'est vrai!* (It's true—it's true!)

Naturally, the bullet lodged in my spine also got sucked up and flew straight into the guitar and also vanished. Poof! *Aussi vrai!* (Also true!)

I can only thank Donnie the Dentist for replacing all my gold fillings (he was into porcelain so, *so* early), otherwise Goddess only knows what would have happened to my jawline (and you could have said good-bye to my cheeks as well).

As I clung to my morphine drip (thank Dow it was made of plastic), a flash of bright light filled my head. Suddenly the time continuum folded inward and it was September 21, 1956 (like today, another autumnal equinoctial morning). Our apartment faced south, and from my window I could look down West End Avenue. (I don't know why I remember that—it has nothing to do with the story.) A fat-faced little Jewish boy wearing a checked shirt (a definite bridge-and-tunnel kid) ambled in and sang in the squeakiest of voices, *"The Mississippi Delta's glowing like a national guitar, I'm going to Graceland, Graceland." M'aider ainsi!* (So help me!)

You know how great lives are shaped by great events? Well, from that moment on, I knew—I MEAN, I REALLY KNEW—I was meant to be president of the Upper West Side Chapter of the Paul Simon Fan Club.

As fate would have it, the next day I was fitted with my very first bra, and as soon as I walked out the door, I had another calling far more primal (more like a whistle, actually)— and well, six divorces later, here I am.

Of course, now that "oh miracles of miracles" has occurred, and I'm up and walking again (and ready TO KICK SOME ASSASSIN ASS), I see clearly that I—*me*—*Cheryl*—born a Ginsburg (*pronounced* Du Pont) Girl—has been given a second chance. (Everything comes to she who wants—isn't that the truth.)

Naturally, I have to give my next steps, however wobbly, some serious consideration, so I'm thinking—*Shirley! Shirley, Shirley bo Birley, Bonana fanna fo Firley, Fee fy mo Mirley, Shirley*—NO, NO, NOT THAT—I'm thinking, and hear me out—being president of the Upper West Side Chapter of the *Neil Diamond* Fan Club might be a better career move, and my real destiny.

Of course, one thing is perfectly obvious—you're only as happy as your richest relative.

A l'année prochaine! (Until next year!)

Love,

Cousin Cheryl, A Very Proud Mom

Shirley! Shirley, Shirley bo Birley, Bonana fanna fo Firley, Fee fy mo Mirley, Shirley!

P. S. Remember… *El amor nos guardará juntos.* (Love will keep us together.)

SING IT LOUD! SING IT PROUD! SING IT NOW!

From: Bubbeh.E@Ourmail.us
Date: Wednesday, September 21, 2005, 6:00 a.m.
To: Cheryl.G@Ourmail.us
Cc: US@Ourmail.us
Subject: *Mazel Tov!*

Mein darling Cheryl,

You're walking again! *Mazel Tov!* So much *naches* in one day, I have to sit down . . . Your poor *Bubbeh's* (*pronounced* Granny's) heart can't stand all this happiness. Not that I ever doubted you wouldn't, for you see, my darling Cheryl, our magnetism is well documented in the *Second Book of the 999 Books of She Who Brings Forth Life, the Great Baleboosteh Ginsburg* (*pronounced* Eleanor of Aquitaine), fourth psalm, second chapter, first verse (written in her own hand, and genetically imprinted on our magical gifts—visible only to us after vigorous rubbings of Oil of Olay while repeating the mantra *There once was a man from Nantucket who kept all his gold in a bucket. But his daughter, named Nan, ran away with a man, and as for the bucket, Nantucket.*) And I quote from this sacred text: *Acquiris quodcumque rapis.*

You acquire what you reap. She Who Brings Forth Life, the Great Baleboosteh Ginsburg (*pronounced* Eleanor of Aquitaine) knew a thing or two about attraction!

Of course, you all have heard me speak many times of Franz Anton Mesmer, whom I met at the Herbal Essences Expo in 1800, when Paris was Paris, and having a trunk show meant something less grotesque. He was a cheeky, tricky little frog who could put any woman under his nasty spell. His technique was simple, but oh, so fiendish. What Franz would do was to attach tiny magnets to his body, and then attach himself to an attractive young woman. When the unsuspecting maiden momentarily looked away to inspect the shoes of a rival, as young woman the world over will always do, Franz would spike her drink with a tasteless, fast-dissolving mega iron pill. When the woman became totally charged, the poor thing simply couldn't resist his pull, and would follow the smarmy *mamzer* anywhere.

Once this sneaky little toad got the magnetized creature back to his lair, he would lead the young lovely into his bedroom and deftly place her face up upon his bed, under which he deviously placed powerful magnets strategically arranged in the form of a life-sized cross.

Franz would then disappear behind Curtain Number One, where he could safely remove *his* own magnets. While Franz found this lecherous arrangement quite satisfying, many of his victims were more adventuresome and quickly grew tired of the crucifixion position. Even if I hadn't suggested it, it was only a matter of time before he would plant magnets on the walls, ceilings, and chair backs. But, as usual, I am jumping ahead of my story.

When I arrived for the Herbal Essences Expo, Franz's hypnotizing powers were the talk of all Gay *Paree*. Thanks to my special infrasound capabilities, news of these seductions quickly reached me, naturally piquing my interest, as well as raising my body heat. As I was as notorious a seducer as Franz, when he learned *I* had a booth at the Expo, he made sure he brought a large supply of extra-strength iron pills. *A chazer bleibt a chaser*—excuse my French—a pig remains a pig.

Poor Franz thought he could put one over on me, but I was no weak sister. On the contrary, my *electrifying* affairs with André-Marie Ampère, the very freaky Michael Faraday, and Heinrich "Tiny Hiney" Hertz, brought each to *their* weakened knees.

Like all Ginsburg (*pronounced* Du Pont) Women, I am modest to a fault and hesitant to take credit for the scientific discoveries of these "great men of current." That said, they couldn't have done it without *me*. And these words are not mine, but were uttered verbatim, in more or less the same way, by each of these "Wizards of Ohm" in their own words. (FYI, Ohm—"Ohmy the Lonely" as I loved to call him—gets his own chapter in next year's book.)

Everyone knew, André-Marie had to be chained up against the wall whenever I entered his laboratory, otherwise, we'd be instantaneously fused in a passionate embrace, which could lead to a life-threatening eating disorder if the servants couldn't hear our screams. Of course, the idea of two paralleling currents attracting is now in every sex and home-improvement manual, but back then nobody understood the concept unless they happened to have an unexpurgated copy of *Electrical Outlets and Other Sexual Portals the Government Doesn't Want You to Know About.*

Naturally, I saw the commercial possibilities, and while *some* in the Family Ginsburg (*pronounced* Du Pont)—bingo, if you guess *That Putz*—thought ice would always be kept in wooden chests, I held fast to the worldwide rights, and can point with pride to the numerous members of the Family Ginsburg (*pronounced* Du Pont) who have used the royalty checks from our refrigerator-magnet holdings to secretly purchase large areas of the Jersey Shore.

"Freaky" Faraday may have made my hair stand up whenever we swapped spit, but when he squeezed my buttercups, showers of sparks flew out our ears, even when he wore those cute yellow rubber bodysuits. There was no question, electricity was in the air when we made whoopee, but if he hadn't stuck his finger where the sun don't shine, he wouldn't have gotten the shock of his life, and we'd be all still living by candlelight.

By the time I met "Tiny Hiney," my lovemaking was even more extraordinary. So when Heinrich and I sailed up and down . . . and *down and up* . . . the Rhine, we made beautiful waves together, and with such frequency "Tiny Hiney" Hertz turned into "Mega" Hertz. Heinrich never forgot what I did for him, so when he finally caught the last wave to the Big Radio Station in the sky, he kindly willed his rights over to me; and that is the long (radio) and short (microwaves, infra-red, visible light, ultra-violet, x-rays, and gamma rays) of it—unless, of course, you want to count those royalty checks from AC/DC.

Poor Franz, was he ever in for immortalization. For openers, I told Mesmer unless his last name was *pronounced Hypno,* which I already knew it wasn't, why on earth should he name his technique *hypnotism?* Like they say . . . *Duh!*

I said, "Look, Froggy,"—tough love being the only thing a Frenchy understands—"use your own name, because it's all about branding." Naturally, Mesmer was *mesmerized*. When Franz finally got over himself, he foolishly thought he could nail me to his cross in mesmerizing fashion. *Farbrecher!*—excuse my French—what a con artist, that one!

You should have seen the *putz* when I polarized his *toches* and flipped the little *pisher* over on his backside and rode him like the broken beady-eye buckaroo he was. Oh yeah, HE WAS MY MESMER!

Mein darling Cheryl, there is so much wonderful wit and wisdom to lay at your feet, and starting in the New Year, believe you me, I want us to spend more time together so we can relive my many lives and loves.

In the meanwhile, *mein* darling Cheryl, each morning why don't you look to your own lovely ones with fresh eyes and a hand mirror and carefully read a single chapter from one of *The 999 Books of She Who Brings Forth Life, the Great Baleboosteh Ginsburg* (*pronounced* Eleanor of Aquitaine and written in her own hand, and genetically imprinted on our magical gifts—visible only to us after vigorous rubbings of Oil of Olay while repeating the mantra: *Some boys take a beautiful girl and hide her away from the rest of the world. I want to be the one to walk in the sun. Oh, girls, they want to have fun Oh, girls, just want to have fun*).

I would start in Book Twelve of the *999 Books of She Who Brings Forth Life, the Great Baleboosteh Ginsburg* (*pronounced* Eleanor of Aquitaine), first psalm, first chapter, first to fiftieth verses: *Audentes fortuna juvat.*

"Fortune favors the brave:" With these words begin the revelation of how She Who Brings Forth Life, the Great Baleboosteh Ginsburg (*pronounced* Eleanor of Aquitaine) first came to discover the powerful magnetic forces that resided within her magical gifts.

During the 404 years (give or take), that I have lived large, I always found it titillating that just a little glimpse of Ginsburg (*pronounced* Du Pont) Girl cleavage could attract men from nine to ninety-nine, and immediately force them to their knees so we could grab them by their nose and lead them right to Cartier.

Mein darling Cheryl, in the reading of that psalm, you also will gain knowledge of the Islands of Ginsburg (*pronounced* Du Pont), powerful pools of liquid magnetism covering one third of the moon that can be seen by the naked eye when that mysterious orb is in our second house (usually in the Hamptons).

You'll come to appreciate how, when listening to CCR, these supernatural force fields, nocturnally activated and powered by the ocean tides and our own neocortex, flow in the form of droplets riding on moonbeams into their genetic twin isles located deep within our magical gifts.

I know you must already sense this phenomenon, otherwise *mein* darling Cheryl, *mein* pretty one—you would not sing "Who'll Stop the Rain?" every time you watch The Weather Channel. *Farshtaist?*—excuse my French—Duh!

I love you all as only a Bubbeh can!

Bubbeh Esther (*pronounced* Granny Smith Apples)

From: Sylvia.G@Ourmail.us
Date: Wednesday, September 21, 2005, 8:07 a.m.
To: Cheryl.G@Ourmail.us
Subject: Just trying to help…

Dear Cuz,

Well, I still don't understand why you got so pissy when I told you I signed you up for AsianBoysForOlderGirls.edu. Now that you're out of that horrid wheelchair, I think it's about time you started going out and having some fun again. And, don't give me that guff about *not having your sea legs.* Cheryl, darling, let's face it—you and I have never been able to have a dozen martinis and then walk ten feet without falling down.

If you're so concerned about your walking, why don't you do what I do, and get yourself an ex-football-player-turned-ex-sportscaster-turned in-between-jobs-limo-driver. These Big Apple Tarzans will carry you in, gently lower you into your seat, and for no extra charge, plant a nice long kiss on your lips. Take it from someone who knows, it makes for a grand entrance when your escort is six-five, two-fifty, and has dreadlocks down to his shoulders. Yum!

Once you're safely ensconced, you order a stiff one, and wait for your "'Have Some Dim Sum' Stud Muffin'" to show—*you always arrange it so you get there before he does.* Oh, and make certain you're on your cell while you're gulping down your martinis. You definitely do not want to be the *only* woman in the room *not* pretending to be important.

If this East meets West doesn't lead to belly to belly, at least you've had a few drinks, learned how to say *"shaken, not stirred"* in Mandarin, and are that much nearer to the next *Close Encounter of the Hard Kind.* What's so difficult about that?

And tell me, Cheryl, darling, why did you get so uppity when I brought over Mike Tyson? Just because *that's what I called him,* didn't mean you couldn't change his name. I bought him for *you.* He was going to be *your* dog. You could have named him *Cream Puff* for all I cared. I just thought because he came from a long line of champion, ear-biting, pit bulls—well—giving him to Bermuda is a better idea. I need a ciggie and a pee.

OK, I'm back! I'm back!

Look, I'm feeling a little hormonal right now, and that makes me very vulnerable. And let's face it, Cheryl—when you took two shots at me and yelled, *"Die bitch-bastard, die,"* well, it brought back a rush of childhood memories that—OK—may have clouded my judgment a bit. Why in heaven's name wouldn't you let me clean your wound? What was that all about? Instead, I had to walk home wearing one shoe. What—you thought I could hop it, and that would save my $175.00 Wolford Sheer Ebony and Ivory pantyhose you discovered *can't be re-ordered*?

If you wanted my beige alligator slingback Manolos you should have come right out and said so, instead of just sitting there, with the four-inch heel of my right shoe imbedded in your forehead.

We've been cousins and best friends for too long to let a tiny misunderstanding turn us into someone we just nod at at weddings and funerals; and that's what will happen, if you continue to put black mambas in my bed. I would be dead now if the fire hadn't fried the slimy sucker.

The Big Pecker thinks this all happened because you got it into your amygdala that I was trying to steal your morphine drip, but I only wanted to read the label because my source is now smuggling dogs—*that's how I got Mike Tyson*—and the dealer he recommended is outside my group drug plan.

You will be happy to know I took your advice and didn't mention anything to The Big Pecker about his sicko camp relationship with my deviant diva of a husband. Cheryl, darling, I must be honest with you, because honesty has been the basis of our friendship—right from the time we were four, and my loving father locked us away in a closet for six hours—*remember*? Well, a failed and misguided shooting shouldn't change that, should it?

I confess, once The Big Pecker took out his penis-envy-pipe, I couldn't resist making several veiled prison references—you know, just throwing in some jail jargon I picked up watching "Oz." Guess what, he didn't flinch once, although I swear, I thought I detected a tiny smile cross his swollen Botoxian lips when I said, "Bend over, *you is my bitch now.*"

Well—I shouldn't be surprised. He's always been one to see your head as half empty, and that kind of negativity, while sure it can turn you on sexually, probably accounts for the reason he doesn't smile much.

I'll tell you what kind of a prick The Big Pecker is. Remember, when you called to tell me about Neil Diamond coming into your apartment and getting you to walk again, and how I fainted because at that very moment they were playing the second of two back-to-back Neil Diamond songs on AM 100 Easy Listening? You heard it, right? It's funny how our brains immediately pick up on connections like that, and in the seconds before I lost consciousness after falling and bouncing my head against the hardwood floor, I heard the words of my like-a-guru Sari Sarigatchamoneynow echo in my head: *Wear a helmet, wear a helmet.* He knew, like, all the great ones who chanted in the nude while locked in an industrial freezer—*Nothing is by chance.*

Well, when I told The Big Pecker about it, he couldn't stop laughing—that is until I peed in my La Perlas. I thought he was going to throttle me! He recently had his office totally redecorated, and I was sitting in his brand new, zebra-covered Pygmy chairs with matching arm rests, which he had just finished telling me "were on backorder for five fucking months."

I'm sure he dislocated my shoulder when he yanked me up and hurled me through the door; why else can't I lift my left hand away from my side? I need a ciggie, a pee, and a Percocet.

OK, I'm back!

Of course, he immediately let go and had to cover his eyes when my nose started spitting blood, which according to the *New England Journal of Medical Malpractice,* isn't a magic trick, and occurs more than we like to know in families who have a late-model blue SUV, and to anyone who's invited Satan into their nasal passages. I have to thank

Cousin Tenderly for this information, because it was only on account of her incessant nudging that I finally gave in to her threats of bodily infection and signed up for her End of World Emergency Updates, which now include medical oddities, freaks of nature, and recaps of the latest episode of "24."

Naturally, I signed up my lovely Bermuda, who is under so much pressure these days that I worry she's going to nose-spit herself to death before she can find a nice condo in South Beach. In fact, I urgently wanted to address this issue with The Big Pecker at today's emergency session, but the Neil Diamond *thing* just took control of my essence and overwhelmed my precious being.

As soon as I mentioned my *essence* and my *precious being*, I should have known the session would turn to shit, and The Big Pecker would let loose with one of his uncontrollable psychobabble tirades and destroy the office. That's why he got the tiny furniture—so he can make his patients feel *even smaller*.

But I was so vulnerable and I guess, in the back of my mind, I was thinking, *Well, he just redecorated, why would he fuck it all up by throwing his shit all around the room?*—but before I knew it, there went the antelope-skin Swingline stapler, smashing into his Guadalcanal Medical School-Like diploma, shattering the glass into a thousand tiny pieces. Next, he's hurling his giraffe-skin desk lamp with its adjustable neck, but I was ready, and agilely ducked out of the way, and watched it sail over my head, hit the wall, and smash into bits.

Finally, I saw sailing above me his collection of one-of-a-kind millstones (by then I had taken refuge on the floor). There were twenty in number, all made by his father, and all found around the old man's neck when police scuba divers pulled his bloated body from the Hudson for, according to The Big Pecker, one of "Law & Order"'s best episodes. When I asked why *twenty* millstones, and what did the *$10,000* inscribed on the bottom of each meant, The Big Pecker said the number stood for the years it took for him to pass the New York State Psychiatric Boards—and the $10,000 the amount each lost year cost his father.

Would our fathers ever have done something so beautiful? I THINK NOT! I need a ciggie and a pee, and another painkiller.

OK, I'm back!

Can you tell me why certain people can't let go? Oh, sure, Sari self-immolated, but hell, by then I'd been arrested on arson charges what—five, six times? Shit, there'd be a forest fire in North Dakota and the NYFD would be at my door. Innocent until proven guilty, *my ass*.

Why can't my psycho psychiatrist see that, and let me be sorry, for Sari? I tell you why. The Big Pecker is blinded by his unnatural love of his childhood summer-camp bum buddy Book 'em Dano, my gunrunning husband whom my daughter loves more than me. Sure, *sure*, now I can see that. But this morning, *this morning*, all I could hear was Sari's chanting: *Wear a helmet, wear a helmet.*

Oh, Cheryl, darling, let's go for a walk up Madison Avenue, but only in the Sixties. Let's get out into the fresh air and take in the Java Chip Frappuccino Tuna Tartar wafting from the Starbucks that conveniently occupies every fourth store on every city street. From now on, let's live every moment of every second of every minute! We have the money for drugs, so what's stopping us?

Love,
Cousin Sylvia

From: Sylvia.G@Ourmail.us
Date: Wednesday, September 21, 2005, 8:10 a.m.
To: US@Ourmail.us
Subject: Sharing my happiness

Dear, dear Family Ginsburg (*pronounced* Du Pont),

I don't know what I was thinking, but these seasonal emails shouldn't just be about boring old me. Please forgive me, my Family Ginsburg (*pronounced* Du Pont), for being so thoughtless. Allow me the honor to bring you up to speed and tell you about the most wonderful things that have happened in the last three months, which is another way of saying, give me ten minutes of your time and I've give you . . . *Bermuda.*

Yes—my honey lamb has suffered unspeakable hardships, but let's talk truth here. Ever since she was a little girl, Bermuda has looked trouble in the eye and stared it down in the best tradition of all Ginsburg (*pronounced* Du Pont) Women. We would expect nothing less.

I know this is something Bermuda doesn't want me to make public (she has a shy side that's so sweet), but I want everyone to know that I agree wholeheartedly—the public *is* ready for a remake of *My Favorite Launderette,* and my baby's decision to change the location and obviously the title, is both brilliant and inspired. Again, we would expect nothing less.

That said and put out of the way, I would like to add my two cents for whatever that's worth and say, Bermuda, after looking at the footage you logged it into Final Cut Pro 1500, I feel and more strongly than ever that you should seriously consider doing the entire movie in Spanish. (I guess I'm just a postmodernist in a "Back to the Sixties" housedress.)

I know you're in love with the title, because as you say, "The blood-and-guts market is shit hot." Darling Bermuda, I also know it's your dream to have one of your films open the Tribeca Slut and Slushie Film Festival; what's more, to have a film with the title *La Sala de la Belleza que Tomó mi Pelo* naturally has nicer film noir ring to it than

The Beauty Parlor That Took My Hair. I need a ciggie and a pee.

OK, I'm back!

I also want you to consider this. Last night, Lou Dobbs announced that salsa is now the number-one condiment in the U.S., proving beyond anyone's xenophobic paranoia that muscular Mexican day laborers are hot, and their equally sizzling women have a love-hate relationship with their hair.

Darling Bermuda, your film-school professors will not believe their eyes because your surrealistic approach to atheism, as it takes shape in *The Day in the Life of a Beauty Shop*, looks just like it was shot in Panavision.

You probably don't see it because you're so close to it—and true *artistes* never recognize their own genius, or the difference between film and video—but, I believe this incredible cinematic gift of *mise-en-scène* comes from your childhood disillusionment with the way the matzo and gefilte fish were so unashamedly displayed in bodegas along Amsterdam Avenue during Passover—a corruption of our Jew-like religion that has compelled you to expose it so pictorially as it manifests itself in the rinsing of anorexic and bulimic Rumanian trophy wives. Wow, that was a mouthful, but I got it out!

Naturally, the comparisons to *L'Age d'Or* will be made, and if Buñuel had your father and me as parents, and the access to a digital camera and portable quartz lighting as you did, one would see the comparison makes perfect sense.

I want to also congratulate my daughter for handling this Lulu-Lu Crawford creature in a way that brings credit to the Family Ginsburg (*pronounced* Du Pont) Name. Such grace and dignity is, of course, a Ginsburg (*pronounced* Du Pont) trait and tradition, but I know Cousin Tenderly's daily End of Days Last Alert Wristband and Heart Defibrillator Updates were a source of inspiration, as were the concealed-weapons training and garroting demonstrations. I want to thank Cousin Cheryl and Cousin Bea respectively for that.

I haven't seen much of my boys, Hill and Dale, since they got their own reality series. Of course, the mother is always the last to know.

I had to hear it from of all people, *That Putz,* who is making sure everyone knows *he's* the one making sure that all the building supplies come from one of the family's twenty-five thousand (give or take) shell corporations.

Don't ask me why, but the boys have always leaned forward in favor of the male figures in the Family Ginsburg (*pronounced* Du Pont) for as far back as I can remember. Of course, I would have buried these disturbing family memories in the trash bin of my brain if my lovely Bermuda hadn't photographed, 24/7, each and every little thing we did. Unfortunately, she did, and there it is—as it first reared their ugly little heads in 8-mm sound and color: Hill and Dale dressing up in Bermuda's undies in celebration of some fucking "ER" month and then hopping up on their grandfather's knee.

Goddess knows what lies the dirty old buzzard whispered about me as he stroked their beautiful blond locks. It probably had something to do with his sneaking away from me while I was looking for sable in Zabar's, and then me running across Broadway to track him and his brothers to the Russian steam room hidden in back of the Woolworth's Five & Dime. (I couldn't pry those little devils out of there for love or money.)

At least I have one thing to be thankful for: my sons didn't buddy up to their father, who was always too busy hugging Clayboy to give his own flesh and blood the fatherly touch boys need to stay straight. Oh, sure, Book 'em Dano paraded them before his cronies over at Paul Stuart. Thank Goddess, Hill and Dale didn't want to look like Pat Boone clones. Dressing up like all the other prep-school robots in their dark-blue blazers, white bucks, matching pink socks and shirts was not to their taste—not that my two Adonises wouldn't have made Narcissus look their way. No, my boys were individualists, and they had their hearts set on something with an A-line.

Of course, their dress code changed in only the way lives change when you leave your zip code, and the cab drops you off in front of the D&D Building instead of your dentist's building, two blocks up on Third. Suddenly, they saw that cross-dressing was just going to be something you do on the weekends, but picking out furniture, fabrics and carpeting would be your life, and the salvation of so many insecure women who married well, but unhappily. I need a ciggie and a pee.

OK, I'm back!

Where was I? Hill and Dale and interior design—that was it, wasn't it? Oh, I'm not saying I'm not thrilled with their success, because there isn't a prouder mom on my floor than me, so let me set the record straight on that one.

Look—coming up with the most beautiful powder room in a competition pitting them against twenty of New York's most famous interior designers in the 2005 Big Apple Show House Shootout with the winner getting their own Show House Shootout reality series makes them *numero uno*... *But*—and this is a big *but*—I still think that before they accepted ABC's offer, they should have gone to Bubbeh Esther (*pronounced* Granny Smith Apples), instead of *That Putz*, because in my heart of hearts, I know they would have had more creative guidance had they taken the Fox offer. Let's face it, does the title "Desperate Decorators" tell you it's a show about how to redecorate after a hurricane destroys your home? Duh!

Oh, sure, "Hurricane Makeovers" is a title that has been used to death, but when you couple it with *Right Wing*—then, *then* it has a patriotic *Reaganesque* quality. And—*and*, imagine how it would grab ratings during news coverage of the Iraq war. *Hurricane Right Wing Makeovers! Hurricane Right Wing Makeovers!*

The more I say it, the more I hope it's *my* company-owned Florida house or condo that's destroyed during the next Category 3, so Hill and Dale can come on in primetime, in front of a national audience, and fix it up, free of charge. (I guess I'm just a deconstructionist dressed up in a "Back to The Seventies" mother's housedress.) I need a ciggie and a pee.

OK, I'm back!

Tell me, where was Oprah in all of this? She's supposed to be their new best friend—OK, MOTHER FIGURE!

"Mix 18th-Century French with IKEA modern, you're so black even if you're white," she says the last time she had them on her show.

Well, then WHERE THE FUCK WAS SHE when my boys needed some reality series advice, HUH . . . HUH . . . HUH! I need a ciggie and a pee, and another Percocet!

OK, I'm back!

Before I spit blood, I'm going to stick a wad of cotton up my nose and examine my lovely ones, because now that I'm clean and sober, I think I'll spend some time with *The 999 Books* and reacquaint myself with the words of She Who Brings Forth Life, the Great Baleboosteh Ginsburg (*pronounced* Eleanor of Aquitaine).

I only hope I have some Oil of Olay; otherwise, you know what a bitch it is rubbing your gifts when they're dry.

Love,
Sylvia

From: Bermuda.G@Ourmail.us
Date: Wednesday, September 21, 2005, 8:30 a.m.
To: Sylvia.G@Ourmail.us
Cc: US@Ourmail.us
Subject: What a mom!!!!

Mama, Mama, *Mama* . . .

Can anyone have a more supportive mama than me? I don't think so. From the very first time you went into a coma, I knew I was born to direct and have in my DNA the natural instinct for correctly framing a shot as evident in the through-a-closet-darkly peephole sequence. I realize you enjoy comparing me to Fassbinder, and I must admit, if Daddy and Clayboy hadn't kept falling down drunk I would have shot my now infamous Father's Day Breakfast Scene in one continuous *Marriage-of-Marie-Braun*-take instead of two that is more reminiscent of eating scenes in *Ali: Fear Eats the Soul*. All in all it was a seminal event, and *the first time* Mount Sinai permitted a recidivist coma patient to critique a rough cut using REM; and that, is something no one can rob from me—or *you*.

You know what else, Mama? After watching Daddy and Clayboy do The Carioca Scene, I share your admiration for the rock-steady way I hand-held the Bell and Howell and captured every erotic hand gesture. Of course, Mama, I could not have done it without your support. No matter how fast or slow, or how suddenly I stopped or started, you held fast to my waist. You were my human Steadicam as I raced back and forth over the darkened rooftop.

I can't count the times I stayed up 'til dawn watching *Flying Down To Rio* so I could choreograph that number, *a lá* Fred and Ginger; but when you have two naked, toked-up dandies flitting around on a moonlit 100-by-100 roof garden, and you're across a fifty-foot alleyway with an short-lens 8-mm crank job, you have to concede that even a Henry Mancini score could not garner a PG rating. Although, when I cut it to "Moon River," I had the version Roman liked best. I just wished you could have met Mr. Polanski, because you always identified with *Rosemary's Baby*, but the truth was, you were still recovering from your nineteenth failed suicide attempt, weren't you?

Of course, it *was* my fault, Mama, and don't think I don't blame myself. If I hadn't provided a running commentary, you wouldn't have known what Daddy and Claymore were doing and consequently leaped off the parapet, leaving me to shoot their final embrace with one hand, as the other desperately reached behind me and grabbed a handful of air—for, if you recall, *you had already disappeared over the edge*. I can only thank the heavens above for the nor'easter, for if that buckling awning hadn't cushioned your fall, you would have broken *both* your Harry Winston heels.

Speaking of lucky times, remember, Mama, immediately after we screened *Atlantic City*, you invited Aunt Cheryl and Aunt Clarice over for a reading, and had the bright idea to add tequila to the lemon juice? Ever since I was a little girl, I enjoyed taking turns reading from each other's D-cups, but that time, instead of using Oil of Olay, we rubbed one another with a daring new mixture—pretending, as we chanted, we were Susan Sarandon staring into her mirror while from across the alleyway Burt Lancaster watched her rub her gifts. Well, *that was something special, wasn't it?*

I recall we read from ninth psalm, ninth chapter, ninth verse of *The Ninth Book of the 999 Books of She Who Brings Forth Life, the Great Baleboosteh Ginsburg* (*pronounced* Eleanor of Aquitaine, written in her own hand, and genetically imprinted on our magical gifts and visible only to us after vigorous rubbings of Oil of Olay while repeating the mantra*: It don't mean a thing if it ain't got that swing!*), and I quote: *Dum vita est, spes est.* Where there is life, there is hope!

Cheryl immediately called her bookie, and we all played *666*.

You got me so hysterical, I could hardly hold the camera steady when you kept screaming at Cheryl to stop rotating her head, which was really cool on the 6 train, but after the hundredth time, got to be old hat.

I know you're a traditionalist, but I'm weighted down by nostalgia, and confess every third day, and on the obscure Lutheran holiday, I put away the Oil of Olay and make myself a tequila-and-lemon moisturizer. Perhaps it senescence, but my lovelies feel dryer, and I have to load up on the tequila if I want the any residue to lick off my fingers.

Mama, thank you, *thank you, thank you* for Mike Tyson. You were absolutely right—having him next to me is pure joy, and his antics are just the distraction I need. Another thing, Mama—I must be totally candid, and tell you that just before I boarded, I did take a Librium to go with the Ativan I had to have during that dreadful trip through the Mid-Town Tunnel. Don't fret, by then I had already peed out the get-out-of-bed Xanax, and thus prevented my sensory organs from picking up sounds of the East River seeping into the tunnel, a constant reminder there's infrastructure trouble in River City.

I look at Mr. Mike Tyson—I added the *Mr.* because he appears so gentlemanly—and simply cannot imagine anyone betting forty thousand dollars on him. Mama, to clear up the mystery, please check with your dog smuggler to make sure this is *the* Mike Tyson? Not that I intend to return him, or anything, but if Mike *is* the notorious pit that bit off the ears of the cocker-mastiff mix when it won Cuba's Fight Dog Of The Year Award—well, I would like to make some mention of that on the matching his-and-hers diamond studded chains Uncle Jules will implant in our necks.

Oops! *That was to be a secret!* Sorry, Uncle Jules, I know you wanted to be the one to announce your newest canine jewelry implantation line.

Well, to ease your mind, Mama, I arrived safely, *and not in air marshal handcuffs*, and want everyone to know I am now ensconced at luxuriously South Beach Ginsburg (*pronounced* Du Pont). I followed Bubbeh Esther's (*pronounced* Granny Smith Apples's) instructions and registered as Notorious Big Ones (*pronounced* Dame Joan Sutherland). Befitting my rap sheet, I was immediately given the Royal Rapper Suite—the one fully stocked with Cristal and assault weapons. (FYI—a shout-out to Shirley, who hand-loaded the ammo.) The suite has one master bedroom for Mr. Mike Tyson and me, and two adjoining rooms for my Rent-a-Miami Dolphins

Linebackers-turned personal posse bodyguards.

No question, Mama, as a Ginsburg (*pronounced* Du Pont), I could have had the crib on the cuff (one of our twenty-five thousand [give or take] shell corporations owns the place—The Blind Trust and Shell Game of Dubai, LLC, if you must know), but sometimes a girl just wants to have fun.

Mama, I just love South Beach. To reunite with so many of my long-time customers from New York plus, my fame has preceded me and created quite the buzz. This morning, the next mayor of South Beach made an appointment, then minutes later the next Broward County Police Chief and his next wife, who just so happens to be the next State Attorney General. Jeb is in Riyadh picking up his summer wardrobe, but his office called and booked next Wednesday.

Oh, listen to this Mama. I'm playing phone tag with Fidel again. He simply won't let go and accept he bet against Mr. Mike Tyson and lost $5,000. I left a message telling him to just get over it, or I won't bring him any more jawbreakers.

Mama—I don't know if doing this film is the right thing. After all, starting over again in a new place is tough enough without worrying about foreign-distribution rights. Oh, I know Bubbeh Esther (*pronounced* Granny Smith Apples) just purchased the Napa and Sonoma Valleys, which gets her controlling interest in Lockheed Martin through a blind trust and ten million shares of Snapple, translating into sole ownership of The Mississippi and all her tributaries including Viacom, and, well—Viacom is *well—Viacom* . . .

I do know one thing, Mama—doing a reality show is off the table. I did not spend my prepubescence in art houses watching films by Ozu and Satyajit Ray so I could do TV.

And Mama, I'd sooner die than compete with the Brothers Hill and Dale for their Wednesday, 8:00 p.m. time slot. I owe them that—after what they did for me when I was doing time up in Danbury.

And no, Mama, I'm not giving into pressure from the Red Army, because once you win Best Foreign Film, you get theater distribution, whether you have product placement or not. Besides, I already have

The People's Republic of China's Third Armored in two scenes, and I will not interrupt the *mise-en-scène* just so the Russians can show off how many long-range missiles they have to sell. Tell me—isn't it enough that thanks to Daddy, President Putin finally was able to get his eldest daughter, Svetlana, out of the house? (FYI—that's "Big Svetlana" to her friends.) I hear she would love to bring it on—on "WWF SmackDown"—or at least have her own line of steroids. Well—if she's sleeping with your enemy, Daddy should make that happen, don't you think?

Mama, what you have heard i*s true.* I've only talked to President Putin that one time—(FYI—when he came into my shop five weeks ago)—but in the time it took for me to give him a rinse, I got the feeling he thought it was the media that blew the entire situation out of proportion. In fact, he swore to me there never were any missing WMDs, therefore, no one for Book 'em Dano to betray . . . ergo, no ballet company to stomp him, or our family. Incidentally, he swore decapitation was never the Russian way, unless you happen to be in Japan for their annual Odd Jobs' Bowler Toss.

So, Mama, after all this, one question remains: When does a Ginsburg (*pronounced* Du Pont) *Girl* become a Ginsburg (*pronounced* Du Pont) *Woman*? Wait! That was only a rhetorical question. You see, after looking into Mr. Mike Tyson eyes and then joining him in song, I knew the answer.

Bermuda, Bermuda, Bermuda shorts, Bermuda, Bermuda, Bermuda shorts —hey baby, hey-yay dig them shorts . . .

Now *I* need a *ciggie and a pee. . .*

Until next year. . .

Love you,

Bermuda

From: Laverne.G@Ourmail.us
Date: Wednesday, September 21, 2005, 9:30 a.m.
To: US@Ourmail.us
Subject: Life on the run

Hi, gang!

Well, it's me again, Laverne, from the On-the-Run Clan of the Family Ginsburg (*pronounced* Du Pont). I sold three sculptures from my *American Outlaw Family Series,* with the last one on hold, but the cash I did get went to bribing the guards at the trailer park. I made an executive decision: I'm through with using empty propane tanks. I need full tanks for my work if I'm going to be true to my new subject, *American Outlaw Family–Reloaded.* You like the name? The kids thought it up after watching *The Matrix Reloaded.* Uncle Jules thinks it's a winner—don't you, Uncle Jules?

Since Marie's been on the FBI's Ten Most Wanted Women, she can't get a dime out of her Mary Kay franchise, and forget about collecting on any of my dad's trailer insurance. You're in empty hands with Allstate when the Feds got you, you can bet on that. To put a little cash in our pockets, Marie and I have taken on the identities of Sly and the Family Stone. It'll only be for another few days; then we're thinking of becoming the Mormon Tabernacle Choir.

The Daughters of Adam and Eve are trying to help, and they give us apples from their garden, but they're all electronically tagged, so we can't poison them and resell to KillYourSpouse.com.

William's endorsement money is pouring into his Cayman account, and as a parent of a celebrity, I could access it, but heck, every so often you have to do what's right, or else the kid'll be penniless when the fame turns into flames. You know what I mean—right?

The kids have their own credit cards and I try to hold onto them and give 'em out only when they need 'em, but just when I think I got 'em all, some banking fella turns up at the candy counter and slips 'em a new one with a must-have, cartoon-figure logo. Say what you will about the banking industry, they do stand for family values. Let's face it, without credit-card debt, kids would have all the money, and then could you never bribe 'em to go to sleep.

I'm a little blue 'cause everyone has terrible head colds, and we just keep giving 'em back and forth to each other. We're a little better off now we're out of the Winnebago. I can't say enough good things about our "Winnie on Wheels," but it's a mobile Petri dish, if you ask me.

Remember how all I did was bitch and moan about how hot and humid the South was? At least there, I could park the kids at NASCAR and let the fumes clean out their sinuses. Plus, there's no better place than 100,000 drunken Johnny Rebs and their Mountain Mommas to sharpen your pickpocketing skills

Up here in Pennsylvania, the weather's changing every day, and I swear, I don't know how to dress 'em. And boy, do they miss getting their Big Kid's Chew Tobacco at the Piggly Wiggly. Somebody at the last filling station said the 7-Eleven just east of Dover has the flavors they love, so maybe that's where we'll go after The Daughters of Adam and Eve get us settled at the safe house.

You probably saw it on CNN 'cause I saw Anderson just after the meteor flattened the Staples, so we're staying at the Petco up on Mule Rd. We weren't sure it would be available, but The Children of Divorced Dog Owners completed their sit-in, so the place will be all ours.

The kids are looking forward to the change, even though they'll miss the copying machines. Cousin Younger the Elder by Twenty-Three—the kids want to talk to you about getting 'em some venture capital so they can make it a real business. I don't know all the details, but judging by the $500 bucks worth of candy they got at Walmart, the Sly and the Family Stone Music Visa Cards look authentic. You're probably wondering why they forge 'em when they're getting stacks of real ones? I know I did. You know what they said? *All the kids are into making their own, and they don't want to be left out.* Well, we were all kids once so we know how that is—right?

You know when they say a meteor sounds like a freight train falling from the sky, well—hell—it sure as hot diggity do. What really pisses me off is this morning, when the kids were talking to Reverend Robinson about their co-op marketing deal, he never said word one about the meteor strike. It was just about nine later that night when the f'ing thing hit. Willie and Clara were putting away the Chutes and Ladders. Marie just finished wiring up the time delay on the exploding handbills. I was on the throwaway having a three-way with Conrad and Judith Ann, seeing if Jerry truly was walking and was the one aiming a grenade launcher at our window or just one of The Daughters of Adam and Eve out on patrol.

Daughter Eve, our Dover Welcome Hostess, said the last time Reverend Robinson sent a meteor, *Gorillas in the Mist* was playing at the RKO, and in Pat's own words, "would show them Darwins a thing or two about the survival of the fittest."

Daughter Eve, who is married to Daughter Eve's (not the Dover Welcome Hostess Daughter Eve) brother, Daughter Adam, said she remembered the first one because she saw it hit the RKO square on, and the only reason Pat's prediction didn't come true was a mouse ran up someone's leg, and they had already emptied out.

This time Daughter Eve (not the Dover Welcome Hostess Daughter Eve) said the Lord would get his wish, and the lawyers from "Boston Legal" would get theirs when "Pat's Meteor Too" (that's what they called yesterday's event) would flatten the Days Inn, in her words, "flatter than a stack a flapjacks run over twice by an 18-wheeler."

Unfortunately, according to Daughter Eve (the Dover Welcome Hostess), Pat must have been staying up late reading scriptures, otherwise, his eyes wouldn't have been so darn tired and his aim a sight better. Marie said the next time old Pat calls on the wrath of Goddess, he better check with MapQuest, 'cause she uses them all the time, and she's never mistook a Staples for a Days Inn.

Willie and Clara laughed themselves silly, and I thought the two Eves were going to kill us right there. I quickly calmed the Eves Gone Mad by saying the kids were suffering from post-dramatic syndrome. Let's face it: how many people can say they escaped being crushed by a meteor thanks to an exploding handbill sending them out the front window, and into a flatbed filled with shredded unpaid IRS tax bills?

I sternly reminded Willie and Clara that when a woman joins The Daughters of Adam and Eve she takes a solemn oath never to tell a knock-knock joke, draw a smiley face, or see humor in anything we think is funny. I believe they then saw I meant business, and that this was no laughing matter.

Clara saved the day when she showed everyone how far she could spit tobacco sideways while lying flat on her back. Goddamn, she may be a demon child, but it's times like this I'm glad Willie kidnapped her and I let Marie convince me to take her with us.

I was shaking in my Hush Puppies after the two Eves left, because these Eves will kill you soon as look at you. I told you I learned that the hard way when I threw salt over my left shoulder during our first all-you-can-eat-communal-sit-down—you know, so I wouldn't get the acid reflux—and the next thing I know my cheeks are getting a machete massage.

Now, before I eat with these hell raisers, I take five spoonfuls of Pepto and make sure during the meal I stay away from their Low-Cal Garden-Fresh Adam and Eve Organic Apple Preserves, or their Low-Cal Adam and Eve 100% Garden All-Organic Fresh Fermented Apple Juice

I feel a little guilty because I should be spending more time with Conrad and Judith Ann, instead of with William, even though Willie is my youngest, and needs his momma's full attention during the all-important revolutionary years—that's why I try to speak to Conrad and Judith Ann every day. Although we are running low on our one-time-only throwaway cell phones. (FYI—we're supposed to get a new supply any day.)

I feel Judith Ann is in good hands, and I know the aliens are treating her well. They've made her their designated driver and diet coach, and that's on top of her job as their personal trainer. And get this, they've also promised they'll produce her screenplay, *Who Will Watch The Weight Watchers?: The Guts, The Glory, The Sugar.*

As you know, this is the never-before-told, thrill-a-minute story of Weight Watchers founder Jean Nidetch's personal battle to overcome her secret addiction. Hell, I'm always bitching and moaning about my life, but boy, after you read Judith Ann's screenplay, you just have to thank your lucky stars you've never had to battle the Dark Chocolate Demon. The only downside to the deal is one of the aliens wants to direct.

I talked Judith Ann out of slitting her throat by telling her to play along and you'll get a shot at directing the sequel.

I don't know about you, but I hate a whiny child, so I also told her quit feeling sorry for herself, because Ginsburg (*pronounced* Du Pont) Girls don't feel sorry for themselves. What we do is take responsibility, and make people pay for crossing us.

She's the one who picked the film business. Her high-school guidance counselor said there were a dozen other things she was good at, and Goddess knows, with her body, Judith Ann could have had her pick of any boy who was going into his father's business.

As it turned out, her wanting to leave town was a good thing—what with the poison cloud moving in. While I wasn't too thrilled about her getting involved with aliens, after hearing Tenderly talk, I have to admit, in the long run, moving to another planet might be Judith Ann's best chance of her directing a feature. Even Bermuda agreed.

Then Judith Ann started complaining about how the aliens took her for granted considering all she did for their kids. I have to agree, 'cause not every kickboxing coach could take a bunch of extraterrestrials all the way to the state finals, only to lose because of those judges—the f'ing homers!

Finally—I told her to check her horoscope in *People,* and if that didn't make her feel better, to call me back.

Conrad is the one I'm most concerned about. He's decided to leave school, even though it meant giving up the class presidency, his starting-guard position on the varsity basketball team, and his work in the school printing shop. You know he was the one who got the pictures, designed the ads, and even supervised the missing-children posters, handbills, and milk-carton production.

Cousin Younger the Elder by Twenty-Three—I should let you know Conrad will be calling you today. He said he's solved the dye and paper problems and is looking for some start-up capital so he can get his counterfeiting business off the ground. I think counterfeiting runs in our family, don't you think?

Where was I? Oh yeah—Connie leaving school. He didn't want to, but when all the kids who hadn't been kidnapped went *en masse* to the principal's office and told him they'd burn down the school if Conrad wasn't scheduled to be hanged by the neck until dead—well, Connie saw the handwriting on the goal posts.

I know I shouldn't blame myself, but if William were still barricaded in the house *he'd* be getting all the media attention, and no one would be the wiser because Conrad never confessed, and as long as CSI can't find a body or bodies, what do they have? SQUAT! EXACTLY! And I'm not saying this just because I'm his mother.

So, I said to Connie, let's sue the fuckers! In fact, I told Conrad I was going to call Uncle Abe, and he would know what to do. Speaking of CSI, Judith Ann said she would bring down "CSI: New York" because she felt the evidence "CSI: Miami" uncovered was tainted, even though she and Conrad had speaking parts in all three episodes.

But to Conrad's credit, he said no. He thought those episodes deserved an Emmy nomination, and even though Horatio bitch-slapped him in the last one, he thinks his performance was so moving, the writers will find a way to reprise his character so Horatio can do it again. Let's face it, getting bitch-slapped is something that just can't be taught in acting class. You either have it, or you don't.

Between you and me, I think the real reason Connie doesn't want to go to court is he's afraid the stuff about the Midget Massacre will come to light, and what that revelation would do to Jerry's ability to walk again.

I didn't say a word. Look, no matter how I feel about that son of a bitch, I will never say a bad word about him to our kids, and that includes me telling the world what I know about Jerry's involvement in that infamous game of "Small-Ball Bowling," known all around the Internet as "The Night of the Flying Dead," or "When the Little Guy's Lights Went Out at the Bowl-O-Rama."

You know, I'm always trying to support the kids, even though I got diddly squat from my folks. That's why I told Conrad he shouldn't feel alone, and we could certainly use him here for moral support and to help Marie distribute her new supply of explosive handbills. And let's face it, there's always someone we run across we'd like to see disappear into the night.

I've got to go: the kids are having a tobacco-spitting contest to see which one can knock an apple off my head. It's times like these I got to agree with the folks here in Dover when they say that some biological systems are so complex they could not have evolved through random mutations as the vast majority of biologists teach, and this complexity is proof positive life was formed by an unintelligent designer.

Love,

Cousin Laverne

P.S. Thank you all for the nice things you said about my sculptures

P.P.S. Aunt Bea, I promise—next year in the convent.

From: LawyerUp@AbeSues4You.edu
Date: Wednesday, September 21, 2005, 9:45 a.m.
To: US@Ourmail.us
Subject: Will you stop *hocking* me to death, why don't you?

Enough already with the phone calls and the emails. My Goddess—She should excuse the expression—you people are driving me *meshugeh*! Once and for all, *I got no idea if you should stop eating chicken, or venison.* And, between you, me and the bedpost, I think you should stop talking to dogs, even if one of them is you-know-who. Maybe She's not interested in talking. You ever think She just wants to be left alone, so She can take a nice shit and pee in peace?

Thank Goddess—She should excuse the expression—it's not Easter, or else you'd really be crazy. That's right, the last time I saw Her, She was a *rabbit*—a white rabbit with a blue nose, if you gotta know all the details.

Sure, I tried not to stare, because I never saw a rabbit with a blue nose, not that I know from rabbits. I thought She was cold, but She said, no, it was nice and warm on the balcony, even though we were nineteen floors up, and if I didn't mind, She just wanted to sun Herself awhile. She wants to sun Herself and She asks if I mind—what is She, *meshugeh*?

She did ask if I had any sunscreen, number 30, and then She wanted me to put it on Her back because She couldn't reach it with Her paws, or whatever rabbits have.

She pooh-poohed me when I said I just heard sunscreens didn't work. I was going to show Her my End of Days Last Alert Wristband and Heart Defibrillator and pull up the stuff Tenderly sent me on the subject, but then I saw I wasn't wearing it.

Anyway, She told me to just put twice as much on, and to make sure if She went into the water, to put it on again because, She knew for a fact, none of them were waterproof.

I just nodded my head a few times. That's what you do when She talks to you, even if you don't understand what She's talking about.

I thought She might be upset about my new class action lawsuit—you know the one I'm talking about? Right—the one against Her, on behalf of everyone who never had their prayers answered.

In fact, I thought that's why She was there, and I figured I might as well just bend over and kiss my *toches* goodbye, if you know what I mean? The wrath of Her—I mean—the vengeful *You-Know-Who*—and all that . . .

But you know what, She wasn't—so I didn't.

She—*You-Know-Who*—the Rabbit—looked me square in the face. I don't really remember it all too clearly because I couldn't keep from staring at Her red eyes and Her blue nose, but I do remember Her saying, "A miss is as good as a mile."

I nodded a lot after that. What else do you do when you don't know what the hell She's talking about.?

She said She knew a leopard couldn't change his spots after meeting Her, so She didn't expect much from me. I nodded some more, but I tell you one thing, I knew enough to put Bengay on right after She left, so I wouldn't have a stiff neck in the morning.

She did say I had another thing coming if I thought She was going to show up in court as a chicken, a deer, or even a rabbit. I nodded some more and thought maybe I should drop the lawsuit because maybe She was telling me She was going to come as the Terminator and terminate my *toches*.

She said She liked coming to my condo, and I shouldn't be surprised if She came a lot more, but I shouldn't get the idea I was the only one She knew with a nice ocean view.

I asked Her if She knew about my new TV show, "The 9,999 Club," and She said She'd seen the bus ads, but Her cable was out, so She hadn't seen it yet. She said She was surprised by how many people joined "The 9,999 Club," since filing 9,999 lawsuits can give you carpal tunnel syndrome.

Once I showed Her the Cafferty File Poll numbers, I could see how quickly She processes information and that she saw for Herself, if you want to keep ahead of the daily increases in taxes, tuition, and toiletries, not to mention $1,500 designer jeans with or without holes, you had to supplement your income with money from frivolous lawsuits.

Come on, everyone knows wages don't cut it, not even if you got married and thought sending the wife out to work would do it. Oh sure, marriage is always good if you can get her family to help out, but that's not an automatic gimme anymore. And forget about you holding two jobs—unless you don't care of about never sleeping again. Sure, if you keep your kids living in the house until they die, that helps, as long as you keep them from ordering takeout and forget about feeding their friends and love puppies—unless they're investment bankers, which is every parent's dream girl.

Nope—plain and simple, you want to supplement your income, you play poker online with somebody more unlucky then you; grow marijuana, but don't get high on your own supply; or sue someone, early and often—and let me tell you from learning it the hard way, only one of those three works long-term.

I was lucky I had some salad left over from eating out at Denny's the night before, because She wanted something to nosh on with the Diet Carrot Snapple She'd first made me warm up in the sun because She said cold drinks made Her tummy hurt.

She gave me one of Her funny looks again, and I just shook my head and said, "What?"

She kept looking at me, and I said, "WHAT—WHAT?"

She can get you so crazy sometimes, you just want to tear your hair out. Am I right, or am I right?

Then She says, "*That's all folks*," and I swear, if you closed your eyes you thought it was, you know—not *You-Know-Who*, but the other *You-Know-Who*.

OK, that was yesterday, and today is today, and maybe I'm thinking I won't sue Her, because even a leopard who won't change his spots can see Her in a new light and in a new way, and I'm not saying that because She may be the Terminator, but because She's back—as a chicken—*again* . . .

I just think maybe I'm going to kick back a little and be more, you know, selective. I'm also looking at this from a public-relations angle. How is going to look me suing *You-Know-Who*, when She's over my place a few days a week, eating my food, drinking my Snapple, and using up my cell phone minutes. I know, I'm going to probably disappoint a lot of people, including members of my own family, but there'll be other lawsuits.

Don't think I haven't lost sleep over this, but just the other day, when I was out on my balcony watching Hurricane Rita send that '06 750 Beemer flying by, I thought, *Even at nineteen floors up, that car really looks nice in black . . . but then black cars always look great after a good wash.*

And you know what else? That made me think of all the things I've been missing, and maybe I should be spending more of my time watching cars fly by, instead of being cooped up inside a courtroom all the time.

Don't get me wrong, I got, maybe two hundred other lawsuits I'm not dropping so fast; and I'm not giving up my "The 9,999 Club" and disappointing the thousands of nice people from the Midwest who are driving their RVs down just to be in the studio audience. I mean, you know what kind of a bookkeeping nightmare returning money orders can be, and that's if the Bank of Belize would even do that. Besides, who keeps receipts?

I should also mention it cost me plenty to buy SeaWorld, and do you think it's cheap getting someone to get porpoises to jump off the high dive wearing judges' robes?

All I can say to you, and anyone else who wants me dead, is come down to South Beach and sit on the terrace with me, and see how I am with Her. Of course, I can't promise you'll be able to see Her, but the invitation is there. I don't say come right away, because we got some more storms headed this way, but right after all the power is restored, and they bury all the bodies—come.

Trust me, I'll get you into the show—front seats, so you'll get splashed good by the porpoises—and I'll make sure you'll have a nice

Escalade to share. Know what else? I'll get Uncle Maxie to come by and say hello. We can all go over to Joe's Stone Crab, and I guarantee it'll be fun, because you never know who Uncle Maxie will *think* he sees there.

Anyway, I'm not going to beg. So, before I say goodbye, I want to tell you She shows up this morning and makes a big deal out of not wanting eggs because it won't look right. I don't know who's looking because I'm not expecting anyone, except maybe the handyman, but that's after 12:00 a.m., if the bitch-bastard *mamzer* shows up at all.

I should also mention She's got *shpilkes*, and She can't sit still. You should have seen Her, walking back and forth, back and forth. I told Her I could make Her decaf, but She wanted a triple espresso I had to send out for because I don't know how to work the *farkakte* espresso machine Clarice and Cheryl sent me for my birthday last year.

Thank Her, it didn't rain, because I don't know about you, but I don't want no chicken walking on my white rugs, maybe doing Her business, if you know what I mean—even if She's *You-Know-Who*.

Anyhow, She asked me if I liked Her as a chicken, or if I liked the rabbit better. She didn't bring up the Pekinese, or the deer, so I didn't mention them either. I said I liked them all, but if I had a choice, I'd pick the chicken. I said that because She was a chicken right then. Naturally, if She were the rabbit, I would have said *rabbit*.

I asked Her if She wanted sunscreen, like the other day. She looked at me like I was crazy, but I told Her, sure it was cloudy, but you still could get a burn.

Suddenly, it came to me like a shot—I should shut my mouth, because what if She's a chicken because the rabbit's got a burn, because I missed a spot? You got to think of these things, especially when you're dealing with someone who knows Her way around a lawsuit just as good as you.

Thank Her again, because the sun broke through the clouds, and She said, A little on Her beak would be good—just make sure I didn't get any in Her eyes.

I made toast with Brummel & Brown, and it wasn't until She ate it I told Her it wasn't butter, but yogurt. She made me show Her the container, that's how surprised She was.

She had only half the espresso. She said it was giving Her a little of the reflux, which happens when She's a chicken, so She suddenly turned into the rabbit. She was having trouble getting Her tongue into the demitasse, so I poured it all into the saucer, and She sipped it up, quick as can be.

Love,
Uncle Abe

From: TenderlyThroughMySupremeBanker@MySupremeBanker.him
Date: Wednesday, September 21, 2005, 9:49 a.m.
To: US@Ourmail.us
Subject: Are you going to take it lying down, or what?

Hello and happy holidays to my loving family!

May My Supreme Banker, known by many names and different faces, bring you all love, peace, and harmony, and remind you we are all connected by credit-card debt.

I have so, *so* much to say I almost don't know where to begin.

You might want to pee first, or get yourself a cold one, because once I start, it'll be hard to stop.

I won't open by saying I told you so, because I know how difficult it is for humans to change their ways, even though I warned you all—*over*—*and over*—*and over*—that hurricanes, tsunamis, tornadoes, flash floods, and pandemic pestilence were coming soon to a neighborhood near you.

Arlene (Jun 8-13), Bret (Jun 28-29), Cindy (Jul 3-7), Dennis (Jul 4-12), Emily (Jul 11-21), Franklin (Jul 21-29), Gert (Jul 23-25), Harvey (Aug3-8), Irene (Aug 7-18), José (Aug 22-23), Katrina (Aug 23-30), Lee (Aug 31-Sep 1), María (Sep 2-10), Nate (Sep 5-10), Ophelia (Sept 7-18), Phillipe (Sep 17-TBD), and Rita (Sept 18-TBD) . . .

How many more *dead* members of the Family Ginsburg (*pronounced* Du Pont) are to be named hurricanes this year before *living* members of the Family Ginsburg (*pronounced* Du Pont) get the hint?

Do you think it was easy for me to wash my entire body seven times a day with boric acid until it was so raw I looked like a maraschino cherry on steroids? What about eating food only from the movie *Soylent Green*? And this is coming from someone who couldn't go a day without Goldenberg's Chews and a glass of Bosco.

If you think I enjoy living in the Andes without my Humvee, well—think again. I can't begin to tell you what joy that three-ton camo-covered beauty gave me, especially when I rumbled up to the nail salon and watched all the screaming Koreans run hysterically out the door.

Giving up the easy life isn't easy. In the modern world, snow on your screen just means dialing your cable company. Up in the Andes, it's another matter. Blessed be My Supreme Banker for supplying the Freeman Water Suit, for it has a built-in oxygen tank, so necessary for survival, because once you've been buried in an avalanche it can take upwards of a month to dig yourself out.

Finally, for someone who's never missed a Beyoncé concert—well—I just won't go there right now because it's just too painful and I don't have any more tears to shed.

Dear Family Ginsburg (*pronounced* Du Pont), if you're reading this, that means you're still alive, or at least temporarily off your meds, so I beg you, I *plead* with you—it's not too late to join me up here in the Andes, or to head for your own refuge.

I have attached a list of safe havens, but every day choice pieces of mountain-peak real estate is going into the hands of greedy speculators who think this is the next economic bubble, or location for a reality TV series. I suggest you access your End of Days Last Alert Wristband and Heart Defibrillator for hourly updates.

Even as we speak, I am being informed unless you marry an Australian or have had a baby out of wedlock with *Crocodile Dundee*, the Blue Mountains are off limits.

People are always saying, "Tenderly, I know the world is going to hell in a handbasket, and I should go down to the basement with my family and drink a Jimmy Jones Kool-Aid cocktail, but it's holiday time and I want to go on vacation. Can you help me? P.S. I always heard that Paris at Christmas time is so, *so* romantic."

It's this kind of adventurous spirit that makes *us* great shoppers, and *me* proud to be an American. However, if you want to go to *Gay Paree* you're a century late and a euro short. The City Of Lights has gone dark, thanks to a newly discovered tear in the ozone layer located directly above the Eiffel Tower.

According to CountdownToTheEnd.com, the increased amounts of chlorofluorocarbon have turned the Eiffel Tower into a super ionic breeze air purifier. Millionaires directly related to Louis XIV are immune; however, those who speak enough French not to be laughed at, found a working cell site in the last ten minutes, or bought something from a Sharper Image catalogue in the last year are asked to seek medical attention immediately. All others are asked to bend over and kiss their *derrière au revoir.*

It has also come to my attention that lupus is rampant amongst anyone returning from a stroll along the *Champs-Elysées*. Obviously, the French police, like New York's Finest, are unable to stop the proliferation of fake Louis Vuitton designer bags, and whether we want to accept it or not, the lupus pandemic is already decimating a generation of savvy shoppers.

Under ordinary circumstances, Venice would be my next choice, but because of Hurricane Katrina, anyone who has watched more than twenty hours of CNN coverage is liable to suffer serious psychotic episodes when surrounded by that much water.

A little closer to home, Puerto Rico has always been a favorite holiday getaway of mine and still is. The pluses of course are the wonderfully friendly, fun-loving people, the terrific weather, and the close proximity to Miami Heart Hospital.

The chance of contracting the Black Death from sand fleas are nonexistent, however, I would stay off the beach after dark when traveling circus performers are believed to conduct sybaritic rituals using circus fleas.

I don't know about you, but when I think of Puerto Rico, I also think of those huge cruise ships, and again, many of you have asked me, "Tenderly, are cruise ships safe, or will crew members rape and murder me?" No, no, and *no*! You are more likely to be raped and murdered by a family member or a bipolar polar bear than somebody who works on a cruise ship.

If you have already bought cruisewear and have booked your cabin, stay away from all dairy products, eat only the fish of the day (if you saw it caught by a New England fisherman), and eat as much salt as possible for salt is the natural enemy of botulism.

I suggest plenty of McDonald's French fries, but make sure they never leave your sight from the time you bought them to the time you disembark.

If you're thinking of a road trip, perhaps to a romantic bed and breakfast, make sure you go to DeathByDriving.com for the latest info on where and when automobiles are more likely to self-immolate.

Like human beings, holiday time brings severe depression, and the family car is not immune to self-destructive behavior. Fender benders, inferior gasoline, being manufactured in Detroit on a Friday, no Sirius Radio reception—these are just some of the factors that cause a car to suddenly burst into flames at Christmas time.

I guess what I'm saying is—if you're determined to get away for the holidays, I advise you to head for the highest hills and get a jump on the rest of humanity before it's too late. And let me tell you, once Oprah picks mountain peaks as one of her favorite holiday gifts, you'll have no choice but to remain in low-lying areas, and be killed by Earth's deadliest of diseases that every second are rising to the surface to destroy us.

For those of you holding out the hope the polar ice caps will melt and cause massive tidal flooding that will sweep away all disease and pestilence, I have only five words for you—*your boat ain't big enough.*

I know some of you have asked if this is Earth's way of getting even with humans for building strip malls but, I для одного, on the eve of the holiest of holidays, do not want to get my feet wet in that moral cesspool.

My Supreme Banker didn't make me his media rep, and soon-to-be his exclusive sports agent, simply to bring ill tidings to my family when—as My Supreme Banker teaches—*what we need most is more credit-card Debt with a capital D.*

Before I talk about other holiday choices, I do want to warn you about toys that kill. SaveMyWorthlessAss.com, the worldwide nuclear reactor watchdog site, is posting the names of over 500 toys capable of blowing up large sections of a small city.

I know you know about battery leakage and what it does to your bones once it burns through your skin. You must impress upon your boy children that "batteries not included" is a good thing, and if they just push and scream *WHOOSH,* they can make a car zoom around a room at the speed of light. As for your little girls, I for one am tired of hearing Barbie telling me she needs to take a crap.

WhatJewsEatOnXmas.com lists restaurants serving pork specials, and in the spirit of ecumenical love, the Ginsburg Family (*pronounced* Du Pont) should warn our friends of the Christian faith to be on the lookout for people who have read *The Da Vinci Code* and want to sell you Yule logs that are not 100% virgin wood.

I have only one more word to say on the subject of holiday awareness: FRUITCAKE!

As you are well aware if you've read *They'll Have To Kill Me If They Want Me to Die,* by Jack LaLanne, you know within the fruitcake (the older the better) lie a myriad of remedies, from curing the common cold to sustaining an erection until she cries for mercy, even if you wear Depends.

Speaking of longevity, pick up a copy of *Autopsy Today*— their end-of-the-year issue is, as usual, a killer. This year's main article, "Death by New-Car Smell," features the most extraordinary Morgan Freeman photos, and we all know what a genius he is around the morgue. For those of you who don't see the magazine at your medical examiner's office, you can get single copies or a subscription at AutopsyToday.com/subscribe.html .

As you know, this is a site I can't live without. In fact, if you're at your computer now, or wearing your End of Days Last Alert Wristband and Heart Defibrillator, you'll see my burning-bush icon alerting you to the image I just sent that I pulled off their site showing several people leaving the Eiffel Tower, their hair ablaze and their skin bluish in the afternoon sun. It is an absolutely incredible photo, and one I'm thinking of using as a screensaver.

As the voice through which My Supreme Banker speaks, He does want you to see the glass as half full. He points to all the many

Ginsburgs (*pronounced* Du Ponts) who gave both time and money to aid tsunami victims, in particular to businesses we own in Dubai. He gives a special shout-out to those Family Ginsburgs (*pronounced* Du Ponts) who hurried off to areas devastated by hurricanes, risking life and limb so they could hug Anderson Cooper. Unfortunately, there is nothing anyone can do to reverse the fact that your hair turned gray.

Finally, I salute those Family Ginsburgs (*pronounced* Du Ponts) who took advantage of the George Foreman rebates and purchased his grill before the first of the year. As you know, My Supreme Banker, through George Foreman, is battling against time to get Americans to grill more, for it is only through grill-awareness we can save the planet.

Love from My Supreme Banker through Tenderly

P.S. When the time is right, I'd like to explain why the heart is a lonely hunter.

From: Lulu-LuCrawford@PleasureIsWhereYouFindIt.org
Date: Wednesday, September 21, 2005, 10:49 a.m.
To: Bubbeh.E@Ourmail.us
Cc: US@Ourmail.us
Subject: I seen the white light and it seen me!

Well, B. E., I, like, sure as hell ain't ever seen storms like this, and if I never see nothin' like it again in my earthly lifetime, that'll be too soon, lemme tell you. B.E., I, like, never been too religious—what with church folks not takin' too kindly to those of us with two different-colored eyes—but, like, that don't make no nevermind now when death was starin' me in the face, and me with no bars on my cell, and my End of Days Wristband and Heart Defibrillator lost in the woods someplace.

I was, like, halfway up into the hills to see the folks, when ole Becky Mountain Road was, like, washed away, and what with me with it. I seen a movie once where, like, a car went off the mountain, and turned over, like, a dozen times, and no matter how many times I rewound the tape, the car always burned up and all. That's a fact, and you know what else? The two in the car, the convict tryin' to go straight and his pure-as-the-driven-snow girl always get themselves fried up crispier than Aunt Aspellina's Fourth o' July Fire Cracker Chicken Tenders—she's got my eyes, so I know we're kin. Pay for your sins, I say—you pay for your sins...

Anywho, I tell you another thing, tradin' in the pink T-Bird was the smartest thing, 'cause goddamn it, like, nobody can save your hiney like those German SUVs.

I always, like, have my seatbelt on since Uncle Fructose Varicose—he's got my eyes, so I know we're kin—went through the windshield and got his head, like, decapitated and eaten up by bears. Yep, that's the story townsfolk tell, cross my heart and hope to die. Still—since that was the day a the nuclear explosion—nobody actually saw he'd, like, gone headless. Me—don't see how bears be dumb enough to come to town what with the radioactivity in the air and all.

B. E., my gut says if anyone ate Uncle Fructose's head it more likely be one a the People's Girls—Two Peoples, or her older sister, Four, would be my guess. I used to walk to school with Four Peoples, but, like, she was quiet and all, and never took off her muzzle, even when she drank from the water fountain. Two Peoples hardly-used roads, so you'd never seen her 'til you were, like, sittin' in class, and she'd be, like, comin' through a window. Four Peoples used to sit in the front row 'cause she had somethin' matter with her eyes, but Two, she be, like, pacin' back and forth, back and forth, and I tell you what, you never looked back there and stared, 'cause if you did, she'd be waitin' for you out in the woods like she did with Little Billy Missing Two Fingers.

Funny how you remember things like that, huh? You know what else I recollect? Right from first grade on, Two was real good at doin' numbers in her head, and, like, if she had a mind to, could spat out the formula for the rocket fuel they made down at the plant, or. like, give you the odds for any hog fight in the county. On the other hand, her sister Four, could really, like, sew up a storm, so you knew she'd be the one to clean up after Two.

When I was, like, rode outta town on a rail after being tarred and feathered by everyone wasn't kin, Two and Four were the ones, like, found me, patched me up, gave me some clothes and the twenty-five thou in cash, and kept me goin' 'til I met Bermuda at the ladies' bar in Chelsea.

B. E., it just goes to show you, like, never know what peoples are really like 'til the shit hits the fan, which man alive it did big time when ole Becky Mountain Road, like, washed out, and I, like, slid down the mountain like I was a greased hog at a water slide.

B. E., you know they say your entire life, like, flashes right before your eyes—well—that's a fact. See—just before the lights went out in my brand-new mechanical head, yours truly remembered every single hand job, lick, fuck, and blow job clear as day—like it just happened—and you know what else I remembered? Exactly *who* paid me *what*—and *when*. That's another fact. Was that, like, weird, or what?

Funny, like, just before I crashed down that ole mountain, I was thinkin' how fun it was drivin' with my new mechanical head 'cause, like, it has its own navigational system, and, like, I could upload stuff like satellite images offa MapQuest. Stuff I couldn't do in the Benz all 'cause of some silly NATO gripe they got against the Germans. And, like, the T-Bird didn't even have anythin' 'cept ole greased-up gas-station maps.

B. E., things are sure different now 'cause, like, no matter what car I'm drivin'—even a rental, or say I'm walkin'—no matter how thick and black the smoke, I know exactly where I'm goin' in Hogs Breath 'cause my mechanical head, like, always gives me a heads-up. Get my meaning, B. E.?

Sure, last month folks, like, caught a break, used the fires from the plant, but that's, like, hit or miss, 'cause you'll have explosions for, like, a few days, then, like, nothin' for a week, plus no tellin' how the wind can change and really mess you up.

I didn't want to, like, ruffle the Finest Doctor's feathers, like after all he's given me my mechanical head,—go complain about anythin'—especially about Nurse Miss Sweden who took care of my hair real well after the operation. Guess if I never had a Benz maybe I wouldn't know any better, but gee, after you, like, hear their navigational system talk to you, you just can't, like, listen to no one else without gettin' a little lovesick, you know what I mean?

The Finest Doctor has a SL65 AMG and a 500 SUV AMG like the one I totaled, so he knows what I'm sayin'; and between you and me, he's got a bit of a hard-on for her, too—so I guess he won't mind me bitchin' a little like I'm doin'.

You see, the Finest Doctor did, like, some investigatin' and discovered Mercedes got her wrapped up so she can't use her voice, even if it's not in a navigation system, and in say, like, someone's mechanical head. B. E., that's, like, so unfair, ain't it?

And B. E., lemme tell you the Finest Doctor was doin' all this research 'cause he knows his mechanical heads would be so much better usin' *her* voice, like, instead of Nurse Miss Sweden, who sounds a little like my Uncle Mental—he's got my eyes, so I know we're kin—who gets to sing-songin' when the still fumes backs up on'em.

B. E., I was gonna ask you to see if you do somethin' 'bout it 'cause I know if you don't own it, you knows who does 'cause you people, like, own everythin' but—listen to this—like, the Finest Doctor *actually talked to Miss Benz about me,* and she says I sound really interestin' and would like to meet me, but first *Schneeflocke*—that's her name in German . . . it means, like, snowflake—needs a little time to get over her last relationship—some jerk from Düsseldorf who was, like, real bad at takin' directions.

Gettin' back to my little misfortune, what saved me was, like, the lightnin' strike caused the air bags to smack my head, and, like, knocked me silly.

Anywho, I'm gettin' a little ahead of myself like I normally do 'cause a my chemical imbalance, but there's just so much to tell—like how my pet hog, Noodle-May, saved my life.

Who would have thought Miss Tenderly's contraption worked in, like, animals, but hogs are smarter than most people I know, so Noodle-May had no trouble usin' the Vital Signs Telemetry Feature in her End of Days Last Alert Animal Wristband and Defibrillator that, like, started up the resuscitation life-support gizmo and, like, got me outta there—otherwise, she'd a had to do her hog's breath on me in combo with Jaws A Life to get me outta there, like, before the Benz exploded.

Course, I didn't see any of this stuff, but when she, like, showed me how the movie playback worked, I could' a kicked myself in the butt 'cause if I, like, read the directions, I coulda, like, used my End of Days Last Alert Wristband and Defibrillator and got the whole crash.

The first thing I remember is, like, somethin' whackin' me in the face, and I'm thinkin' it's Bermuda, and she's bitch-smackin' me 'cause, like, I won't whip her bee-hind, so I'm yellin': "Take off the fuckin' mask and maybe I can see your ugly ass!"

Jumpin' Jiminy Cricket, how can you, like, whip somethin' you can't see—right B. E.?

Then, like, I see it ain't Bermuda 'cause the second time it happened,

I, like, seen the lightnin' comin' right outta the sky and head straight for me. I remember thinkin' this ain't no dream, and, like, I better move my head before I get blown up but—*WHACK, SMACK AND SIZZLE*—and suddenly Noodle-May's, like, peein' all over me, and I don't smell fire no more, and then, like, I hear, "*Go two blocks, make a right, and then another left,*" and, like, I turned my head, and there she was—*Schneeflocke*—my *Snowflake*—the voice of my Mercedes Navigational System, blonde, blue eyes, and sweet as a German Mechanical Lady Angel can be when she's a smellin' like hog's breath, and I'm smellin' like pee.

Well, B. E., that brings us up to date, and as of this moment, with me, like, pegged up against a tree by a lightnin' bolt stuck through my head, waitin' for Noodle-May to, like, wash her hooves. I figure it's been, like, two days, but I think they got their act together, at least that's what the Finest Doctor says, only it ain't easy to, like, hear him 'cause the sound quality in the Talk-You-Through-It-Self-Surgery-Module of End of Days Last Alert Wristband and Defibrillator is, like, for shit.

B. E., don't you cry for me, Alabama, 'cause if anyone can pull this here lightnin' bolt outta Miss Lulu-Lu Crawford's brain, rewire, and then do, like, a virus scan on my frontal lobe circuits without a DSL connection, it's the hog I saved from drownin'.

Love you like the mama I ain't had . . .

Respectfully yours,

Miss Lulu-Lu Crawford (*pronounced* the way it looks), via Voicemail. Module of End of Days Last Alert Animal Wristband and Defibrillator

P.S. I was, like, countin' on Four Peoples to do the stitchin' up, but she's a glowin' so bad nobody can get close without, like, goin' blind.

P.P.S. To Tenderly:

Noodle-May, like, just wants to inform you she ain't mad at you for, like, shootin' your End of Days Last Alert Animal Wristband and Defibrillator from the helicopter down into her ass, 'seein' it hurt like fuckin' hell, and say hey—you think we're all, like, double-jointed, or you don't know a hog's ass from her wrist.

From: Clarice.G@Ourmail.us
Date: Wednesday, September 21, 2005, 10:51 a.m.
To: Cheryl.G@Ourmail.us
Subject: You ruined my life

What I can't f-ing believe—what I can't wrap my poor aching brain matter around is—the fact Neil Diamond saved your pathetically paralyzed ass!

Every time I played "Girl, You'll Be a Woman Soon," you stuck your fingers down your throat, locked yourself in the bathroom, and listened to the sound of your own throw-up.

Remember when I bought "Cherry Cherry," you tried to stab me with your f-ing protractor? To this day, I don't know what made me turn around in time.

What about "I Thank the Lord for the Night Time"? You probably don't remember because you told everyone you were sleepwalking, but I've never heard of a sleepwalker trying to take out her sister's eyes with an f-ing can opener.

Maybe it wasn't Neil Diamond who put your tits in a ringer, but the fact is it was me, Clarice, your younger sister, who wrote the songs that make the whole world sing.

Can you please explain to me why my songwriting talent made you so jealous when you, you precocious bitch, were so f-ing great at everything? When you were three, you could translate the *New York Times* into *lingua Latina,* and me . . . when I got to be three, still couldn't ask for a cup of water without people tickling me under my chin and saying, *"Goo goo, goo goo."*

Do you remember when I was eight, and Mommy and Daddy rushed me to the neurologist all crazy and everything, thinking I was brain damaged just because I couldn't thread a needle without jabbing myself in the check? You know, don't you, it was your fault—*yes, it was*—*you only-child wannabe,* making those f-ing ten-foot origami title cards while acting out the f-ing *Teahouse of the August Moon* in Japanese—they put those f-ing electrodes in my f-ing cerebellum?

Thank Goddess, Bubbeh Esther (*pronounced* Granny Smith Apples) pulled them out before any real damage was done. Bubbeh Esther (*pronounced* Granny Smith Apples)—she was the only one who saw my songwriting talents, and it was she who encouraged me to *dream the impossible dream.*

You were in Washington then, showing off your knack for forgery to the president. Bubbeh (*pronounced* Granny) was the one who arranged that, and you thought she would have gone with you, but she was selling Tin Pan Alley and had to be in New York that day for the closing.

Bad luck for you. Good luck for me.

I remember the events as if it were yesterday. Do you?

It was just a few weeks after Bubbeh (*pronounced* Granny), using the magic magnets she wore around her ankles, pulled the electrodes out of my head. It was a glorious day for me when my protector came by the apartment to take off my bandages and undo my restraints and then had the brilliant idea I needed to get out of the house for a little fresh air. It was also her idea we should walk to the closing, because that would be the very thing to get the circulation going again in my paralyzed limbs.

So, off we went to the Brill Building. The closing was in an office that once belonged to Irving Berlin. We took the elevator up to the twenty-fifth floor, and as we walked along the narrow corridor toward our destination, I could hear people singing and playing the piano. Bubbeh (*pronounced* Granny) explained that all the best songwriters of the day hung out there, and she promised she'd tell me how when she wasn't seeing Irving, she and Ira came up with *Porgy and Bess.*

When we got to Irving's old office, she took me over to the piano and began playing "Swanee River." It was only later, when she was playing "Goddess Bless America," and I was backing her up on the conga, that she recalled the time Irving and she wrote the tune during one of their lovemaking romps on the Cyclone at Coney Island.

It was there, at Irving's old Steinway, that I had a musical epiphany and instinctively knew I needed only two chords to write a hit rock-and-roll song.

When you came back from Washington, Mommy and Daddy didn't pay much attention to me when I played some of my songs, although they did look strangely at each other when I pounded out "Why Do Fools Fall in Love?"

No—all Mommy and Daddy could do was rave on about how *you* sat down in the oval office and wrote out the entire Declaration of Independence, including the fifty-six John Hancocks in seventeen minutes flat, and how, when the President held them up side by side, not one member of Congress could tell the copy from the original.

But *you*—older sister—*you* noticed "Heartbreak Hotel," plus the five hundred other tunes tacked to the walls that I'd written that day, didn't you? Nothing got by your jealous scene-stealer eyes, did they? No—my talents, meager and measly as they were, pissed you off royally, and you just couldn't wait to get even, could you? *Only-child wannabe!*

Oh—I know it was you, big sister Cheryl, who forged the love letter to The Elephant Man and signed it Bubbeh Esther (*pronounced* Granny Smith Apples). And then, when he wrote her back, you so cleverly left a series of clues leading Bubbeh (*pronounced* Granny) to search behind my life-size Paul Anka poster, where she could discover what you placed there, and what the ASPCA Crime Lab determined were the *rough drafts* of said love letter.

Oh right, Bubbeh Esther (*pronounced* Granny Smith Apples) soon forgot what she called *my menstruating mischief*, but our relationship was never the same after that, and you soon replaced me as her favorite. That was your plan all along, wasn't it? *Only-child wannabe from hell!*

I wrote "Breaking Up is Hard to Do"—then buried my woes by writing the twelve tunes that made Neil's first LP go gold. I guess if Neil played the guitar instead of the piano, he might have come to your rescue, too, huh? I supposed that's his gift and your tragedy.

For my sixteenth birthday, you made a five-foot cake out of my melted gold records. Oh, I know everyone blamed Cousin Sylvia, but she loved Sam Cooke in a very unhealthy teenage way and could never have set fire and melted my records on the wall, or done anything to hurt her cousin, the composer of her two most favorite songs in the world— "Chain Gang" and "You Send Me."

When I was seventeen, you hatched one of your more insane plots against me when you grabbed Carole King outside the Brill Building. You thought Carole was my biggest rival, and if you offered her a *Strangers on the Train* murder deal, she'd jump at the chance to destroy my career.

What you didn't know, because you never cared to send the very best, was that Carole and I bonded when the movement of the earth under our feet caused us to simultaneously jump off the subway grading.

Do you remember the time I was voted into The Songwriters Hall Of Fame for being the only songwriter in history to write all one hundred of *Billboard's Hot 100* songs—three consecutive months in a row? Huh ... HUH ... HUH ... ?

So, what did you do? You—*you*, jealous *only-child wannabe*—forged twenty thousand, phony, pissed-off listeners' letters and sent them to Cousin Bruce, all demanding he stop playing my songs because when you played them backwards, they all sounded like Laurence Welk was telling them to have sex with their fathers.

It just so happened I was at the station that day, helping the engineers rewire the control room, otherwise, I wouldn't have been able to divert the mailbags over to the Staten Island Landfill.

So, why is it I'm the one feeling guilty, mixing Fiorinals and Saki and singing "We Are F-ing Family" until the wasabi kicks in, and I collapse?

You've had six failed marriages and hundreds of encounters of the worst kind, and I'm saying to myself ... would things have turned out so *Lamborghiniesque* if I had made *you* memorize the lyrics to my *relationship* songs?

Then I ask myself—what if I had acknowledged the possibility, remote that it was, that in fact *you were the reincarnation of Anastasia* and were actually suffering from *Royal Family Massacre Syndrome* some eighty-seven years and one continent away later? Would I have still thrown up at the sight of blennies, or joined your frightened silly ass in your closet when the shooting started?

Then, there are the pods in the closet—not that I believe that's where the manicurists at Princess Leia Nails come from—even though they all look like Dana Wynter.

I guess what I'm trying to say is—now that you're back on your feet—you should choose your weapons and meet me over at Shirley's Sister's Ex-Mother-in-Law's Market for some unfinished sibling ribaldry.

Time to rumble in the jungle!

Love,

your sister, Clarice

From: Maxie.Ruthie.4Ever@Ourmail.us
Date: Wednesday, September 21, 2005, 2:00 p.m.
To: US@Ourmail.us
Subject: Better than ever!

Hi, everybody!

I just got a nice new pair of gray slacks at Urban Outfitters—size 32! I've been a 32 since I was twenty. Can you imagine? *Emes!* No bullshit!

I was over there getting a cyst taken out of my *toches* and I said to myself, *Maxie, buy yourself something . . . you deserve something nice today.*

They got Hurricane Rita sales on all windbreakers and rain hats. On top of that, I get the Dr. Green Surgical Cyst Discount, so my clothing co-pay is like almost nothing. Can you imagine? *Emes!* No bullshit!

I wanted the windbreaker in green, but they went during the Hurricane Katrina sale. I almost didn't get anything, but when I put on the yellow hat everybody came over and wanted my autograph. They said I looked like the guy from "Gilligan's Island." Can you imagine? *Emes!* No bullshit!

You could hear the *farkakte* wind blowing and blowing and the fire alarms kept going off, but everyone was too busy looking through the racks because this was some sale. The only time someone looked up was if they heard their car alarm go off, but that didn't happen too much because most of us were driving Mercedes, and they don't go off unless somebody without money goes near them. Can you imagine? *Emes!* No bullshit!

So, the wind is blowing, and then this woman came running in, all *farblondzhet*, yelling, "Rita just blew the roof off the Cineplex. . . Rita just blew the roof off the Cineplex!"

Suddenly, a sales guy started singing and dancing, *"Lovely Rita, meter maid, where would I be without you?"* You know that *cockamamie* Beatles' song?

My ass felt OK, just a little sore if you touched it, so you weren't gonna catch me dancing and having somebody touch my *toches*, but when the sales guy (who was also the nurse who gave me the anesthetic in the operating room) grabbed me and spun me around, well—I showed him how the Brooklyn Boys from Bushwick danced the Lindy.

I had on a pair of nice white Bermuda shorts I got over at Old Navy. I picked them up the last time I saw Dr. Green. They were $28.50, but with The Dr. Green Annual Checkup Discount, my copay was something like $18.20. Can you imagine? *Emes!* No bullshit!

I was wearing them because they were a little big in the backside, and when I called for an appointment, his Cyst Hostess said that's what I should wear on account of the bandages were really bulky. She also told me to bring a pillow for my car. I told her the seats in the 2005 500 SL were 12-way adjustable, and it was like sitting on air. She said she had the same exact model, and I should bring a pillow anyway.

I think I mentioned her before? Miss Universe 2003? She's Cuban, or maybe Swedish. You know, the one who hands out the Polo for Men over at Bloomingdales? That's where Dr. Green does all his cysts. I only went over to Urban Outfitters because they didn't have any slacks in my size at the Polo shop. Everything was picked cleaned during Katrina except his cashmere socks, because they never go on sale.

You know, Ralph was gonna buy the penthouse in my South West Tower, B Line, but then he bought himself an island, maybe Jamaica; no—Bubbeh Esther (*pronounced* Granny Smith Apples) bought that, didn't she?

I see him all the time over at Joe's Stone Crab, and I always say, "Ralph, remember me—Maxie—from the time we met at the dance at the B'nai Jeshurum on Friday night, May 25, 1957—and you were with Fifi Rice, and I was with Carole Jacobs?"

He's always giving me his card and telling me to call his office, and they'd give me a list of the sale dates—but you think he'd put the socks on sale, even after I told him how much I love the purple ones?

What—it'll kill him to give me a discount? It's all the Ferraris he owns. It's made him *meshugeh ahf toit!*

You can't believe how many people were at the mall today. I think they all figured Rita was gonna keep everyone inside and there wouldn't be much of a wait at the doctors' offices.

I figured that, too, but what I didn't figure was that Dr. Green would be late for my surgery because he couldn't get off of Star Island because the bridge was blocked by those nuts, you know—what do they call them . . . *paparazzi* . . . yeah, *paparazzi*. They were taking pictures of Rosie O'Donnell. Can you imagine? *Emes!* No bullshit!

She was showing her kid how to wave at the passengers on the cruise ship that just capsized across the causeway in the Port of Miami. Maybe you read about it? At first I thought, it's the Going Overboard Cruise Lines, and they're killing everyone, but then I remembered they got to be a hundred miles off shore before they knock anyone off.

Anyway, when I got the news he was running late. Danka, the hostess, said I had three options: I could reschedule. I could wait for Dr Green, but there were three cysts ahead of me, so that could be all day. Or, I could have one his associates do it. I need to wait like I needed a *luch in kup* but then guess what—Dr. Green called. Can you imagine? *Emes!* No bullshit!

She put him on the phone, and he told me, "Maxie, don't worry, you're gonna get Dr. Trujillo-Trujillo (*pronounced* Steinberg-Steinberg), who just so happens to be the Fox News Cyst Doctor." Can you imagine? *Emes!* No bullshit!

When I got home, I looked him up on the computer, and you know what—he owns a four-bedroom in the condo I just built on 46th Ave. Eighteenth floor, A Line, South West Tower of the Ginsburg (*pronounced* Du Pont) South Beach Emerald Green Towers. Can you imagine? *Emes!* No bullshit!

I thought I recognized him from when he came over to my apartment and paid in cash, but then I said to myself, *Maxie, it was probably just a dream because you know they stick a needle in your arm and shoot you full of drugs and one Trujillo-Trujillo (pronounced*

Steinberg-Steinberg) looks like the next, but now, I'm sure it was him—telling me none of the bills were in consecutive order, and how he was thinking he'd like to buy another apartment for his parents if they could be on the same line and he could pay in Krugerrands.

Remind me, I got to call the rental office.

I think I got my cyst from the colonoscopy because, I remembered afterwards, I had such an itch. I was scratching so bad, my *toches* looked like a strawberry. Can you imagine? *Emes!* No Bullshit!

I almost missed the Foot Locker sale, that's how bad it was, and I would have—only I started looking for a pharmacy for some baby cream, because I knew I wasn't gonna make it home, when I saw the nurse who took my blood when I went for my annual—and guess where he was working? You got it—Foot Locker! Can you imagine? *Emes! No bullshit!*

Right away I figured he'd know where I could find the baby cream. Listen to this, he tells me they were selling a foot cream he swears is great for ass itch. He's a body builder, so he knows what he's talking about. So then—he says how he remembers what a nice guy I was when he was taking my blood, so he's gonna slip me a few samples.

It was Dr. Green's Flavored Aerated Steroid Foot Gloss—you know the one Italy banned because a whole bunch of soccer players died from licking their toes?

He said my other choice was Barnes & Noble, up on the second floor, where they just put in a combination pharmacy and Starbucks Coffee Boutique.

I thought I was gonna jump out of my pants. Can you imagine? *Emes!* No bullshit! So I took the samples and went into the men's room.

That's when I saw how red my *toches* was. When I came out, I saw the sale. I was feeling a little better, so I sat down, and Brad, that was the nurse's name, he showed me the 500 Series in white: $170.50, but with the colonoscopy and Katrina discounts my co-pay was $57.50. Pretty good, right? That was the best co-pay up until this one.

You know down in South Florida, New Balance never goes on sale, so I bought two pairs. I have very wide feet, so I can't wear anything else. I don't think they look so wide, but Ruthie—may she rest in peace, *aleichem sholom*—used to make fun of them and called them "Clarabell feet." She should talk, what with those corns of hers, the bitch-bastard. You should have seen her feet yesterday. They looked liked goddamn flippers. It was the humidity. You know, from the hurricane. Everything on her swelled up. She looked like one of Macy's Thanksgiving Day balloons when she went off the terrace. I never saw a wave come twenty-five floors up like that except in the movies. Can you imagine? *Emes!* No bullshit!

The ropes, you know, that were supposed to hold her to the railing while I aired the place out, snapped like twigs, and off she went up over the side.

I happened to be inside at the time looking at "Law & Order"—you know, the one where Lenny is eating a pizza in the car—when I hear this *WHOOSH,* so I grabbed my cell phone and snapped off twenty or thirty shots of Ruthie—may she rest in peace, *aleichem sholom*—flying away, the Saran Wrap and the aluminum foil peeling right off like it was tissue paper.

In the pictures it looks like she's swimming, or maybe paddling, you know—like surfers when they get on top of a wave. I don't see how, because, Ruthie—may she rest in peace, *aleichem sholom*—couldn't surf.

The only thing I can think of is it must have been the grease from the chicken fat, because in the pictures you can see it pouring out of her body. That also got to be the reason she kept getting thinner and thinner as she went out to sea. She was speeding up, too. I never seen somebody paddle that fast. Can you imagine? *Emes!* No bullshit!

Before I knew it, a Coast Guard helicopter was flying over. One of those big orange things with white stripes! What great timing. I told them to drop my Mercedes right onto the terrace and I'd drive it into the spare bedroom and park it next to the Lamborghini. These guys are the best. I *shtup* them a thousand dollars a week, and they take my car out and bring it back up. Sure, I got to give them some notice, but that's not a problem.

Oh, did I tell you Lenny—I mean Jerry—Jerry Orbach's staying with me now? What a nice thing for the holidays. Can you imagine? *Emes!* No bullshit!

Love,
Uncle Maxie

From: Jules@JewelerToTheStars.us
Date: Wednesday, September 21, 2005, 2:00 p.m.
To: US@Ourmail.us
Subject: Laverne—share my joy!

Laverne, my sweet, creative and kindred spirit,

I've been up for nearly ninety-six straight hours, so please forgive me if I'm not making much sense. I have never before been a witness to such an outpouring of love for my work as I have these last two magical days. I believe The Jewelry Organ Giveback Katrina Flood Relief Telethon raised over ten million dollars for hurricane victims, and the phones are still ringing off the hook.

I don't know whom to thank first. I guess I should start with Condi, because she was the one who brought me the presidential pardon. When she and Madonna came into my cell, I thought I was hallucinating. I hadn't eaten since lunch and was still suffering from the after effects of the triple espresso I finished moments before. And strange as it seems, I was still having phantom neck pains from being hung.

Well—Condi said the president loved *The Pope's A-Poppin' Series*, something I already knew because he called me right after his private tour; however, we decided we'd get more donations if we kept that secret, and he pretended he was seeing it for the first time just like the TV audience at home.

Of course, I was disappointed to leave jail, because every day I stayed sold more show tickets; but when your president calls—you must answer, especially when it was *your* brilliant idea to be the one to personally show him how to open the Pope's stomach.

I also have to thank Brand Nubian, Spoonie Gee, and Carl Rove for being the first to sign up for the telethon. I don't believe there was a single one of my clients who didn't immediately volunteer to have their gold organ(s), orb(s), or limb(s) removed and tossed into the melting pot; and those with precious stones—my Goddess—they were literally knocking down my door to have me remove them right in front of a worldwide audience.

I don't know if you saw the tears behind my surgical mask as I plucked the sapphires out of Sarah Jessica Parker's orbs, or removed Letterman's solid gold testicles.

Obviously, we couldn't have done it without the giveback program initiated by the Coalition of Custom Jewelry Prison Evangelists who service the many who couldn't attend in person. The same holds true for The Association of Divorce Lawyers and Jewelry Appraisers of Los Angeles, Reno, and New York, who released dozens of my customer from escrow. Without this philanthropic gesture, many organs, limbs, and in one case an entire platinum skull, would have remained in limbo and prevented clients embroiled in nasty alimony and custody cases from giving of themselves, for which the poor Katrina victims are eternally grateful.

I don't want to leave out the tens of patrons sporting my jeweled bottled-caps rings and implants. Clint tops the list, and was a hit when he came out as Bronco Billy, riding the very horse he rode in the film of the same name.

Do you know Clint wasn't using a stunt double when I removed the green-and-blue topaz caps from his chest without a local? The audience went wild. What a man—and what a great American.

Did you happen to catch Queen Elizabeth and Prince Phillip parachuting into Shea? I don't think I've anything as exciting since the Beatles—back in 1966.

From the time this lovely royal couple purchased their Snapple Rings, we have never missed exchanging holiday greetings, so I know how hard it was for them to give up their rings; but as they confided, this romantic duo once spent a calorie-filled time stuffing their faces with Cajun Kringles at Haydel's and knew in their hearts they wanted to give something back to the community that allowed them to be, if only for a fortnight, two silly overweight kids from across the pond.

Speaking of the Beatles, Paul and Ringo were there, and both gave two pints of their gold blood. It was only thanks to the diligence of the Shea Stadium Police that more middle-age women didn't jump from the upper decks—but who could blame them as they watched the telethon on the jumbo TV screen set up in centerfield?

Laverne, before I forget, I want to go back two weeks—to that dreadful day when my last thoughts were of you as that angry mob of nuns pulled me from the museum and dragged me outside. I thought the National Guard would step in to save me, but they falsely believed it was part of the publicity campaign, so they used their bayonets to prod the nuns on.

I remember being lifted up and passed over the heads of a sea of black veils and thinking, *What a strong bunch of women these old nuns are.* It was indeed a dark moment for people like us. I thought of Jan van Eyck, the first artist to use oil paints and consequently be boiled to death in them because he didn't paint by numbers. What about Sandro Botticelli, thrown overboard and drowned by fishermen who believed he ruined their business because customers didn't want clams on the half shell unless they contained a naked young lovely named Venus?

The list of martyred artists goes on and on, and when I felt the rope being placed around my neck I was reconciled to my name joining that fabled group. They say your entire life flashes by in an instant (see Lulu-Lu's last email) and it's a fact. Metropolitan Museum of Art colored buttons of the day I used to resell on nearby street corners filled my head.

I saw the faces of the clients who still owed me money, and I couldn't believe how many Academy Award winners had stiffed me because they thought celebrity meant getting everything free.

Then there were all the artist supplies on order, money gone from my checking account and never to be recouped because the items were on sale and not returnable.

I vowed, there and then, if I ever got out of this alive, I would immediately give up my jewelry biz and devote my entire life to art projects that would help the starving masses like the *Eat a Peach Pit Series,* inspired by the Allman Brothers' unsuccessful battle on behalf of Harley riders with eating disorders.

I must have blacked out, for the next thing I knew, I was laying on a cot in a cell in Federal Prison just a few miles away from the museum. Clint, giving me his best Dirty Harry imitation, stood over me, and I thought, he's really sore because I didn't give him any anesthetic. But no—he wasn't angry. He proceeded to show me his neck and the marks from being hung in *Hang Em 'High*—saying he wished he had had my gold neck when they shot that scene in Spain. It was then that I realized the hanging was *really a publicity stunt*. The nuns had participated in the ruse so they could get their *Wandering Habit Retrospective, March Of The Penguins: The Real Deal,* into the museum this coming spring. A little quid pro quo, if you know what I mean?

I recall touching my golden neck and realizing how lucky I was I hadn't chosen the softer platinum, for that would have left a bruise that wouldn't photograph half as well.

Then I remembered my pledge, to do something for humanity. Laverne, I know how difficult it is for outlaws to find time to do their art, that's why I hesitated to burden you further, but you must join me in an opportunity of a lifetime, for you see, my prayers have been answered. Together with my scientist friends who are still quarantined at Two Mile Island, I am taking Dada into the 21st Century and creating *Eada*—art that will insure no one will ever go food shopping as long as they have wall space.

What is this thing called *Eada?* In simple terms, *Eada*—or Eadaism—is art that produces food by connecting the dots of DNA, RNA, and the secret ingredients of Coke (my office sponsor).

My first piece is entitled *Fruit in a Bowl With Cheese Frame.* Exciting, isn't it? At the moment, the food has to be eaten with special 3-D glasses, but we hope to develop LASIK surgery that will enable the diner to eat without eyewear. (FYI—we currently only offer complimentary Jarlsberg and Parmigiano Reggiano cheese frames).

There is more to tell, but my neck hurts.

Love,
Uncle Jules

P.S. Any chance you guys can slip across the Pennsylvania state line, and see my show before we leave for Rome? Let me know. I'll make sure to leave passes at the door. I know the kids would love the exploding birth canals.

From: YoungerTheElder23@Ourmail.us
Date: Wednesday, September 21, 2005, 2:10 p.m.
To: US@Ourmail.us
Subject: Update from Your Humble Servant

Dear Members of the Family Ginsburg (*pronounced* Du Pont) Family,

It is almost 2:00 a.m., and I am still at the office working on the family portfolio. You know I am not just saying this simply to blow my own horn. I am only the faithful and most humble servant of the Family Ginsburg (*pronounced* Du Pont) Family, as was my father and his father and his father before him, all the way back to Younger the Elder by One Ginsburg (*pronounced* Du Pont), may he be inscribed in *The History of the World: The Book Of Ratings,* Chapter 11, The Great CPAs of History.

Moments ago, I finished decoding FEMA'S most recent message, and I am happy to announce we have been completely successful in our attempts to purchase all the flooded coastline properties in the Louisiana territories for ten cents on the Katrina.

I will compose a coded letter of thanks to our friends at FEMA, an agency I had the foresight this past May to rent with an option to buy. I say this in all humility and not simply to blow my own horn.

The success of our Louisiana purchase is due in no small part to the role of our friends, the Plaquemine Family (*pronounced* Bonaparte) of Plaquemines Parish and St. Bart's, and their indebtedness, by marriage and sports betting, to the *Mangia! Mangia!* (*pronounced* Thomas Jefferson! Thomas Jefferson!) Family of Cicero, Palm Beach, and where home really is—Palermo, Italy.

Obviously, none of this land grab could have been accomplished without the help of our own insatiable Mr. Nicholas Graham. He may be deported, but he is certainly not forgotten, especially if you read Liz Smith Apples, watch "South Park," or are a fan of regicide.

I think any discussion of the King's water-balloon mishap must be tabled until Nicholas's coronation, at which time, I will email the

Family Ginsburg (*pronounced* Du Pont) Family Members (who have a high-speed Internet connections) a QuickTime version showing, in slow motion, the errant throw striking the monarch's head, the valiant attempts made by Saul the Seal to revive his fallen playmate, and the seal's suicide subsequent to watching the video replay.

Monaco and its people mourn a great King. Cartier mourns a great spender, and Sea World mourns a great entertainer. The Family Ginsburg (*pronounced* Du Pont), of course, gets us another country.

To return to the land grab at hand . . . as you most certainly remember, it was Nicholas's twin brother, Nicholas, who broke his thirty-three-year vow of silence to alert Nicholas (referred here as Our Nicholas) to the real-estate opportunities that were forming when Katrina first appeared on the southernmost edges of his Doppler Radar Screen. While Our Nicholas's brother Nicholas's job description is to handle PR for Levi's and to make sure whenever a Levy gets married, or a levee breaks anywhere in the world, reporters on the scene wear Levi's, use the correct pronunciation (Levi's instead of Levy or Levee), and tell viewers they can get 25% off on their 501s . . . I have to remind you that this Nicholas continues to owe half a million dollars to Our Nicholas for backing his chain of New Deli Delis—and ultimately has a fiduciary responsibility to the Family Ginsburg (*pronounced* in Southern Asia as Buddha, Buddha and Gandhi), CPA, Southern Asia, because we fronted the money, the cold cuts and the India Ink.

As an aside, Our Nicholas wants me to tell everyone in the Family Ginsburg (*pronounced* Du Pont) that his brother has been awarded The Naan White Bread Award, India's most important outsourcing honor. When I spoke to Our Nicholas, he also informed me his brother, Nicholas, would be listed in the next edition of *The Guinness Book Of Records*—a feat every hard-drinking Englishman would gladly die for. The only sour note is that Our Nicholas's brother, Nicholas, would have loved to have set the record for "answering the most consumers' phone queries in the history of the world," in his own hometown of Surrey, England . . . but then, how would over twenty million surprised Americans say when connected to their local bank, "But you don't sound like you're in India?"

I can't tell you how proud Our Nicholas is of his brother, Nicholas, and well he should be, because their relationship goes deeper than skin. You see, when Our Nicholas and his brother, Nicholas, were born, they were joined at the head, and without any help, they broke free of each other; however, those twenty-years of drinking out of the same feeding tube created a bond that can never be broken.

Kudos also must be handed out to Uncle Maxie and Uncle Abe for assisting my efforts in securing the Dade and Broward County's soon-to-be-waterfront properties. I speak from experience when I say how hard it is to get eminent-domain status without identity theft.

Uncle Maxie and Uncle Abe also deserve much of the credit for structuring the deal allowing the Family Ginsburg (*pronounced* Du Pont) to acquire huge tracts of then-soon-to-be-ocean property from our Caribbean neighbors in exchange for the exclusive gambling and renaming rights to Ginsburg (*pronounced* Du Pont) Mountains, better known as the Catskills.

I am assembling a little family album and spreadsheet that graphically illustrates how much money we ultimately washed when Collins Avenue was washed away. I know this is still a sore spot because South Florida was a vacation paradise to generations of the Family Ginsburg (*pronounced* Du Pont) Snowbirds. I, for one, still deeply cherish the time, before credit cards, when the hotels we owned along that glorious avenue of sun-drenched real estate were cash cows, and all we had to do was ship the bags of money offshore to our friendly Havana bankers.

However, as the Family Ginsburg (*pronounced* Du Pont) accountant of record, it is my sworn duty to notify you of each and every uncontrollable force of nature and explain how they financially impact on property values we intend to buy on the cheap. We CPAs may have started out as uninvited and insignificant guests of this planet, but thanks to our unique body type that allows us to squirm through the loopholes in the United States Tax Code, in just a few short centuries we created global warming, and with this meltdown comes the ownership of the *new* Collins Avenue, now located *west* of what used to be the Intracoastal Waterway.

And next year, imagine as CNN reporters lash themselves to trees, South American despots madly bidding on the next strip of beachfront property that we own! To reap the hurricane winds and measure our rising off shore assets by the rising tides and tidal waves is a watershed event, and a gift that keeps on giving! I only hope and pray the small part I played in this defining moment will, once and for all, wash away the bad blood some members of the Family Ginsburg (*pronounced* Du Pont) have toward the Ginsburg (*pronounced* Du Pont) line of Younger The Elders by One to Twenty-Three, may they all be inscribed in *The History of the World: The Book Of Ratings*, Chapter 11, The Great CPAs of History (except for me, of course).

Oh, don't pretend you don't hate me. I tap phones, too, you know. I hear what is said about me. I may be a CPA, but I do have real feelings and I have a name and it's not—*That Putz*.

Well—*That Putz* didn't spend ten years in opium dens in Chiang Mai with Mr. Nicholas Graham and not learn a thing or two about keeping two sets of books, and how easy it is to empty an offshore account when you have access codes. Put that in your pipes and smoke it!

No longer humble, or your *servant,*
Younger the Elder by Twenty-Three

From: SisterChanelSize4@SistersOfTheRuinedFeet.com
Date: Wednesday, September 21, 2005, 2:41 p.m.
To: US@Ourmail.us
Subject: Your forgiveness is all the love I need

Dear Family Ginsburg (*pronounced* Du Pont),

Working behind the counter at the Starbucks Café and Confessional, in the main chapel of the Sisters of the Ruined Feet Sanctuary, has put the spring back in my step, and I joyfully await the day I am to be given the Golden Shoe Horn.

Everyone here believed yesterday was going to be the day I was to fulfill 3b of the *Three Prophecies of the Golden Shoe Trees*. Unfortunately, our Mother Superior, Sister Prada Size 6, was called away on a mission of extreme urgency and will not return for another ten days. She took with her Sister Susan Bennis Size 10, Sister Novitiate Tayrn Rose Size 4, and Sister Fendi Size 10. In her absence, I have been chosen to be the Acting Mother Superior. This is an exceptional honor and fulfills 3c of the *Three Prophecies of the Golden Shoe Trees*.

It now appears the chosen day will fall during the last days of the year, so in keeping with the holiday spirit, we are all going to wear our party outfits. For the blessed event, I have chosen a bright-red pair of patent-leather Chanel pumps with a 2-inch heel. Tomorrow, I am going to take a little walk around my cell and break them in. In the past, I have discovered Chanel pumps can pinch the big toe on my left foot just a smidgen and cause a blister to form. You all know how that can be painful, so I am going to put a thin piece of surgical tape there to protect the area. Why it is always the left foot remains a mystery. Sister Chanel Size 10 says the same thing happens to her, only, it's her *right* foot. Oh, the mysteries of feet—are they not mysterious?

I am still in a state of shock resulting from the outpouring of love and affection my loving Family Ginsburg (*pronounced* Du Pont) has showered upon me these last few months.

I was particularly touched by the intervention organized by Cousin Tenderly. I know what a disappointment it must have been for you to be turned away after trekking down to us from your Himalayan mountain retreat. I am also amazed Bermuda was able to get away, particularly during the holidays, and to be accompanied by her mother, who I thought was under house arrest because of the arson charges.

Neither words, nor the check for $1,000,000, will ever atone for what happened when you attempted to enter our sanctuary. I think you can excuse the Mace attack because Sister Novitiate Gucci Size 8 and Sister Novitiate Miu Miu Size 4 were a tad overzealous and wanted only to make a good impression.

What *was inexcusable* was Sister Forzieri Size 7's use of the stun gun when the surveillance videos clearly showed the Mace had blinded you while, at the same time, Sister Givenchy Size 4's first burst from her fully automatic AK47 had also put you down—and even though you were wearing Wolford silk bodysuits under your fur coats, it was clear to anyone with eyes that the rubber bullets found their mark and had inflicted enormous pain. If the images of your uncontrolled writhing weren't enough proof, your high-pitched screams certainly made us wince, even though we were wearing the new-generation JB1000 custom-molded Noise Protectors.

You can be sure there will be a full investigation and the necessary punishment meted out to the individuals involved. Furthermore, a new set of instructions will be issued dealing with how and when small arms fire can be used when repelling invaders.

We have managed to control the media coverage and spin a story that keeps Sisterhood and its purpose secret. However, news of this incursion has leaked out into the clandestine world of Mercenary Women's Shoes, and we can see it is already adversely affecting our recruiting efforts that traditionally begin this time of the year.

I want to go on record as saying there are still openings for Israeli paratroopers, Japanese ninja warriors, and American roller-derby queens. We cherish those among us now—all of whom, I might add, behaved exceptionally well during the recent skirmish. However, if we are to successfully spread our message throughout the world of spoiled, self-indulgent women who have an uncontrollable addiction to overpriced shoes, we cannot lower our admission standards and let anyone who cannot defend herself with a No-Limit American Express Platinum Card join the Sisterhood.

Then, there are the legacies to consider. There would be catastrophic consequences if the sisters around the world were to get the idea we have somehow gone soft on violence and can't even terminate, with extreme prejudice, three unarmed women who sought to breach the perimeters of one of our most heavily guarded and important sanctuaries, perhaps even reaching the sacred tomb of Imelda, and helping themselves to our holiest of treasures.

Would the sisters then get cold feet during our annual winter fundraising drive and decide to end their yearly gift-giving because it was no longer their intention to send their progenies to follow in their crooked footsteps?

A precipitous drop in alumni contributions that account for more than fifty percent of our income stream would be particularly injurious to us at this critical juncture when the *Three Prophecies of the Golden Shoe Trees* is about to come true and money is needed to finance my trip and the opening of the Madison Avenue worshiping venue.

We can only hope Mother Superior's trip wasn't in vain, for with her rest the hope and future of our order. Just this very morning, she called from the Manolo Blahnik factory in Parabiago, Italy, where for the past week she has spearheaded a drive to get his shoes to the women who couldn't get to his sale because they were watching coverage of Hurricane Katrina.

"Shoes for Hotties," as dubbed by the media, has received lots of coverage in the *Christian Shoe Monitor, Modern Catholic Shoes and Handbags,* and the *Jewish Foot Forward,* but the real news event will be when Oprah arrives and donates her entire Manolo collection. According to our sources, this will happen during the segment of her show when Oprah picks the Sisters of the Ruined Feet Sanctuary as one of Oprah's Ten Christmas Sanctuary Favorites.

As you know, when Oprah picks your sanctuary, well—all I can say is, we won't have to charge for coffee in our Starbucks Café and Confessional.

CAN I HAVE AN AMEN!

A happy and healthy New Year, and to Tenderly, Bermuda, and Sylvia—even though you are all unconscious and not expected to live the year out . . .

Your forgiveness is all the love I need.

Sister Chanel Size 4, Formerly Known as the Aunt Named Bea

www.ingramcontent.com/pod-product-compliance
Lightning Source LLC
Chambersburg PA
CBHW051747040426
42446CB00007B/262